Patrick J. O'Connor

Living in a Coded Land

Names of Places 8

Signatures of People 20

Signs and Symbols 28

Irish Landscape Series no. 1

Oireacht na Mumhan Books

Published in Ireland by
Oireacht na Mumhan Books
Coolanoran
Newcastle West
Co. Limerick

Printed by Litho Press Co., Midleton, Co. Cork.

Living in a Coded Land

For Aisling

Living in a Coded Land

—— You will uncode all landscapes
By this : things founded clean on their own shapes,
Water and ground in their extremity [1]

Ireland has been shaped by the human hand and dominated by the human wish for millennia, and as we look around us to-day, we cannot but contemplate a land grown old with humanity. Multiple layers of occupancy may be discerned. The leavings of past cultures may be distinguished. Deep feelings may be entertained. The prospect is therefore an inviting and challenging one. Moreover, the landscape itself is instinct with signs, material and mystical. The more we look and see and think, the more the realisation grows that we live in a superbly coded island on the edge of the Old World.

How then should we seek to address an island domain that is at once both strange and familiar? The task is difficult, even daunting. However, we could scarcely make a better start than with the names of places. These are the names by which landscapes may be envisioned. Their bestowal is a humanising act. People name places, and since any landscape encompasses a net of places, their names provide culture clues for anyone who knows how to read them. Secondly, we may focus upon an island landscape marked by the signatures of its makers, past and present. Since time immemorial people have signed their own distinguishing features onto the face of the land. They have thus issued their own particular spatial comments and studying these affords a better insight into the nature of their creators. All such signatures share a common bond : they serve as cultural markers. Thirdly, we may consider an increasing number of signs and symbols in the landscape, and seek to comprehend their complexities of meaning. All landscapes and all kinds of space express meanings which reflect their power over

7

our thinking and perception. Such meanings may be spiritual, or mythical, or monumental, imbued as they are, with the cumulative culture of our perceptions. Generally speaking, the Irish landscape is a text to be read, a much written over manuscript. It is representative of many authors and a mirror of many histories.

Names of Places

Nothing, no country, can be really owned except under familiar name or satisfying phrase [2]

To recollect the place-names in certain regions was to remember the ancient tribes and their memorable deeds. How different it was with the planters round about them. For them, all that Gaelic background of myth, literature and history had no existence. They differed from the people in race, language, religion, culture; while the landscape they looked upon was indeed but rocks and stones and trees [3]

Writers in all cultures have shown an awareness of the power of place-names to evoke and to forge landscapes. In Ireland we need only refer to such luminaries as Joyce and Yeats. Using a net of named places, Joyce creates his own literary landscape, and in the process, transforms Dublin into a universal symbol. Places as diverse as Sandycove and Glasnevin, Sandymount Strand and Nighttown (alias Monto), Mountjoy Square and Eccles Street, are all woven into a topographic tapestry of great imaginative intensity. Here in a city standing for all cities, the life experience of modern man is envisioned.[4] Yeats, in contrast, invokes the incantatory power of rural place-names in conjuring up his vision of an atavistic, and perhaps ultimately mythic, landscape. This is a kind of dreamland. It may even be an escape into fairyland.[5] And yet for all that, his vision merges imperceptibly with reality and gives a Yeatsian *frisson* to such places as Dromahair, Lissadell, Scanavin and Lugnagall. In the larger sense, Yeats succeeds in forming a landscape of the mind in that intimate and alluring setting of Sligo and its Leitrim borderland. His spirit, like that of the English poet Wordsworth, pervades an area in which our imaginations respond

8

Plate 1.1.The lake isle of Innisfree, Yeatsian possibilities, and a beautiful lady

to the stimulus of familiar names. Ben Bulben and Knocknarea, Innisfree and Dooney, Glencar and Drumcliff, all evoke that landscape and its Yeatsian possibilities.

Other modern writers also invoke place-names to stake out the landscapes with which they seek identity. The poet, Nuala Ní Dhomhnaill, for example, does this with stunning simplicity when she imaginatively engages *Baile an tSléibhe* and an associated net of places in the far west of Corca Dhuibhne, Co. Kerry. [6] Another poet writing in Irish, Mairtín Ó Direáin, avails of the framework of his native Árainn, onto which he fits a lifetime of lyric vision. However, landscapes fenced out with names find their clearest expression in the work of northern poets. These are led out by Patrick Kavanagh, the poet of drumlin country. Kavanagh, unlike Yeats, uses place-names to mark out a landscape that is unencumbered by the burden of history or etymology. For him, ordinary places like Drummerril and Drumnagrella, Mucker and Mullahincha, Shancobane and Shancoduff, sustain life as it is lived by the smallholding community of south Monaghan. He lays his hand on the landscape : inside the townland net everything becomes personal, actual, known, and immediate. Ordinary people bestow ordinary names such as Brady's hill, Cassidy's haggard, Caffrey's plantation, and Rooney's meadow, while the fine print of their landscape emerges in such features as a cart pass in

9

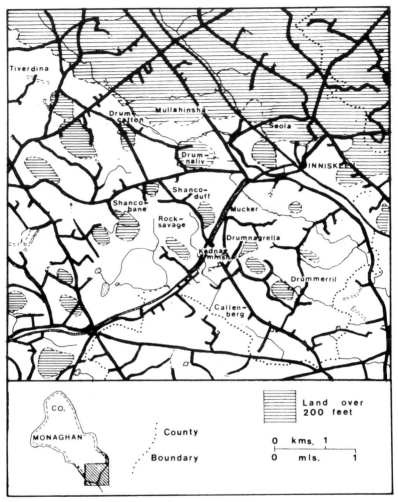

Fig. 1.1.   Countryside around Inniskeen, Co. Monaghan, transformed by the
poet, Patrick Kavanagh, into a minutely authored landscape

Drumnagrella, a field in Rocksavage, and an array of intimately known
ruts, tracks, gaps, laneways, ridges, furrows, headlands — . There is
movement, light, colour, people. Everywhere the marks of human
endeavour merit the tag of a familiar name. In short, for the here and now,
Kavanagh's Monaghan is a humanised landscape perfectly envisioned.

Further north, we may skirt by the great sheet of water, that is Lough
Neagh, and head on for the home ground of Seamus Heaney, between
the villages of Castledawson and Toome in south-east Derry. The road
we traverse takes us from Kavanagh's Mucker to Heaney's Mossbawn,
from one man's cradle to another's. Each in his way renders filial

obeisance. First, Kavanagh pays homage to Mucker. This is a place abounding in pigs in its original Gaelic form, and a lived-in townland where the name has caused much aesthetic heartaching for its inhabitants. Still, despite an obvious capacity for obscene rhyming, the place has kept its name, and Kavanagh has forged for it a masterly paper landscape.[7] Heaney equally cherishes the little known farmland of Mossbawn, and he too explores its meaning. For him, the syllables of home stand as metaphor for the cultural dimensions of Ulster.[8] He teases out the possible nuances. *Moss* is a Scots word of probable planter origin and *bawn* is the name English colonists gave to their

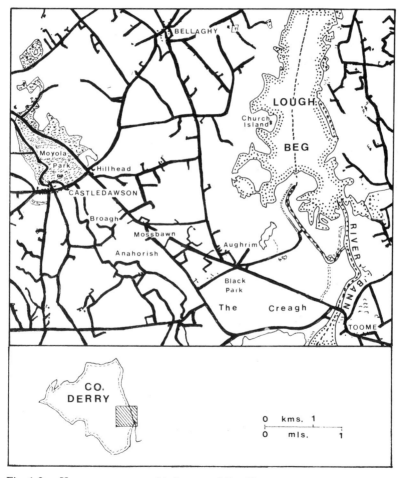

Fig. 1.2.   Heaney country with its net of familiar names spreading like an apron to the shores of Lough Beg

11

fortified farmhouses. These combine to signify the planter's house on the bog. However, local usage overrides Ordnance Survey spelling to render bawn as bann or *bán*. So the place may mean the moss of bog cotton or simply the white bog! Is it therefore a metaphor for the split culture of Ulster, or a layering of all possible worlds - Gaelic, Scots and English ?

Whatever about Mossbawn, there is no ambiguity about the bordering townlands of Broagh and Anahorish. These are resolutely Gaelic, and their original forms of *bruach* (the riverbank) and *anach fhíor uisce* (the place of clear water) signify the close world of Bannside, while also yielding a throaty, forgotten music. It is a music that harks back to an ancient civilisation which was shattered in the early modern period, when bawn and demesne wall came to proclaim the new order of planter in the landscape. There is thus a depth charge to Heaney's place-names that is not found at all in Kavanagh's. There is also a variety of etymological forms to be encountered near Bannside, unlike the exclusively Gaelic underlay of south Monaghan. Heaney is alive to all this. For instance, looking across the fields of his youth he is drawn imaginatively to places such as Grove Hill and Back Park. These are names that evoke pastoral serenity and perhaps reach back to Old English origins. Moyola Park on the other hand, the demesne of Chichester-Clark, stands for the New English order. Field names recall a record of occupancy compounded of the Gaels, the Scots, and the English. The landscape is therefore finely coded. It takes a sharp eye to see the subtleties and a keen mind to comprehend them.

Heaney is possessor of both. As well his feelings flow into familiar places and in return an accumulation of feeling filters back into his consciousness. Everywhere he finds a prospect to engage the mind, whether it be the forbidden ground of his native moss spreading out like an apron towards water's edge; or light among the bluebells on Grove Hill; or the rattle of Orange drums on Aughrim Hill; or the spire of Church Island in Lough Beg. He pegs out a landscape laden with the resonances of its place-names and he marks out the boundaries. To the east Lough Beg serves as limit, while to the west Slieve Gallon, irradiated in song, takes the eye out over grassland, ploughed land, and woodland. Within, as Heaney reminds us, we step across one of the oldest inhabited areas in Ireland. Hoards of flints and fishbones by the River Bann furnish the necessary proof. Appropriately in this old humanised region, the moss-holes are bottomless and the layers of culture that the poet grew up beneath are deep and intricate. Heaney sounds out the living landscape. He has allowed us to hear the music.[9] The vision, in contrast, remains his own.

Next we may turn to the work of John Hewitt, a poet from the planter tradition who has sought to cultivate a regionalist identity for Ulster. Although born to the suburbs of Belfast, he is frequently drawn by instinct and by taste to the countryside. He is acutely conscious of his roots and has a refined sense of the legitimacy of the planter's place in Ulster.[10] The quest for origins draws him back to Armagh orchard country. Kilmore is the place where his mother's people are hearth-rolled and on the church-topped mound there half the tombstones bear the Howard name. This all signifies the density of Hewitt's roots in what he refers to as planter lands. Moreover, lines of continuity from the seventeenth century mean that the poet feels at home in Northern Ireland and that he ranges freely over it in his imagination. During the relatively untroubled times of the 1950s he invokes in a pastoral vein a whole range of Ulster place-names and in his mind's eye visualises the associated landscapes or townscapes. Later on in 1984 his mental map of the province becomes blood-stained and torn as places like Banbridge, Co. Down; Ballykelly, Co. Derry; Darkley, Co. Armagh; and Crossmaglen, Co. Armagh take, on dark and compelling resonances.[11]

Through good times and bad, he maintains a special affinity with a particular region. This is the north Antrim countryside where his spirit ranges from over the moss between Orra and Slievenanee down into the glens, the source of much of his best verse. Here he is at home as co-inhabitant but not as kin with the natives. He probes the secrets of their farming world, while seeking to make his own of it. In the process, he fixes place-names like burrs in our minds. He marks out the middle glens - Glendun, Glenaan, Glenballyemon, and Glenariff - and his weave of places stretches from high Trostan (1817' O.D.) down to the braes of Layde, while fanning out to embrace the Craigagh wood, Garron Top, and Red Bay, as well as the townlands of Ballyvooley, Cloughglass, and Tieveragh. In *The Glens of Antrim* the poet sketches in a peopled landscape where each dispersed homestead may be marked and named, and where the round of the working year may be set off against the kaleidoscope of the seasons. In *The Glen of Light* on the other hand, everything is apt to be transfigured.[12] For the seeing eye, it is a glen replete with all kinds of transcendental possibilities.

From the Glens of Antrim we may cut lastly to the Clogher valley of west Tyrone to find a poet skilled in the use of place-names as a tool for reading the landscape. This is John Montague, another words-smith deeply mindful of his roots. For him, everything that counts begins in the townland of Garvaghey (*garbh achaidh, a rough field*). He is struck by the appropriateness of the name. The landscape is harsh and

Plate 1.2. At the head of Glenariff, the queen of the glens beloved by Hewitt

haunting in this wedge of ground between whin-bound hills. All around Montague finds shards of a lost culture in cabins only recently deserted and he is captivated by the names of the places that take him out from Garvaghey. These all betoken a lost tradition. Glencull, where he went to school, he renders as the *glen of the hazels* and the nearby village of Clogher, an old diocesan centre, as the *bishopric of the golden stone*.[13] Knockmany, which on the face of it derives from *Cnoc Maine,* is rendered locally as *Áine's Cove,* and this for the poet is a throwback to the earth as the mother goddess of ancient civilisation. Images abound therefore in the world that nurtures John Montague. Indeed, for him, the Irish landscape as mediated through its place-names, is a kind of primal Gaeltacht that reaches back beyond the oldest theme in Irish literature, the *dinnseanchas* or lore of places. The whole landscape is a manuscript, he maintains.[14] To stand any chance of reading it aright, we need to sound out , as he does, the Gaelic underlay of its place-names.

Ultimately we may be drawn back to the nature of early Celtic culture and how it influenced the toponymy of our island setting on the edge of a continent. That culture appears to have been remarkable for its

14

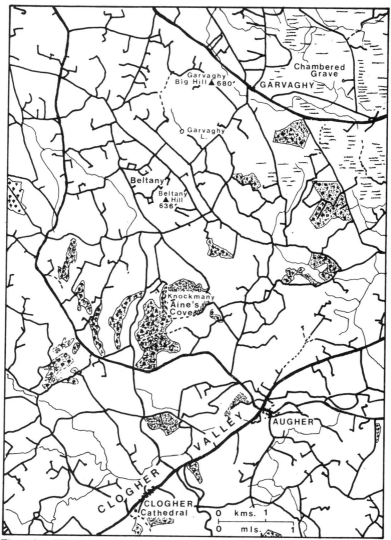

Fig. 1.3.   West Tyrone landscape interpreted through the medium of its place-names, and seen by the poet Montague as a kind of primal Gaeltacht

exclusiveness, to judge from the constant repetition of the same place-name elements throughout the country.[15]   One element alone - the ubiquitous *baile*, 'place' - occurs in one-tenth of our total complement of over 62,000 townland names and other strongly recurring elements include *cill*, 'church'; *cluain*, 'meadow'; *cnoc*, 'hill'; *doire*, 'oakwood'; *lios*, 'fort'; and *ráth*, 'fort'.   Putting matters to the test at regional level, we find that in north Co. Kerry, for example, a dozen

15

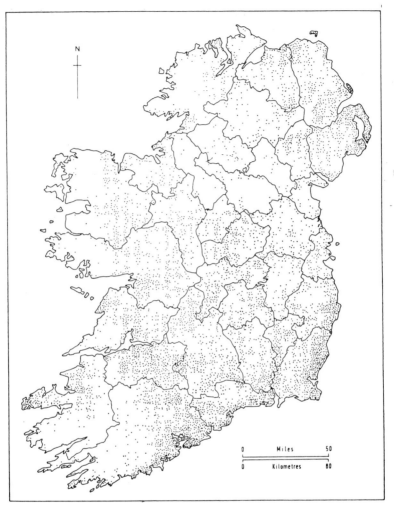

Fig. 1.4. *Baile* as prefix and suffix in townland names (after Jones Hughes, 1970)

elements feature in the names of one-half of its constituent townlands.[16] Of these, *baile* with 219 occurrences displays by far the leading pattern of recurrence, followed by *cill* (96); *cnoc* (90); *gleann,* 'glen', (47); *gort,* ' field', (47); *druim,*' ridge', (38); *maigh,* 'plain', (33); *lios* (32); *cluain* (31); *fearann,* 'land', (28); *cathair,* 'stone fort' (27); and *ráth* (26). Further evidence of exclusiveness is furnished in this region by the fact that more than 45 per cent of the total number of its townland names contain elements which refer to toponymic features of either a topographic or a botanical nature, and a further 43 per cent are indicative of the types of land unit and some of the leading settlement items that were characteristic of early and medieval Ireland. No doubt this same kind of underlay to our modern network of place-names could be replicated for many other regions in Ireland.

Not for everywhere, however, because the challenge offered by the Anglo-Normans greatly modified the pre-existing pattern in the areas successfully colonised by them. We may recognise a zone of enduring Norman settlement and it had as its basis in place-names the suffix *town,* the Old English equivalent of the Gaelic *baile.* The *town* zone stands out in north Leinster where there is a close relationship between

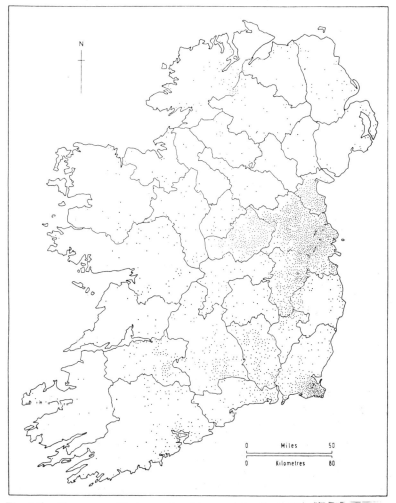

Fig. 1.5. *Town* as suffix in townland names (after Jones Hughes, 1970)

its location and extent and that of the medieval Pale. It embraces most of the counties Dublin, Meath and Louth, as well as east Westmeath and east Kildare. The zone belongs to the realm of desirable boulder clay plains and it is set sharply against the drumlin edge of Ulster, while it tends to fade away towards the wet lands of central Ireland. It furnishes us with the landscape *par excellence* of motte-and-baileys, stone castles, monasteries, and manorial villages and towns. These all occur with the kind of frequency that ensures continuity of status for the zone as Ireland's metropolitan region. Away from north Leinster the suffix *town* only occurs again with comparable if not greater frequency in the baronies of Bargy and Forth in south-east Co. Wexford.[17] Here the element *town* in townland names is found alongside a great variety of other Old English forms. This differentiates it from north Leinster. So also does the generous admixture of *town* and *baile* place-names, and together these characteristics suggest the evolution of a truly mixed community in the medieval period. The associated landscape is noteworthy for the distinctiveness and richness of its material culture, including windmills and elaborate vernacular farmhouses.

There are also extensive hybrid areas where the two cultures, Gaelic and Norman, met, mingled and strove for supremacy. We may include among these the strongly Normanised county of Kilkenny, as well as east Waterford, east Cork, south Tipperary and east Limerick where the two elements *baile* and *town* wax strong and appear to have been interchangeable in place-names. In these areas which would count among Europe's finest, cultural fusion gave a lustre to life and landscape. From an early date emphasis was placed on productive agriculture and on the close integration of rural and urban settings. Another set of areas comprising north Tipperary, east Clare and east Galway saw a marked intermingling of *baile* townlands and those incorporating Old English elements other than *town*. The most prolific of such elements would include *castle, court, farm, field, grange, grove, hall, hill, land, mill, park* and *wood*. The romance element *park* or *páirc*, for instance, is especially prominent in east Galway, where it may often have been substituted for *baile* or *town*. This kind of interchangeability shows how thoroughly the cultures of the Gael and Norman fused in the hybrid areas during the course of the later medieval period, and along with the place-name evidence landscapes studded with tower houses may provide the keenest attestation to the identity of such areas.

Later contributions to the toponymy of our townland net were slight. Indeed if we leave aside nineteenth century anglicisation, the vast majority of the place-names we have inherited may be said to be residual from the middle ages. The New English in particular did little, apart from the bestowal of names which endured near the major early centres of anglicisation. These would include estate cores and their surrounding aureoles, and the hinterlands of cities and towns. Fresh elements such as *brook, dale, lawn, lodge, mount,* and *ville* were especially favoured and these along with the re-deployment of older English elements such as *castle, court, demesne, grove, hall, hill* and *park* served to convey the resonance of a landscape made in the image of its owners. New names for old were invoked to complete the metamorphosis but the limited nature of the replacement is clear from a recent comprehensive survey of the place-names of Co. Limerick,[18] and might, by extension, be confirmed for the country as a whole.

Such a general survey would prove the integrity of the old Gaelic substratum, especially towards the north and west. Towards the north, the drumlin belt stands out as a distinctive toponymic region which features the prefixes *druim* and *corr* in large numbers in names that are altogether Gaelic. These provide the most telling appraisal of a landscape of little hills, especially in counties Fermanagh, Monaghan, Cavan and south Leitrim. Beyond the drumlin belt much of the flavour of Montague's primeval Gaeltacht may be savoured in the etymology of the place-names of counties Tyrone and Derry, while Ulster as a whole possesses the toponymic credentials of being the most Gaelic of the Irish provinces. This proves that names, once bestowed, may prove enduring, no matter how sweeping the subsequent ethnic changes or how hopelessly they may be transliterated into another language.

Turning to the west, we face into a harsh Atlantic world of stone, moorland and bog, and accordingly place-names all the way from north Donegal to west Cork feature a very high ratio of toponyms. Constantly recurring elements include *carraig, cnoc, cúil, gleann, inis, mullach* and *tullach*. These are spread over extensive sections which experienced some of the latest lived-in landscapes in Ireland. However, there are also landscapes in the west which wear the accoutrements of longstanding human occupancy. Such a living landscape may be encountered in the townland of Kilgalligan, the *ultima Thule* of the Erris Gaeltacht in north-west Mayo, and the repository of nearly 800 place-names.[19]

Signatures of People

*As a poet of the historic consciousness I suppose I am bound
to see landscape as a field dominated by the human wish — A
landscape scribbled with the signatures of men and epochs* [20]

*Ineluctable modality of the visible : at least that if no more,
thought through my eyes. Signatures of all things I am here to
read, sea-spawn and seawrack, the nearing tide, that rusty
boot. Snotgreen, bluesilver, rust : coloured signs — Am I
walking into eternity along Sandymount Strand?* [21]

Our most distinguished geographer, E. Estyn Evans, makes a bold and
imaginative choice from among the myriad of signatures left by
ordinary people on the face of Ireland. As he sees it, there is no more
diagnostic feature to be encountered than the bundles of abandoned
cultivation ridges that are part of the rural scene of many areas.[22]
Evans takes these spade-turned ridges - the so-called lazy-beds or
iomairí - to represent the face of an old Ireland, a face that is much
wrinkled by their tracks. He details their great antiquity and continuity,
their supreme adaptation to Irish soil and climatic conditions, and
depending upon age, their graphic or muted expression in the
landscape. There can scarcely be a more humanising mark on the land
than one which seeks to tame it and to till it in a time-honoured way.
Hence we may ponder at some length the possible significance of the
spade-ridge in Irish life. If we come to the same conclusion as Evans,
then like the poet of his own Welsh borderland we will see that 'the
works of man / are mortised in the cultured wilderness' [23]; we will see
that the signature of the humble spadesman may net whole worlds with
its associations.

Such worlds may be as old as Newgrange. Here by the bend of the
Boyne in Co. Meath, ample proof is furnished of the capacity of
Neolithic man to slice sods and to incorporate them into the most
celebrated of our pre-historic funerary mounds. From slicing sods to
turning ridges is a small transition, and for the evidence, we are drawn
to the recent daring exposures from beneath western bogs. In counties
Kerry, Clare and Mayo, for example, whole fossilised landscapes have

Plate 1.3. Fossil ridges providing the tell-tale accompaniment to traces of a long abandoned farm cluster near Manor Kilbride in west Co. Wicklow

been uncovered after the lid of the peat has been lifted by the archaeologist and the turf-cutter. The spade-ridge is an integral part of these pre-historic landscapes and striking lay-outs have been revealed at locations such as Bunnyconnellan on the north-west slopes of the Ox Mountains in Co. Mayo, and at Belderg and Carrownaglogh in the same county. Fossil ridges occur too in situations as diverse as the thin limestone soils of east Connacht and the western flanks of the Wicklow Mountains. On the one hand, their skeletal outlines may show inside older enclosures within modern walled fields; on the other, they may provide the tell-tale accompaniment to traces of long-abandoned farm clusters.

For their most vivid expression, however, we must confront the swollen demographic conditions of pre-Famine Ireland and the responses elicited from among the land-hungry and the impoverished. A wholesale assault was provoked on to marginal land where the needs of potato-growing, in particular, were met by the spade-ridge. Scrawny hillsides all over the country tell the same story of desperation etched in tracks almost as fresh as when they were first turned more than 150 years ago. At the extremity of Corca Dhuibhne in Co. Kerry, or at the heart of the Partry Mountains in Co. Mayo, or on the doorstep of Dublin at Ballinascorney gap, the same mute testament to the rapid comings and goings of poor people is quilted under heather and bracken, and cast into sharp relief. In contrast, scarcely anything may be visible of older examples. It may take a low sun or a veneer of frost

21

or snow to throw them into profile. Once on a January day when visiting the farm village of Glencullen in south Co. Dublin, an enthralling scene was enacted before us. Snow flaked down gently and in minutes the whole microtopography around the village was rigged in ridges. The snow stopped. Then the sun's low trajectory emboldened and illuminated the signatures of ancient spadesmen. It was all so entrancing. The face of old Ireland had come to captivate us for a little while.

From a timeless theme of old Ireland, we may turn next to the signatures that make for synthesis in one of our many hidden Irelands. This is the small farm country of the drumlin belt and for a lead-in guide we may summon up the poet, Patrick Kavanagh. The signatures of people abound in Kavanagh country. Here around Inniskeen in south Co. Monaghan, community life is etched in an intensive carve-up of the landscape. Symptomatic of this is the network of little fields, the tangled skein of lanes and by-roads, and the relative concentration of houses. Onto a topography of hills tumbling away to the horizon, the smallholders have grafted their mosaic of high-hedged fields that lead down to the bottomlands, where lakes gather and streams sneak away. Kavanagh writes of the grip of these same irregular fields that no one escapes.[24] They furnish the essential setting for the pursuit of livelihood and as such are well trodden and well known. Signatures are writ large upon them in the form of cart-tracks and cattle tracks, guttery gaps and guttery headlands, and the innumerable marks of landworking. Beyond the ambit of familiar fields, turf-banks are 'stripped for victory' when it is timely, while alongside home the detailing eye may pick out the ricks, the sheds, the cabbage garden, even the stones of the street.[25] All in all, Kavanagh has succeeded in turning his borderland of hungry hills into a minutely authored landscape.

The American ethnographer, Henry Glassie, has sought to do something similar in another part of drumlin country. Glassie tunes in superbly to a farming community passing the time by Upper Lough Erne in Co. Fermanagh, and through a combination of insider/outsider perspectives, he puts a hitherto hidden landscape on view. He offers to the world 'the startling richness of one small spot in Ireland'[26] which he calls *Ballymenone,* an amalgam of townlands strung out to the north of the Arney River and bounded by the lakeside and by roads. The signatures of people are everywhere to be read over this area of four square miles, embracing the realms of home, clay, moss and bog.

To start, the architecture and artefacts of home are lovingly depicted, and such is the attention to detail that the eye may range from the thatch on the roof to the latch on the door, and out over outbuildings edged around the street, the haggard and the lawn. We may encounter thatcher, John Drumm, busy at work on Bob Lamb's roof, or find Ellen Cutler lavishing attention on tasteful home environs at the top of Gortdonaghy Hill. Beyond the realm of home, hills of sticky clay roll and tumble where old spade-ridges may reside awaiting a snowy revelation, but where green grass now prevails. The clay is signed away into fields, into grazing and meadowing, for this is the realm of cattle. Wish fired by will dictates the look of the land. Meadows may be smooth or rough, hedges may be trim or overgrown, trees may be in or out of line : either way, the landscape of pastoralism is cast in the image of its people.

The realm of the moss is low-lying, devoid of rocks, and is often cut-away bog where the needs of drainage are paramount. This is where gardens are formed. ' The spade is the weapon for the moss ground' [27] : here its wielder comes into his own. He turns ridges along twine-struck lines to conquer wetness and to maximise accessibility for the growing crops. He shepherds potatoes and cabbage through their growth cycles, and he comes back every spring to the same emblematic ground. The most marginal of the realms - bogland - also exerts its pull as spring flows into summer. Here the wielder of the turf-spade or *slèan* inscribes his signature and sets the pace in the winning of a peaty harvest. The bog is a strange and elemental place where the hand of humanity abides. Finds in the cut-away may be as wondrous as the stumps of great oak so perfectly aligned that they could only have been planted by people.[28] As well, the realm of the bog is ruggedly utilitarian, and we move from the edge where turf is cut to the hearth at the centre where turf burns. Thus the people of Ballymenone impose their will from core to margin. Their's is a world of intimate realms where they pass the time and scribble out their names.

Moving south again across the border, we may repair to a part of the drumlin country which is scarcely known at all. This is a neighbourhood lying asleep among the low hills, some three miles to the north of Ballinamore in Co. Leitrim. As ever the prefixes *druim* and *corr* introduce the lie of the land, and townlands such as Drumbad, Cornageeragh and Cornacreeve exemplify it fully (fig 1.6.). Life is much depleted now relative to a generation or so ago. The houses have been swept out of the back lanes; the young have been vacuumed up by Dublin, London or New York. Smithy and school have gone. Signatories to the landscape have grown old and isolated; the community has reached a stage of terminal decline. In this kind of situation much is consigned to memory awaiting the occasional *céilí*

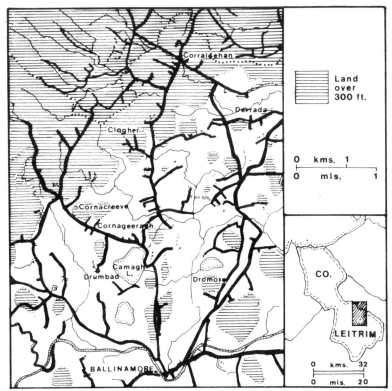

Fig. 1.6.   Land of the little hills around Ballinamore, Co. Leitrim

when neighbours may recall Micky 'Sammy' (McKeon) of Drumbad
and his freshly baked cakes, cloth-wrapped and steaming and smelling
deliciously, and left out on the window sill to cool; or the Brady men,
father and son, out spraying potatoes with bluestone on the black
ground at the bottom of Cornacreeve; or Maggie Anne Gilheany of
Clogher out 'on the briar', picking blackberries for sale by the stone; or
a willing assistant with an unwilling pony poised perilously over the
lane at Cornacreeve, while raking the hill meadow.

This is a neighbourhood in which the forester has stamped his
presence. At Skerahoo and Doon, the old outreach of the bog has been
ceded completely in favour of maturing Sitka spruce. It is impossible
to find a locational bearing anymore for those who may have tasted the
pleasures of Skerahoo on Bilberry Sunday or knew where 'Paddy the
Bog' lived high up in Doon. The forest has swallowed up whole
swathes of the countryside, taking in contours, place-names, old
signatures —- everything. It has spread downslope too where it is
sometimes met by the whin displaying all the fertility of sin. It tops the

24

round hill of Cornacreeve, having obliterated the holdings and habitations of the Creamers and the Beirnes, and it hovers threateningly above the last inhabited farm in the townland, where Florrie McKeon, a widow in her seventies, lives. She alone has withstood an exodus that has seen off all of her own family and all of her nearest neighbours, and after her there is no one to forestall the bland hand of the forester. Sadly, the prospect of the same bland signature hangs over the entire neighbourhood.

If the area around Cornacreeve stands for a hidden rural Ireland - a loaded metaphor if ever there was one - then we must go elsewhere in search of the signatures that denote a new and modern Ireland. Inevitably we are drawn into the ambit of an urbanising world, given people's preference for life in and around our expanding cities and towns. Urban dwellers have by now decisively eclipsed rural dwellers and this is compelling enough reason to look to the urban scene for markers of identity and modernity. We shall certainly find them there. It is only a matter of looking, seeing and selecting, and of following along intuitive lines. In our quest for urban signatures we find ourselves drawn persuasively northwards by a modern poet's vision of the modern city. Ciaran Carson is the poet and Belfast is his city.

Carson's is a much written over city. At times he feels that every inch of Belfast has, in a literal sense, seen a succession of writing, erasure and re-writing. [29] There is a plethora of messages to behold. In a divided society these may proclaim liminality as in 'WELCOME TO PROVO LAND', or they may be directed specifically at insiders as in 'WE SHALL NOT FORSAKE THE BLUE SKIES OF FREEDOM FOR THE GREY MISTS OF AN IRISH REPUBLIC / NO

Plate 1.4. A message proclaiming liminality in a city where Carson, the poet, invests the spatial order with the meaning of the moment

25

SURRENDER', or they may be aimed at patrolling British soldiers as in 'When you came to this land / You said you came to understand. / Soldier we're tired of your understanding. / Tired of the knock upon the door. / Tired of the rifle-butt on the head. / Tired of the jails and the beatings. / Tired of the deaths of old friends. / Tired of the tears and funerals - / those endless endless funerals. / Is this your understanding ?' [30] There is also a spate of Loyalist and Republican acronyms which are painted on walls and which may sometimes accompany elaborate murals. Painted curses are directed outwards; political imperatives are meant to firm the resolve of insiders. But most of all, Carson sees a succession of ordinary names and nicknames emblazoned across the face of his native city. He finds litanies of signatures on gable walls, all asking to be remembered.

Plate 1.5. Signatures of insiders writ large in Glenalpin Street in south Belfast where everything is in a state of preparedness for the annual Twelfth of July celebrations

Carson tunes in sensitively to one of the major themes of urbanisation - the capacity for perennial renewal. The old insignias of his city are disappearing daily.[31] For instance, the imposing Victorian facade of the Grand Central Hotel which dominated the whole of Royal Avenue and which later saw service as an army barracks, was in its place one day and gone the next. The levelling hand simply erases everything that was, and instead novel arrangements are cobbled together in the urban wilderness. Carson enumerates these markers of transition - pizza parlours, massage parlours, night-clubs, drinking clubs, antique shops,

26

designer studios - which invade and succeed. However, these too will vanish with the dawn. Everything is apt to be revised. Familiar pubs bearing familiar names give way to a miscellany of land uses. The tangled net of streets known as Pound Loney came to be transformed into the Divis Flats in accordance with the high-rise optimism of the 1960s, only to be falling asunder in the 1980s, and fit again for replacement. Gerry Hunter of the Birmingham Six returns home to a birthplace that no longer is; everything he had known has been erased by a new estate.[32] The city as a whole is a kind of palimpsest which bears the up-to-date signatures of its people.

Such are the dynamics of change that the map as guide is unreliable. In a long-troubled city it fails to capture the moment posed by ramps, barricades, diversions, peace lines. Carson explores the inner urban being : ' The city is a map of the city / Its forbidden areas changing daily,' [33] and like James Joyce he is on hand to read all kinds of signatures. That of the bomber may be signalled by an avalanche of glass and cast into relief by casualties. That of the rioter may litter a whole street with half-bricks, broken glass and battered artefacts. That of the gunman may be etched in blood on doorsteps. Those of a stricken people may be reflected, as we remember them in August 1969, by hastily erected barricades of buses and bakery vans and felled trees on and off the Falls Road, and by poor souls on the move with their possessions in whatever mode of transport they could muster, desperate in their quest for sanctuary. Carson takes in much of this in the course of his peregrinations through the city. All the while on his bike, he is testing observation against memory, noting change, and decrying the limitations of the map. He might well append the signature of a geographical *manqué* to the results of his urban explorations.

As Carson sees it, brick is the hallmark of Belfast.[34] The city is built on *sleech* - alluvial or tidal mud - and is built on sleech, metamorphosed into brick. Moreover, the city devoured its source as the brickfields themselves were built upon. Brick underpinned the great building cycles of the nineteenth century; the painter Paul Henry, for instance, could recall no more familiar sight from childhood than 'the unending procession of carts of bricks with which Belfast was feverishly built.' [35] Carson also invokes the subversive half-brick which has seen service in the hands of generations of rioters and the coal-brick or *breek* being hawked on a hand-cart through the smoggy backstreets of his youth. He then returns to the theme of erasure as he sees the brickwork of rampant industrialisation - chimney-stack, mill and kiln - crumbling back into the dust. The city recycles itself.

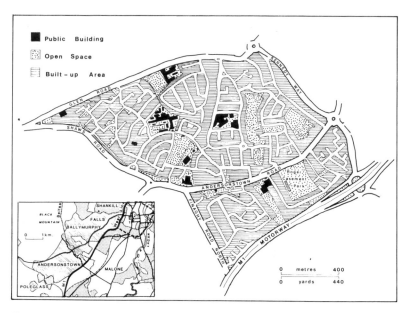

Fig. 1.7.   Andersonstown where brick made its *rustic* début in the 1950s, and which is now a fully fledged suburb of Belfast

Disassembled buildings are poured back into the sleech of the lough shore; sludge becomes *terra firma*. New worlds marked by new signatures again become possible. In the new suburbs too, as in Andersonstown of the 1950s, brick makes its *rustic* début. This is where Carson grew up and where as a boy he built cities of clay by a secret stream. The child may well be father to the man because years later we still find him making and re-making the modern city, while casting and re-casting the signatures of its people.

Signs and Symbols

> *The cumulative culture of our perceptions is like a geological stratigraphy. Thus one considers an increasing number of signs, symbols and significations in the landscape, and their complexities of meaning have caused them to become distinct fields of investigation* [36]

> *Symbols give us our identity, our self-image, our way of explaining ourselves to ourselves, and to others* [37]

Like many of us growing up in the 1940s and 50s, the poet, Seamus Heaney, is able to recall a world then on the wane in which the landscape was subject to reverence. [38] It still held - if only vestigially - the status of a sacral being in accordance with the tenets of an older rite. At every turn there were signs and significations to ponder and behold. For example, on walking to school the young boy was able to pick out Lough Beg from a spot known as Mulholland's Brae, and there below him the spire of Church Island rose out of the trees. This was a local mecca where people gathered on Church Island Sunday in September because, in accordance with a long-cherished tradition, St. Patrick had prayed there. Straightaway associations form and we are reminded of other lakeside or lake isle settings and of their aura of sanctity. These would include such little known islets in midland lakes as Church Island in Lough Owel and Dysart Island in Lough Ennell which lie respectively to the north and to the south of Mullingar in Co. Westmeath, as well as such celebrated places of pilgrimage as Station Island in Lough Derg in Co. Donegal and Our Lady's island in south Co. Wexford. Already by the middle ages Lough Derg had won international renown as a place of penitence, while Our Lady's Island counted among the immemorial holy places indulgenced by Pope Paul V at the beginning of the seventeenth century. [39]

We are reminded too of the cult of St. Patrick and of its far-flung adoption throughout Ireland. This was because later propagandists at Armagh did a superb job in fusing the activities of at least two early missionaries and in raising the name of this composite personage on high. Patrick's *Life* became the text of the greatest, while acting as a kind of mythical dictionary for the rest. Accordingly his name was carried to places he had never visited and venerated among people to whom he had never preached, and as befitted his heroic status, he left his enduring mark in life and in landscape. It is not surprising therefore to find the great hero of early Christian Ireland praying with such intensity that he should forever brand the shape of his knee into a stone in the old churchyard at Church Island, Lough Beg, in Co. Derry; or that he should leave his tracks permanently etched in the ground at Clonarney near Delvin in Co. Westmeath; or that his should be the abiding name associated with our greatest places of pilgrimage, as at Croagh Patrick and Lough Derg. The Patrician cult asserts itself in settlements as far apart as Downpatrick, Co. Down and Ardpatrick, Co. Limerick, in innumerable churches and holy wells, in place lore and in legend. Patrick, the national saint, has indelibly forged his name in the minds of our people and in the landscapes they have fashioned.

Like many of the early saints, Patrick's name is linked with high

Plate 1.6. Possessing all the mystique of a holy mountain, the hump of Slemish in Co. Antrim furnishes us with the genesis of the cult of Patrick

places. The hill of Slane and the hill of Tara in Co. Meath spring readily to mind, as do Croagh Patrick in Co. Mayo and Slemish in Co. Antrim, the scene of his earliest asceticism. On the road to school, Seamus Heaney was able to pick out the well-defined hump of Slemish where a youthful Patrick had tended sheep and had risen in the frosts of winter to pray. In the young Heaney mind, Slemish possesses all the mystique of a holy mountain. It also furnishes us with an example of the potency of the mountain cult, because in all religions mountains play a greater role than all the rest of natural sanctuaries together. [40] Since the most ancient times mountains have been considered a seat of the gods, especially of the heavenly gods and bright powers to whom the people looked up from below, and who gazed down upon the people, blessing them. Their veneration is further echoed in many places in the Bible, where the finest expression occurs in the beginning of the 121st Psalm : 'I will lift up mine eyes unto the hills, from whence cometh my help.'

In Ireland as elsewhere the mountain cult has endured with remarkable tenacity. Holy mountains which abide in the folk memory and which may still be remembered as places of pilgrimage include Slieve Donard in Co. Down, Church Mountain in Co. Wicklow, and Mount Brandon in Co. Kerry. All are layered with meanings compounded out of Christianity and the elder faiths. [41] For instance in the case of Slieve Donard (2796' O.D.), the highest peak of the Mourne

30

Mountains, we find the traditions of a holy mountain shot through by ancient pagan associations. Here a perpetual guardian gives his name to the mountain, Christianity triumphs over paganism, and a pilgrimage takes place on a day associated with Crom Dubh, the old pagan deity and opponent of St. Patrick. At Church Mountain (1789' O.D.), a western spur of the Wicklows overlooking Dunlavin, similar motifs are in evidence. Here at the edge of the settled land of Leinster, a burial cairn crowns a holy mountain where a church was later built and where a pilgrimage was made on the Sunday before Lughnasa.[42] Like Slieve Donard, Mount Brandon (3127' O.D.) is among the most imposing of our tutelary mountains as it thrusts skywards towards the extremity of the Corca Dhuibhne peninsula. Bréanainn mac Fionnlogha, the great seafaring saint, has stamped an imposing presence here and much of

Plate 1.7. Full of the signs of its illustrious saint, Croagh Patrick stands sentinel above the Connacht lowlands

31

the toponymy of the mountain is commemorative of him. Associations also occur with the legendary Fionn, with the triumph of Christianity over paganism, and with a pilgrimage on Domhnach Chrom Dubh. Indeed the mountain as a whole is alive with signs - monumental, mystical and mythical - and known immemorially to the pilgrim and the shepherd.

All the foregoing pale by comparison with Croagh Patrick (2510' O.D.), the most famous of the pilgrimage mountains of Ireland. Popularly known as the 'Reek', it commands a magnificent setting alongside the southern shore of Clew Bay. Here its steep quartzite cone rises abruptly from a narrow ridge, so that for the seeing eye there is no distraction from the pureness of the mountain's shape. The sublime nature of its appearance and its visibility for miles around have helped to make the 'Reek' the holiest mountain in Ireland. From a very early date it was associated with St. Patrick. It is full of the signs of the illustrious saint, whether these be framed in vision or legend, or tracked in pilgrim route, or mounted in summit oratory. As ever traces of the elder faiths linger, and the traditional day for performing the pilgrimage was Domhnach Chrom Dubh, the Sunday before the first of August. Nowadays nearly everything is transmuted into Christian meanings. Thousands pause prayerfully at points on the ascent known as 'stations' and at the summit Masses are celebrated.

Along with holy mountains, heights all over the country have commanded veneration and have acted as places of resort. Sustaining the point, a detailed survey of the celebration of the festival of Lughnasa alone lists a total of 91 heights distributed over 28 counties[43] (fig.1.8.). All are, or were in the past, vivified with signs and among the more notable are Slieve Callan in west Clare, Knockfeerina in mid Limerick, Árd Éireann in the Slieve Bloom country of Laois-Offaly, and Ardagh hill in Co. Longford. Slieve Callan (1284' O.D.) is rich in legend and resonant of the names that betoken the old cult of sun worship. Knockfeerina (948' O.D.) takes its name from the fairy-king Donn Fírinne whose extraordinary powers over the human psyche may be recalled from early in the century when an old man on his deathbed looked out over Knockfeerina and said that he 'would be up there soon on the Black Hill —- where Donn marshals his men.'[44] Árd Éireann (1734' O.D.) merits note for the vast expanses it commands and for the weather lore associated with it. Ardagh Hill (650' O.D.), one of the most famous fairy haunts in Ireland, is steeped in the spirit world, so much so that in modern times a quarry on the hill had to be abandoned because the men working there were mysteriously 'pegged' with stones and sods.[45]

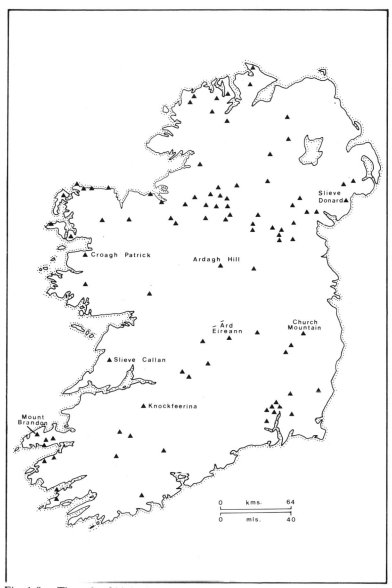

Fig. 1.8. The cult of high places as exemplified by celebration of the festival of Lughnasa (adapted from MacNeill, 1962)

The two great centres of Irish mythology - Uisneach and Tara - both command hill sites and both serve as founts of an Irish state of mind. Although Tara was the centre of political power, the hill of Uisneach (602' O.D.) near Ballymore in Co. Westmeath may once have equalled

33

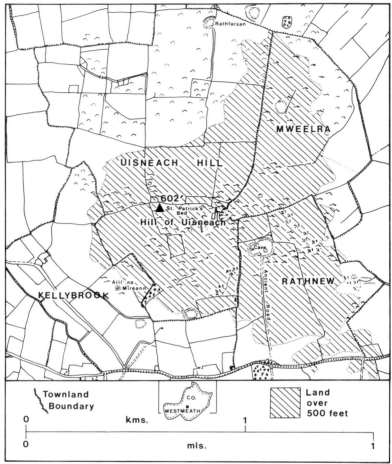

Fig. 1.9.   Uisneach near Ballymore in Co. Westmeath, the accepted centre or
omphalos of Ireland

it in prestige. Moreover, the duality of Uisneach and Tara as ritual sites
is paralleled in other Indo-European cultures as far apart as Rome and
India. [46] It would appear that both sites originally represented
microcosmic symbols and that while Tara evolved as the primary seat
of kingship, Uisneach - the accepted centre or *omphalos* of Ireland -
continued to represent the principle of primordial unity in which all
oppositions are resolved. The landscapes of both are deeply symbolic.
Not only did the provinces and their kingships focus upon these centres
and fuse together, but there was a commonality of such symbols as a
hill, a stone, a palace, a seat, a tree, a well, a fire. Uisneach, for
instance, features a large erratic known as Aill na Míreann (the Rock of
the Divisions) which is said to be the navel of Ireland. Tara counters

Plate 1.8. Tara, Co. Meath, an enigmatic, multi-period site, which will forever
claim precedence as the seat of the high kings

with the Lia Fáil (the Stone of Destiny), the most daring phallic symbol
of ancient Ireland, and a monument which stresses the ritual
significance of the inauguration of kings. In terms of the occupational
and funerary traces they contain, both are enigmatic, multi-period sites,
and while Tara will forever claim precedence as the seat of the high
kings, Uisneach will abide as the home of the druids.

The provincial capitals of ancient Ireland shared many attributes with
those of the centre. Almost without exception they upheld the cult of
high places by standing on hills, or at least on artificial mounds. They
were places of burial and as such were invested with sacred meanings.
Like later churches, they bore dedications to the memory of founders,
who were usually believed to be buried in them. Almost invariably the
founders were female. Thus in the centre we may invoke the names of

Ériu in association with Uisneach and Tea with Tara, while in the provinces we may link the names of the war-goddess Macha with Emhain Macha near Armagh; Nás, the wife of Lug, with Naas in Co. Kildare; and the handmaiden, Cruacha, with Cruachan in Co. Roscommon.[47] Continuing the analogy with churches, most of the Irish centres were archetypal *notre dames* which acted as great places of assembly at sacred points in the yearly cycle. To-day they are potential feeders of our image of Ireland and are emblematic of the provinces they once commanded.

Plate 1.9. With its crown of ruined and desolate buildings, the Rock of Cashel looms in Irish minds as one of our leading totems

None is more symbolic than the Rock of Cashel. This remarkable outcrop rises abruptly from the rolling plain country of south Tipperary, the *Clár Geal Mumhan* of olden song and the hearthland of Munster. With its crown of ruined and desolate buildings, it looms in Irish minds as one of our leading totems and at any time its acropolis-like form could not have failed to strike imagination. Like Uisneach and Tara, its origins are lost in a web of contact with the supernatural world and like them also it features an assemblage of ancient motifs such as a tree, a rock, a fire and a flagstone. It presides over choice lowlands which are accessible in all directions and its pre-eminence stems from temporal as well as spiritual dominion. At Caiseal 'Mumhan the king of Cashel was synonymous with the king of Munster. Here he was guardian of the sacred fane of a rich and fertile region and his influence spread out over an entire province. Cashel had for the south of Ireland a nimbus akin to that of Tara in the midlands, but unlike Tara it was sanctified by Christianity. The Rock of many legends became known as St. Patrick's Rock and Cashel's exalted status was maintained as an arch-diocesan see.

From this cursory survey of the cult of high places, it is clear that the Irish landscape acts as a repository of signs and symbols which have fed imaginations for millennia. It provides, if we like, the layering for a view of the world in which the lore and superstition of the elder faiths was compounded with the thought and practice of Christianity. Once considered sacred, the landscape in living memory still commanded a measure of veneration. Much of the flora of the countryside, for example, had a religious force which was consistent with the root of the word *religare* , to bind fast. Country people have known instinctively the bind of such small trees and shrubs as the rowan, holly, elderberry and whitethorn ever since the elder faiths had endowed these with magic. Going back to origins, the evidence of archaeology and palaeobotany suggests that these plants first established dominion as weeds of cultivation following on from forest clearance.[48] Thus they would bind the psyche of farming peoples and become symbols of the farming year. Their white blossoms signalled the quickening pulse of spring and the end of killing frosts; their red berries held the promise of harvest and the seeds of renewed life.

The lone thorn was singled out for special attention. It bound people to the potent world of fairies and thus was found to command a considerable measure of awe. For example, one researcher reporting from Co. Laois in the 1930s noted that farmers still dreaded the prospect of interfering with a solitary thorn bush on their land [49]; another reporting on the folklore of Ulster in the early 1950s had never personally known of a fairy thorn to suffer interference at human hands.[50] Such reticence is easy to understand in a farming community tied to the belief that the lone thorn - like many of the habitats of an otherworld community - was protected by the sanction of swift retribution should anyone care to tamper with it. Moreover, the stories of retribution were always sufficiently rife to ensure the fairy thorn's standing as a characteristic feature of the landscape. They are to be found in every part of Ireland, but we will see them at best silhouetted against the sky on bare hillsides. E. Estyn Evans was drawn towards Slieve Gullion in south Armagh to sketch a cluster of gentle thorns standing sentinel over the 'hungry grass' [51] and near there also at Cloughinnea at dusk, Michael J. Murphy was struck by the *genius loci* on seeing a fairy thorn rise from one of its rocks 'as if to beat the embers of a burnt-out skyline.' [52]

In our mind's eye we can see the round of the year symbolised in the flora of the countryside; we can see the bonding of people with flora and the eternal verities that were worked out in the interplay between elder and newer faiths. The landscape was charged with meaning. To mark February 1 - the start of the farming year - green rushes were cut and plaited into crosses. This rite of entry bound people to the beneficent spirit of St. Brighid and it bound them into a ritualised way of life. Then on May Eve, blossoms and flowers appeared on doorsteps and window sills as enjoined by the Blessed Virgin and by a pagan goddess before her. The May bush was another token of welcome to the summer as it stood near homes in certain well-defined parts of the country, festooned with flowers and trinkets [53] (fig. 1.10.a). It was

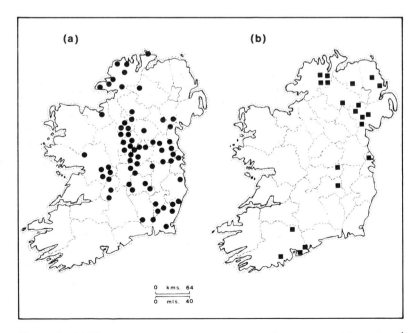

Fig. 1.10. (a) May bush and (b) harvest knot in the Irish folk tradition (after Ó Danachair, 1965)

38

meant to bring luck and protection to the house as well as symbolising the good times to come. When such times came with the harvest there were other rites to be entered into as small ornamental twists or knots of plaited straw were made and worn as a sign of fulfilment. This was a custom known in old tillage country such as Fingal in north Co. Dublin and Imokilly in east Co. Cork, and it was known too in the planter lands of Ulster and Laois-Offaly (fig. 1.10.b). Then on to Samhain Eve at the end of the farming year when more malevolent spirits stirred abroad than at any other time, items such as apples, nuts, cabbages, turnips, ivy and fern-seed were bound into pranks and divination games, [54] and in turn bound participants into the psychic landscape of otherworld.

Plate 1.10. At one time, conifers in a row on the bank of a double ditch are gaunt and gormless; at another, they are silhouetted against a darkening sky, their tattiness gone

Enough has been gleaned from Irish space and time to show that we live in an island laminated with many meanings. In our sensing of it we are bound by countless variables, but most of all by who we are and where we come from. There are only small locales that we can ever know intimately, especially the landscape of home. I live now in Coolanoran [55] where I walk the fields in spring, taking in the signs and trading in some magic of mind that touches on symbols. I pass a lone thorn in a field where the dog always barks, that strange bark, that elicits no known response. Prongs of buds everywhere take hold of the thorn hedges and there is the yolk-yellow splash of the furze to lend an intermittent glow. At one time, conifers in a row on the bank of a double ditch are gaunt and gormless; at another, they are silhouetted against a darkening sky, their tattiness gone. I see a pair of duck, lovers in flight, to the water of life. Earlier on, the cows are corralled in their winter quarters where calves scurry about; later, they graze inside an electrified strip, their flanks still pasted with the glue of over-wintering. I traverse a perfect rectangular field - elongated, insulated, grassy - a micro-world tucked away in cow country. One farmstead turns in upon itself and its suite of outbuildings; another shows a red-brick face to the road and to the world. Their respective spheres abut along the line of bank and master drain where small fields run into big and shades of green collide.

Deep rutted gaps tell of exits and entrances near rushy headlands. Fresh cowshit charts paths of movement through fields carpeted with buttercups. To the east, the line of the road - the N21 - imposes dictates of a different order on life and movement as it becomes more and more a conveyor belt for traffic originating in Dublin, Limerick, Tralee, Newcastle West, wherever! It is an unremitting gatherer of the trappings of modernity, ranging in line of vision from timbered silhouette to illuminated forecourt. Beyond it, the eye ranges over Loghill where O'Faolain came upon *A nest of simple folk* in a time warp by the Deel,[56] and out over a ridge which culminates in Knockfeerina, the fairy hill. To the west past Ardagh, the scene is framed by the hill edge I have known all my life. This arcuate rim has always drawn me to the world of all my paternal ancestors, which it shields. Now on a spring evening, ancestral truths merge with eternal truths as the sun sets behind the hills.

And so this landscape for me has many meanings, in lines received and lines made; in affective signs and symbols; in feeling and in movement. I can only offer it as a token of the coded land which intrigues me now and then : here and in many places.

Notes and References

1. S. Heaney, *Door into the dark*, London, 1969, 21.
2. W. L. Morton, 'Seeing an unliterary landscape', *Mosaic* 3, 1970, 3.
3. D. Corkery, *The hidden Ireland*, Dublin, 1967, 64-5.
4. J. Joyce, *Ulysses*, (Paris 1922) London, 1986.
5. W.B. Yeats, *Collected poems*, London, 1990, 39-41.
6. N. Ní Dhomhnaill, *Selected poems*, Dublin, 1986, 84-5.
7. P. Kavanagh, *The green fool*, Harmondsworth, 1975, 7-8.
8. S. Heaney, *Preoccupations : selected prose 1968-1978*, London, 1978, 35.
9. S. Heaney, *Selected poems 1965-1975*, London, 1980, 58-70.
10. J. Hewitt, *The selected John Hewitt*, Belfast, 1981, 24.
11. J. Hewitt, *Freehold and other poems*, Belfast, 1986, 25-7.
12. J. Hewitt, *The rain dance*, Belfast, 1978, 16-17.
13. J. Montague, *The rough field*, Mountrath, 1984, 34.
14. *Ibid.*, 35.
15. T. Jones Hughes, ' Town and baile in Irish place-names,' in N. Stephens and R.E. Glasscock (eds.), *Irish geographical studies*, Belfast, 1970, 246.
16. P.J. O'Connor, 'Medieval regionalism in north county Kerry : concepts and criteria,' *Journal of the Kerry Archaeological and Historical Society*, 21, 1988, 119-20. North Co. Kerry coincides with the medieval shire and liberty of Kerry, i.e. that part of the modern county which lies to the north of the River Maine.
17. T. Jones Hughes, 1970, *op. cit.*, 247.
18. A Ó Maolfabhail (cag.), *Logaimneacha na hÉireann 1 : contae Luimnigh*, Baile Átha Cliath, 1990.
19. S. Ó Catháin and P. O'Flanagan, *The living landscape : Kilgalligan, Erris, Co. Mayo*, Dublin, 1975, 242.
20. L. Durrell, *Justine*, New York, 1961, 112.
21. J. Joyce, 1986, *op. cit.*, 31.
22. E.E. Evans, *The personality of Ireland*, Belfast, 1981, 40.
23. J. Appleton, *The poetry of habitat*, Hull, 1978, 12.
24. P. Kavanagh, *Collected poems*, London, 1972, 35.
25. *Ibid.*, 31, 68.
26. H. Glassie, *Passing the time in Ballymenone*, Dublin, 1982, xiii.
27. *Ibid.*, 450.
28. *Ibid.*, 483.
29. C. Carson. *Belfast confetti*, Oldcastle, 1989, 52.
30. Cited in J. Darby, *Intimidation and the control of conflict in Northern Ireland*, Dublin, 1986, 107-8.
31. C. Carson, 1989, *op. cit.*, 57-69.
32. K. Dawson, ' The sweet joys of freedom,' *Sunday Tribune*, 17 March, 1991, 1.
33. C. Carson, *The new estate and other poems*, Oldcastle, 1988, 32.

34. C. Carson, 1989, *op. cit.*, 72-5.
35. P. Henry, *Further reminiscences*, Belfast, 1973, 19.
36. S. Quoniam, ' A painter, geographer of Arizona,' *Environment and planning D : society and space* 6, 1988, 4.
37. M. Robinson, ' Presidential inauguration speech,' *Irish Times,* 4 December, 1990, 3.
38. S. Heaney, 1978, *op.cit.*, 132-4.
39. P.J. Corish, ' Two centuries of catholicism in county Wexford,' in K. Whelan (ed.) *Wexford : history and society,* Dublin, 1987, 223.
40. P. Fickeler, ' Fundamental questions in the geography of religions,' in P.L. Wagner and M.W. Mikesell (eds.), *Readings in cultural geography,* Chicago, 1962, 109.
41. M. MacNeill, *The festival of Lughnasa,* Oxford, 1962, 84-105.
42. Lughnasa was one of the quarterly feasts of the old Irish year celebrated on August 1 and later associated with the beginning of harvest.
43. M. MacNeill, 1962, *op. cit.,* 106-242.
44. K. Müller-Lisowski, ' Contributions to a study in Irish folklore,' *Béaloideas,* 18, 1948, 157.
45. M. MacNeill, 1962, *op. cit.*, 242.
46. A. and B. Rees, *Celtic heritage,* London, 1976, 162.
47. *Ibid.,* 167.
48. E.E. Evans, *Irish folk ways,* London, 1967, 297.
49. H.M. Roe, ' Tales, customs and beliefs from Laoighis,' *Béaloideas,* 9,1, 1939, 35.
50. J.C. Foster, *Ulster folklore,* Belfast, 1951 110.
51. E.E. Evans, 1967, *op. cit.,* 297. The ' hungry grass ' was said to be a patch of grass - mostly on hillsides - on which someone might unwittingly walk and thus become afflicted with great hunger. To obviate the effects of the magical hunger wayfarers were obliged to bring some bread with them in their pockets.
52. M.J. Murphy, *Mountain year,* Chester Springs, Pennsylvania, 1965, 31.
53. C. Ó Danachair, ' Distribution patterns in Irish folk tradition,' *Béaloideas,* 33,1965, 104-6.
54. K. Danaher, *The year in Ireland,* Cork, 1972, 214-27.
55. The townland of Coolanoran (Cúil an Fhuaráin, *the corner of the spring*) straddles the low-lying borderland between the parishes of Ardagh, Knockaderry and Newcastle in west Co. Limerick.
56. S. O'Faolain, *A nest of simple folk,* London, 1933, 14.

The Growth of Sociability

H. R. Schaffer

Penguin Books

Penguin Books Ltd, Harmondsworth,
Middlesex, England
Penguin Books Inc., 7110 Ambassador Road,
Baltimore, Md 21207, U.S.A.
Penguin Books Australia Ltd,
Ringwood, Victoria, Australia

First published 1971
Copyright © H. R. Schaffer, 1971

Made and printed in Great Britain by
Hazell, Watson & Viney Ltd,
Tring Road, Aylesbury, Bucks
Set in Linotype Times

To Evelyn, Malcolm and Katie

Penguin Science of Behaviour

This book is one of an ambitious project, the Penguin Science of Behaviour, which covers a very wide range of psychological inquiry. Many of the short 'unit' texts are on central teaching topics, while others deal with present theoretical and empirical work which the Editors consider to be important contributions to psychology. We have kept in mind both the teaching divisions of psychology and also the needs of psychologists at work. For readers working with children, for example, some of the units in the field of Developmental Psychology will deal with psychological techniques in testing children, other units will deal with work on cognitive growth. For academic psychologists, there will be units in well-established areas such as Cognitive Psychology, but also units which do not fall neatly under any one heading, or which are thought of as 'applied', but which nevertheless are highly relevant to psychology as a whole.

The project is published in short units for two main reasons. Firstly, a large range of short texts at inexpensive prices gives the teacher a flexibility in planning his course and recommending texts for it. Secondly, the pace at which important new work is published requires the project to be adaptable. Our plan allows a unit to be revised or a fresh unit to be added with maximum speed and minimal cost to the reader.

Above all, for students, the different viewpoints of many authors, sometimes overlapping, sometimes in contradiction, and the range of topics Editors have selected will reveal the complexity and diversity which exist beyond the necessarily conventional headings of an introductory course.

B.M.F.

Contents

Editorial Foreword   11

1   Introduction: The Study of Infancy   13

2   The Primary Attraction to Social Objects   32

3   Social Signalling Systems   60

4   The Familiarization Process   81

5   Formation of the Bond   106

6   The Nature of the First Relationship   132

7   Stimulation and Deprivation   153

References   177

Acknowledgements   190

Index   191

Editorial Foreword

Over the last few years there has been a marked change in the way that psychologists have studied infants and children. Until a decade or so ago, the literature was dominated by perhaps three main approaches: mapping out the norms and stages of maturation or development, both physical and psychological; theorizing about child development, in attempts to explain personality and abnormality in terms of genetics and early experience, using psychoanalytic or learning theories; and studying the process of socialization by which a child learns the skills, values, beliefs and so on of his society, and relating this study to methods of upbringing and education.

These three approaches are still pursued, but there is now a fourth, rapidly developing approach, which is to study in the child the origins of processes and mechanisms such as attention, language skills, exploration and so on. Such study is carried out using observation and experiment, usually with a conscious effort to resist the kind of experimenter bias which results from holding a theory too strongly. Some of the processes being studied are of particular importance to those interested in the development of social behaviour and personality. These are the processes which ensure that an infant develops attachments to particular people, to other children, to objects, eventually to groups of people, and in contrast remains neutral or even dislikes or fears other people and things. It would seem reasonable to believe that these processes are basic in the development of prejudice, loyalty, affection, taking sides, moral judgement and, paradoxically, parental behaviour.

Professor Schaffer is a leading British investigator of the

growth of sociability. His own experiments on infants and older children are methodologically sophisticated and of considerable significance. He has an international reputation and he himself knows well the related foreign work. Indeed, many of the principal psychologists in this field are personal friends of his.

This book includes detailed studies of crying and smiling, fear of strangers, deprivation, the effects of familiarity, and other matters which are relevant to the formation of the first bonds of affection. It will be essential reading for students taking courses in child development or child psychology. It will also be an ideal introduction to this fascinating study for educationalists, therapists, pediatricians, and anyone interested in the origins of behaviour.

B.M.F.

1 Introduction: The Study of Infancy

At birth an infant is essentially an asocial being. He has as yet no orientation to other people as such; he does not know his mother and cannot differentiate one person from another; and his means of communication are limited in range and egocentric in nature. He cries and his mother attends to him, but he has not yet learned to use this signal in order purposely to manipulate his social environment. Other people, he soon finds out, are fascinating things to watch and feel and listen to, but as yet they do not constitute a class of stimuli distinct from the inanimate world. Indeed, the boundaries between the self and the nonself have still to become established and until this occurs the difference between inner and outer, self-produced and other-produced stimulation remains without meaning.

A year later all this has changed. The child (as Konrad Lorenz once put it) has now joined the human race. He has learned to distinguish familiar people from strangers, he has developed a repertoire of signalling abilities which he can use discriminatively in relation to particular situations and individuals, and he is about to acquire such social skills as language and imitation. Above all, he has formed his first love relationship: a relationship which many believe to be the prototype of all subsequent ones, providing him with that basic security which is an essential ingredient of personality development. In short, the first and most fundamental steps in the child's socializing process have been taken. How they have been taken is the concern of this book.

Our aim is to present a progress report of work undertaken in an attempt to understand this problem. Much of this work is of very recent origin, for it is only of late that an empirical rather than a purely speculative approach has emerged in this field. Indeed, the study of infant behaviour in general has only recently come to be regarded as a feasible topic for empirical investigations. Throughout the ages, it is true, questions have been asked about the earliest stages of development and their role in personality formation and throughout the ages answers have been offered – sometimes tentatively, sometimes dogmatically. Infants, it was held at one time, are essentially 'mind-less' creatures, enclosed in their shells and unaffected by their encounters with the environment. Infants, it was believed at another time, are highly impressionable beings and it is, therefore, the earliest experiences that leave the most indelible marks. Yet none of these views was based on anything but guesswork or dogma, for however great the curiosity the technical problem of studying a speechless organism with only minimal motor capacities appeared insuperable. Even after the emergence of psychology as a scientific discipline the way into the infant seemed closed, and while the investigation of psychological functions of both animals and older human beings forged ahead, the study of infancy remained on a speculative level.

Concepts of infancy

The widely divergent beliefs about the nature of infancy current in the first half of this century reflected the lack of available knowledge. How well organized is the psychological system in the early months of life? William James (1890), for one, had no doubt: 'The baby, assailed by eyes, ears, nose, skin and entrails all at once, feels it all as one great blooming, buzzing confusion.' In this oft-quoted passage James conjures up a picture of disarray and lack of organization, thereby stressing the infant's obvious inferiority in relation to older individuals and implying that such an organism can hardly be a fit subject for psychological inquiry. An essentially negative concept of infancy was thereby fostered and it is no wonder than an attitude of pessimism prevailed among experimental psychologists as to the possibility of carrying out direct studies of such unpromising material. Organization, presumably, comes through experience, and not until sufficient experience has been accumulated and stored in an orderly fashion is empirical investigation feasible. Up to that point only chaos and confusion can be found.

Freud, on the other hand, was convinced that some order and meaning, however primitive, were evident from the beginning – in particular, that the infant was 'set' to assimilate certain types of experience at certain developmental stages and that these experiences had considerable implications for subsequent personality development. On the basis of 'memories' obtained from adult patients in the course of therapy it is possible, Freud believed, to reconstruct the nature of infantile functioning and to determine those experiences to which infants are maximally responsive. Libidinal theory, with its successive stages of bodily preoccupation, delineated the selective sensitivities of children at different ages and pointed to those environmental encounters which leave their permanent imprint in the form of fixation points. Thus from the beginning the infant is, by virtue of his biological endowment, equipped to attend selectively to particular kinds of experience and in this way to impose some order on an otherwise bewildering mass of sensations.

The experiences which Freud considered to play such a formative role were principally of a somatic nature: the struggle of the baby to obtain the maternal breast, the frustrations of scheduling and of weaning, the anger experienced in the toileting situation. A great deal of work went into the subsequent efforts on the part of psychologists to examine the causal relationships indicated by Freud and to find systematic support for his suggestions. Yet, as shown by a number of reviews (Caldwell, 1964; Orlansky, 1949; Sears, 1944), the unequivocal evidence hoped for was not obtained. Parents may be firmly convinced that the particular experiences encountered by their baby will mark him for good or ill for the rest of his life, but when we turn to scientific support for this assertion there is as yet not a single study available which firmly and without ambiguity demonstrates that a specific experience impinging at one particular point of time in early human development will leave permanent effects on that individual. Birth trauma, breast or bottle feeding, type of toilet training, swaddling practices – whatever their effects at the time, the lasting imprint of such events has not been demonstrated. The aphorism that the child is father to the man remains an article of faith rather than a scientifically supported conclusion.

There are various reasons for failure to substantiate Freudian hypotheses – the reliance in many studies on retrospectively obtained data, the many different operational definitions that can be attached to such a term as 'weaning', the difficulties of defining and measuring those aspects of personality considered to be affected by the early experience, the virtual impossibility in human subjects of controlling the course of events intervening between the two points at which measures are obtained. But over and above such methodological considerations a point of view emerges from these studies which was bound to have considerable implications for their findings. This is the assumption that a given experience must necessarily have the same effects on different children, that a particular infant care practice will have identical results on all to whom it is applied. The nature of the experiencing child, that is, is left out of consideration and subject variables which mediate the effects of specific events are thus not attended to. It is probably this factor more than any other which accounted for the failure of the above line of investigations and which has now convinced developmental psychologists of the need to pay attention to the experiencing infant rather than to the subsequent residual of the experience.

What are the forces that come to shape infant behaviour? Here we find one of the major issues that has divided psychologists in the past into, on the one hand, those who see the child as essentially an inert blob of clay that must be moulded by forces impinging upon him from the environment and, on the other hand, those who consider the child preformed and look upon development as largely an unfolding of inherent tendencies. It is easy to assert that heredity and environment must both play a part and there are few who would go against such a safe viewpoint. Yet in practice, and particularly so in relation to early development, we find the divergence of opinion a real and often a heated one.

J. B. Watson, the father of behaviourism, probably represents the empiricist tradition at its most extreme. 'The behaviourist finds that the human being at birth is a very lowly piece of unformed protoplasm, ready to be shaped by any family in whose care it is first placed' (1928). Dedicated to the principle of man's modifiability and with the use of the Pavlovian mechanism of the conditioned reflex as his explanatory tool, Watson confidently set out his recipe for producing superman. 'Give me a dozen healthy infants, well formed,' he asserted, 'and my own specified world to bring them up in, and I will guarantee to take any one at random and train him to become any type of specialist I might select – doctor, lawyer, artist, merchant chief, and yes, even beggarman and thief, regardless of his talents, penchants, tendencies, abilities, vocations, and the race of his ancestors' (1925). His conception of an infant was thus of a *tabula rasa* – of a blank slate on which experience inscribes what it will, of a being that starts life utterly formless and passive, lacking any inherent developmental design and predisposition. Psychological growth is a one-sided process: it is initiated and shaped solely by the infant's surroundings, and behaviour is to be understood purely in terms of the stimuli with which it happens to have been associated in the past. Parents can make what they will of their children; they can take the raw material ('a live squirming bit of flesh, capable of making a few simple responses such as movements of the hands and arms and fingers and toes, crying and smiling, making certain sounds with its throat' – Watson, 1928) and fashion it in ways to suit themselves. Thus, whatever psychological characteristics are to be found in a child are present by virtue of parental treatment. The role of organismic determinants of behaviour was brushed aside.

Equally one sided is the view of early development advanced by Arnold Gesell; only in his case it was intrinsic rather than extrinsic forces that were thought to determine the form, direction and rate of psychological growth. To Gesell the central concept of developmental psychology was maturation and, despite the lip-service which he continued to pay to the role of learning, the child, in his view, developed essentially according to the plan inherent in its germ plasm:

Specific ability in drawing, special interest in music, marked sociality, early facility in language, precocity in the use of generalizations and abstractions, all these manifest themselves in infancy in a way suggestive of native gifts or predispositions. . . . The study of such differences shows that the distinctive human individual traits come not by way of addition to a common substructure, but are laid down in the substructure itself (Gesell, 1928).

Gesell thus pictured early development as an orderly, predetermined unfolding of inherent capacities, affected to only minimal degree by the particular nature of an individual infant's encounters with the environment. The inevitability and certainty of maturation were to him the most impressive features of the early years, leading him to describe maturation as 'the hereditary ballast which conserves and stabilizes the growth of each individual infant'. He doubted whether the basic temperamental qualities of infants can be altered by environmental influence; he could find no evidence that fundamental acceleration of development can be induced by any particular method of stimulation; and he expressed gratitude for the fact that an infant is not a victim of the 'flaccid malleability' sometimes ascribed to him, as this would mean that he would fall only too easily a prey to misguided management.

As it is, the inborn tendency toward optimum development is so inveterate that he benefits liberally from what is good in our

practice, and suffers less than he logically should from our unen-
lightenment. Only if we give respect to this inner core of inheritance can we respect the important individual differences which
distinguish infants as well as man (Gesell, 1928).

Gesell was, however, no mere armchair theorist. His picture of early development derived from an empirical study
of infant development that was both intensive and extensive, and his efforts to map systematically the various stages
of early behavioural growth represent the first large-scale
attempt to provide an empirical foundation for the study of
infant behaviour. Yet, despite the emphasis on the role of
inherent determining forces, Gesell's approach is characterized by the fact that, psychologically speaking, it remained essentially outside the infant. Gesell, that is, was
content to study external manifestations – such as the nature
of eye–hand coordination or the development of vocalization – without relating these to any internal psychological
operations. It is true that he did base such functions on an
anatomical substratum and that he did discuss their physiological counterpart, but at no point did he attempt to relate
them to any internal mental structures. They remained mere
manifestations, the changes in which could only be explained in terms of a *deus ex machina*, the process of maturation. Gesell's infant was thus a creature whose ability to
pick up cubes and to turn from back to side could be observed and related to age norms, but about whose ability
to attend selectively to his environment, take in, process,
categorize and store the information so obtained, and then
carry out action sequences accordingly, no statements could
be made. Gesell, for all his almost lyrical descriptions of
central guiding processes, remained every bit as much outside the skin of the infant as Watson had done.

The traditions of Watson and Gesell are still with us,
though their expressions have changed. The Skinnerian
operant-conditioning model also insists on the need to stay
outside the individual and not to concern oneself with internal structures – psychological or physiological. Its application to infant behaviour has been clearly set out by Bijou

and Baer (1965) and by Gewirtz (1968). The task of the student of infant development, according to these writers, is to isolate those environmental stimuli which function at each growth point in order to control behaviour through the provision of either positive or negative reinforcement. For an environment to be functionally effective and bring about learning it must make available stimuli which can be discriminated by the child and reinforcers which are contingent on his behaviour. The identity of these is a matter of empirical investigation, but presumably any stimulus can be reinforcing if it is seen by the child to be a consequent of his behaviour. An infant, for instance, is more likely to smile if he has learned that his smile can produce certain effects upon other people; he will increase the rate of his vocalization if he finds that various pleasant consequences (auditory feedback from the sounds made by him, his mother laughing or talking back, and so on) regularly follow such behaviour. As long as the child is aware of the contingency relationship involved he will repeat whatever behaviour patterns have been reinforced in the past.

The cognitive-developmental approach

In emphasizing the role of environmental stimuli in the shaping of responses, the Skinnerian model tends to neglect all organismic determinants of behaviour. Yet as soon as one wishes to make statements about change and development, about learning and the effects of environmental impact, one must ask what it is that changes and learns and is affected by stimulation in such a way that future behaviour is altered by the previous experience. To do this, central structures of an enduring nature require to be hypothesized and it is these as much as external stimuli which will determine the form, direction and frequency of behaviour. An organism does not just happen to emit certain responses which then become linked to particular consequences – this is too mechanistic a view. Rather the individual, even in infancy, takes an active part in organizing his experience and in determining those stimuli to which he is exposed –

either by virtue of his genetic endowment or through influences representing the residue of past experience. To account for such organismic determinants, as well as for the ability to store information acquired and, for that matter, for the fact that changes in behaviour may occur under relatively invariant conditions, internal structures need to be postulated. Events under the skin, that is, must be considered.

Cognitive-developmental theory represents one attempt to do this. In fact, a number of somewhat differing views are combined under this one term, but all share three basic characteristics which distinguish them from conventional S–R theories (Baldwin, 1968; Kohlberg, 1968a, 1968b). First, they postulate a coding or representational process which intervenes between stimulus and response. Behaviour, that is, is not merely determined by the physical characteristics of stimuli, but is also to be understood in terms of the mediating structures which an individual possesses for information processing. A stimulus is only a stimulus if it can match or be assimilated to some existing cognitive structure, and the individual must, therefore, be regarded as an active agent in imposing order on his experiences and in moulding them according to his own characteristics. The central structures that transform stimulation are partly inherent in origin, reflecting biases built into the organism, and partly acquired. In particular, as a result of past experience the individual acquires certain internal representations of his distal environment – a kind of model, which enables him to compare and assess present sensory stimulation. All subsequent encounters with stimuli can then become assimilated to the existing cognitive representations and every new experience be checked and responded to on the basis of its fit into the established organization.

In the second place, cognitive-developmental theories do not subscribe to the view that all learning depends on making an overt response to a particular stimulus and that such motor learning can only occur through differential reinforcement. The mere perceptual exposure to stimuli can be sufficient, given the right conditions, to bring about the learning of representations: observational learning, as Bandura (1965) has shown, involving exposure without rehearsal ('no-trial learning'), can result in the acquisition and retention of imitative behaviour patterns. Reference to external motivating forces – hunger, pain, need for approval, and so on – is not necessary, for the mere performance of cognitive activity and its ensuing match or mismatch, confirmation or conflict, is in itself sufficient to account for the direction and intensity of motivated behaviour.

Finally, cognitive-developmental theories assume that progressive changes take place in the course of development in the way in which cognitive structures are organized within the individual. Even the neonate already has a certain structure which predetermines the way in which he will apprehend the external world: but, as a result of interaction with his environment, changes are continuously enforced upon him, transformations take place in the existing pattern of structures and new modes of responsiveness emerge.

The source of psychological growth is, therefore, not just to be found in the maturational characteristics of the organism nor in the moulding influence of external stimulation alone, but in the structured interaction of organism and environment. And as there are a number of fundamental similarities in the structure of all individuals and of all environments, it becomes possible to discern a basic, universally applicable pattern of development progressing through a number of stages common to all.

This latter point has been expounded in great detail in the theory of intellectual development put forward by Piaget (1953, 1955), and indeed much of the original inspiration for the cognitive-developmental point of view comes from this source. Piaget, too, found it necessary to postulate central structures whereby stimuli are brought into relation with responses, though he considered that these 'schemata' (as he referred to them) are primarily of a motor nature. They are initially organized around such innate reflexes as sucking, grasping and visual orientation, which determine how the neonate interacts with the environment and to which features he responds. The possession of a sucking schema, for instance, means that all objects encountered by the infant's mouth are regarded as potentially suckable and that every effort is made to assimilate them to this schema. Yet not all stimuli impinging upon the child correspond to the primitive forms to which the congenital reflexes are adapted – a thumb, for instance, needs a different technique of sucking from that appropriate to a nipple, and as a result the original schemata must change in order to handle new information. This process of enforced change was labelled by Piaget 'accommodation' and comes about because the child, through feedback, becomes aware of the effects that his actions have on objects.

Adaptation to the environment, according to Piaget, is a balance between assimilation and accommodation that reaches a new equilibrium with every successive developmental stage. Events are always selected, interpreted and fitted into the existing pattern of cognitive structures, so that they may result in a coherent, conflict-free, equilibrated system. In the neonate the pattern may be crude and stereotyped, but it does exist and it serves to bring the infant into contact with those aspects of the environment which will ensure his survival. Many lower species never progress beyond this point, but the flexibility of the human being ensures that, as a result of environmental impact, the inborn schemata can change and become adapted to an ever-increasing range of external circumstances – differentiating, diversifying, combining and coordinating with one another and eventually forming a cognitive organization that can handle not merely external stimuli but also their internal representations. In this way the child frees himself from his early 'stimulus-bound' condition and is able to consider events remote in time and space and, eventually, also symbols and abstractions.

However, developmental change can only occur if the stimulation provided by the environment is appropriate to the individual. On the one hand, situations utterly un-familiar and not corresponding in any way to the child's existing schemata will fail to engage his attention. On the other hand, if the correspondence is too great because the situation is too familiar and well attuned to the child's schemata, he will not be challenged in any way and the situation is merely regarded as boring and hence to be avoided. It is the events that can activate an existing schema but do not completely correspond to it that are experienced as challenging and that can enforce change. An optimal degree of discrepancy between existing cognitive skills and external situation is, therefore, required to provide the in-fant with the best opportunities for behavioural growth – the 'problem of the match', as Hunt (1964) has referred to it.

Piaget's conception of early development is clearly very different from and rather more complex than either Gesell's or Watson's. It is not a unidirectional view in which either inherent or environmental forces alone are considered as responsible for psychological growth. It is, rather, an interactionist or epigenetic view, best grasped in Kessen's (1963) phrase that the infant *constructs* his environment. Attention is thereby drawn to the fact that it is the indi-vidual's response to incoming stimulation which brings about behavioural change – not the stimulation alone. Ex-perience is not imposed on an organism; even the youngest is already capable of imposing his own order on experience.

There are, of course, other ways of conceptualizing the mediating structure. One which has emerged from a very different direction and yet has come up with remarkably similar statements to cognitive-developmental theory is an orientation based on systems engineering, the relevance of which to infant behaviour has been specifically discussed by Frank (1966). Just as Piaget has stressed the constructional aspect of development and the quest for equilibrium, and just as he has drawn attention to the way in which the infant's perception of the effects of his own activities comes to modify these activities, so in systems engineering the principles of self-organization and feedback have assumed overriding importance. Instead of the mechanical pull–push models of previous eras, systems are conceived as 'open' with continual inputs and outputs, functioning not as a collection of isolated components and linear mechanisms but as a multidimensional complex possessing a particular pattern of internal organization.

This view, urges Frank, is relevant to psychology in general and infant behaviour in particular – and, as we shall see, has been applied with considerable effectiveness to the understanding of early social behaviour by Bowlby (1969). The human being, it is suggested, may be conceived as a self-organizing system operating with a variety of feedbacks, to which it is inappropriate to apply analytic techniques splitting the organism into linear operating mechanisms. Even for such an immature being as the infant, the role of stimulation is not the traditional one in which energy is solely provided by external sources. Instead, the external stimulus merely initiates a sequence whose outcome may not be at all predictable from the nature and intensity of the stimulus alone. The distinction, Frank points out, is analagous to the difference between power engineering, in which a specific quantity of energy is required to bring about a given effect, and communication engineering, in which a message often involving a minute quantity of energy may initiate a sequence of events, the outcome of which may differ appreciably from one system to another. Thus the response is to be viewed as a function not merely of the message but of the responding organism with its prior experience and particular idiosyncracies. And, as Piaget has also noted, through a feedback mechanism the act of responding will in turn affect the internal organization and thereby alter the response emitted on subsequent encounters with similar stimuli.

It is apparent that both views, the cognitive-developmental and that deriving from systems engineering, share the concept of an infant as a 'self organizing, self-stabilizing, self-directing, largely self-repairing open system which becomes progressively patterned, oriented and coupled to the culturally established dimensions of his environment, natural and human' (Frank, 1966, p. 178). In neither view is self-regulation simply a homeostatic process where imbalance is adjusted by a return to the *status quo*. Together they mark a shift in our concept of early development – a shift which, as Kessen (1963) has put it,

has been from the child who is a passive receptacle, into which learning and maturation pour knowledge and skills and affects until he is full, to the child who is a complex, competent organism who, by acting on the environment and being acted on in turn, develops more elaborated and balanced ways of dealing with discrepancy, conflict and dis-equilibrium.

The endogenous organization of behaviour

If the infant is not to be conceived as an empty vessel but as an organism that brings even to the earliest environmental encounters some kind of organization, it becomes necessary to stipulate the precise form that this organization takes. There are a number of ways in which answers have been sought to this problem: here let us refer to just one which, as we shall see, is particularly relevant to an understanding of early social behaviour.

In a classic paper Lashley (1951) some years ago drew attention to the need to explain the manner in which behaviour is serially organized. 'The control of trotting and pacing in a gaited horse, the rat running the maze, the architect designing a house and the carpenter sawing a board present a problem of sequences of action which cannot be explained in terms of successions of external stimuli', and it becomes necessary, therefore, to find mechanisms within the individual which may account for the intrinsic regulation of time sequences in behaviour. In his paper Lashley argued cogently for the existence of endogenous high-frequency oscillators and suggested that the serial order of voluntary adult behaviour is only explicable if such mechanisms are assumed to be present from birth.

For some time this idea remained purely in the realm of speculation. Recently, however, data have become available from a number of investigations of neonatal behaviour which provide substance to Lashley's suggestion. Wolff (1967), for instance, cited sucking as a behaviour pattern that shows extremely constant rhythmical properties which seem to be endogenously generated. During sleep, infants make spontaneous rapid movements of lips and tongue, grouped in bursts of four to twelve events separated by rest periods. The duration of bursts and of rest periods may vary somewhat among infants, but for any one infant they show impressive constancy over a period of time. Brain-damaged infants show disturbance in the organization of these rhythmical patterns, yet children with congenital oral defects (such as cleft palate or cleft lip) suck at the same rate, in the same pattern of bursts and rest periods, as normal infants. The controlling mechanisms, one must conclude, are thus of central origin and not concerned with motor feedback; moreover, as these patterns are to be found from the earliest days on they cannot be ascribed to experience but must originate in intrinsic regulators of serial order.

Other early response patterns, too, such as crying (Prechtl, Theorell, Grausbergen and Lind, 1969; Wolff, 1967) and eye movements (Prechtl and Lenard, 1967), bear evidence of endogenous organization. Thus, even apparently simple motor patterns are already organized in complex time sequences. Whether, as Lashley believed, these endogenous rhythms persist, to give rise to more complex temporal sequences and thereby influence the sequential arrangement of adult cognitive and motor functioning, remains to be established. What has become apparent by this example is that infant behaviour is a great deal more structured than those psychologists thought who saw only a squirming, randomly moving creature that had to be shaped by externally applied stimulation. Indubitably an infant needs stimulation in order to develop, but this cannot be applied arbitrarily without regard to organismic characteristics. If endogenous control mechanisms exist, the role of the infant in patterning the interactions with the environment in general and the mother in particular can hardly be neglected. The mother, as Richards (1971) pointed out, must adapt to the rhythms of the infant's behaviour and phase her own behaviour accordingly. The issue of providing stimulation to the developing organism is thus not merely one of total quantity but, more vitally, one of phasing and patterning in order to fit in with the organization that is present from the beginning.

The study of early social behaviour

Not only our conception of infancy but also our techniques of study, indeed our very belief in the possibility of the empirical study of so young a being, have changed in recent years. Infants, it was previously thought, are essentially decorticate organisms with minimal sensory capacities, characterized by mass activity from which one cannot obtain stable, measurable response indices other than a few stereotyped reflexes of little interest to the psychologist. The recent increase in research on early behaviour has shown that such indices do exist even in the neonatal period, and stems to no small degree from the technological advances which have made it possible to measure these functions. Some of these indices are physiological (such as cardiac and electromyographic measures), but many others are behavioural in nature, and by such means it has now become possible to appreciate both the orderliness and complexity of early behaviour. Even the neonate is by no means sensorily bereft but is already capable of responding to stimulation with a surprising degree of sophistication, showing at the same time features of individuality that may well be the foundation of later personality structure.

With the new technology a lot of new findings have become available, including data about the early social behaviour of infants. Some descriptive-normative material on this topic had gradually accumulated in the first half of this century, thanks to the efforts of a number of investigators interested in mapping the appearance and manifestation of a variety of early behavioural characteristics – investigators such as Bridges (1931) and Shirley (1933), who carried out longitudinal investigations that were, in fact, more sophisticated and extensive versions of the early, single-case studies of the 'baby biographers' such as Darwin (1877) and Preyer (1882). The data thus contributed referred largely to the more obvious phenomena of early social responsiveness: the appearance of the first smile, the response to 'social overtures' by reduction in bodily activity, the development of various patterns of cooperation or aggression in the interaction with peers, and so on. Such descriptive facts are valuable, indeed essential, but they were treated as isolated phenomena in no way linked together within one developmental framework and they were generally regarded as an end in themselves rather than as surface manifestations of more fundamental processes that needed analysis.

When explanations were sought, they tended to be based on such global concepts as 'herd instinct' or 'gregarious propensity'. These mechanisms were postulated in order to bring into focus a tendency, widespread throughout the animal kingdom, for individuals to approach and remain with others of their kind; yet not only do such concepts fail to act as 'explanations', but they also neglect what is the most distinctive aspect of social behaviour in all but the lowest species, namely its selectivity.

Some sort of association with other members of the species is universal – if only for a brief procreative act. In animals low down the evolutionary scale, such as in many invertebrates and insects, relationships between individuals may be completely impersonal, constituting an 'aggregation of anonymous members', as Lorenz (1966) referred to it. The animals cluster in large herds, flocks or schools, within which bonds of personal relationships simply do not occur. Some selectivity is to be found, in that only members of the same species attract each other; yet within such a supra-individual community there is complete interchangeability of one member for another. Every individual is just as content with one fellow-member of the species as with any other and the need to associate with some rather than others is never felt. Love and affection under such conditions become meaningless terms.

The anonymous crowd, according to Lorenz, undoubtedly evolved phylogenetically long before the personal bond. It would not, therefore, be surprising to find a form of impersonal attraction occurring in the sequence of human development prior to the emergence of more selective relationships — a stage, that is, where attraction is on the basis of universal characteristics within the species, where individuals are interchangeable and friend and foe are greeted alike. It is, however, the development of the personal bond, of the ability to form differentiated relationships to specific individuals, that constitutes the ultimate, essential, most intriguing aspect of early human social behaviour. We tend to regard it is a *sine qua non* for mental health, and its lack in the psychopath or the psychotic fills society with concern. We foster it through parental education programmes and consider its absence among the deprived as a matter of urgent social action. Whether it is true that the first relationship is indeed a prototype for all subsequent relationships remains a moot point; in the absence of any evidence one way or the other we shall not discuss this issue further. Our interest will instead focus on the manner in which the infant forms the primary relationship and on the mechanisms that bring about selective social behaviour, and to examine this development we shall concern ourselves with three basic problems:

1. What is the basis of the infant's initial attraction to other human beings that brings about his orientation towards them in preference to all inanimate features of the environment?

2. How does the infant learn to distinguish among different human beings so that he is able to recognize his mother as familiar and strangers as unfamiliar?

3. What, finally, enables the infant to form a lasting emotionally meaningful bond with certain specific individuals, whose company he will actively seek and whose attention

he will crave, while rejecting the company and attention of other, strange individuals?

These three problems represent sequential achievements that the infant must accomplish if he is to attain mature social behaviour: the differentation of human beings as a class apart from the rest of the environment, the recognition of certain individuals as familiar, and the formation of specific attachments. No complete and generally acceptable explanation is as yet available for any of these, yet sufficient data are now at hand to discern trends and make possible the formulation of hypotheses. To do so, however, it is essential to bear in mind that social behaviour does not constitute a class apart from all other forms of behaviour: the responses that an individual makes to the social part of his environment are based on the same fundamental processes of attention and perception, learning and retention, as the responses he makes to inanimate objects. Cognition and social behaviour are not separate categories: the mechanisms underlying interpersonal behaviour must be related to considerations regarding the initial cognitive structure of the organism, the effects of encounters between this structure and the environment, the manner in which information is obtained and transformed and used to guide behaviour, and other such processes describing the 'cognitive' activities of the organism. Their content may refer to people, but their form is embedded in the total nature of the organism. To study social development without reference to cognitive capacity would impose an arbitrary division that has no counterpart in nature.

2 The Primary Attraction to Social Objects

Children are not born 'knowing' people – let alone specific individuals like their mothers. In the early weeks there is no indication that they are able to categorize their environment into its animate and its inanimate constituents and thus differentiate the social from the non-social. Such differentiation comes only as a result of experience, brought about by an environment which provides opportunities to learn that other human beings as such are, in certain respects, a class apart.

That other members of the species have a special significance from the neonatal period on cannot, of course, be denied. Yet behaviour in the earliest ontogenetic stages is described more correctly as *stimulus-directed* than as *object-directed*. Ploog (1969), in a study of mother–infant interaction processes in squirrel monkeys, made this point when he concluded that the newborn monkey does not regard the mother as a social partner but as a composite of stimuli consisting of fur, nipples, angles, curvatures and warmth. By constructing mother-surrogates containing such stimulus properties it is possible to demonstrate that the young animal still performs almost perfectly. Differential responsiveness thus exists from the beginning, but it is initally elicited by stimulus properties of a wider, more primitive form than specifically parental characteristics. The following response of a duckling can be called forth by any large, salient, moving object and is not restricted to the parent; the infant monkey will cling to all furry objects and not only to his mother's body; and similarly the human baby is attracted by certain features of his surroundings that are by no means exclusive to people. He will, in the early weeks of life, smile as readily at dots painted on a sheet of paper as at his mother's face; he will suck at any nipple-shaped object and not only at the maternal breast; and his crying may be inhibited by various kinaesthetic, visual and auditory stimuli that do not necessarily emanate from other people. He is thus equipped to respond to certain simple stimulus configurations that, in the 'average expectable environment', are provided by his parents but which, initially, encompass a much greater range than parental characteristics as such. Quite soon a narrowing-down will begin to take place in that the infant develops a number of learned preferences – dots and sounds no longer suffice and human faces and human voices must instead be offered if the infant is to be satisfied. But before this occurs, people as such cannot yet be said to exist in the infant's world. As Escalona (1969) has pointed out, it is the observer who classifies the mother's touch as 'social' and the touch of the blanket as 'impersonal': in the first four weeks at least (according to her observations), no such behavioural discrimination is made by the baby.

The secondary drive hypothesis of sociability

How does it come about that infants are increasingly drawn to other people? What are the sources of attraction that impel the young to others of their kind?

Up till recently the most convincing explanation available appeared to be the 'secondary drive hypothesis' of sociability. According to this view, the interest in other members of the species and the wish to be in their company are the result of being fed by them. There are, it is maintained, a number of primary somatic drives in the individual, stemming from the nature of his physiological make-up – drives concerned with hunger, thirst, sex and bodily comfort, and every aspect of behaviour even in the mature individual can eventually be traced back to its association with drive-instigated behaviour. Thus the infant's emotional dependence on others stems from his physical dependence: being motorically helpless he cannot gratify his own needs but must rely on the caretaking activities of others. In this way he comes to associate the presence of other people with the alleviation of unpleasant tensions such as arise from hunger, until in time a self-supporting social drive emerges whereby the child demands the company of other people for its own sake.

This view stems to a large extent from Freud's emphasis on the feeding relationship as the context within which the infant develops a dependency relationship to the mother. Orality, that is, provides not only the first means of making contact with the mother but also accounts for the mechanism whereby the infant develops such intense motivated striving towards her. Dollard and Miller (1950) have made this mechanism even more explicit in their attempt to translate it into Hullian learning theory:

In the first year of its life the human infant has the cues from its mother associated with the primary reward of feeding on more than two thousand occasions. Meanwhile the mother and other people are ministering to many other needs. In general there is a correlation between the absence of people and the prolongation of suffering from hunger, cold, pain and other drives; the appearance of a person is associated with a reinforcing reduction in the drive. Therefore, the proper conditions are present for the infant to learn to attach strong reinforcement value to a variety of cues from the nearness of the mother and other adults. . . . [It] seems reasonable to advance the hypothesis that the related human motives of sociability, dependence, need to receive and show affection, and desire for approval from others are learned.

Social dependence thus develops out of physical dependence.

The secondary drive hypothesis has, however, come increasingly under attack of late, for the data from a number of lines of inquiry have failed to support it:

1. In the first place, studies of social development in precocial birds have shown that social attachments ('imprinting') are generally formed by the young in the absence of any form of physical gratification. The formation of such attachments in these birds takes place very soon after

hatching and before any parental' behaviour has occurred. The most likely explanation is that the young animal learns to follow a particular object on the basis of its perceptual salience and not because it has been provided with food and warmth by it.

2. A similar conclusion comes from the work of Harlow (1958) with rhesus monkeys. Infants were reared on inanimate mother surrogates which were constructed either from wire-mesh or covered with terry cloth. Half the infants were fed on the cloth mother and the remainder on the wire-mesh mother. Far less time was spent in contact with the wire-mesh mother, even when she also provided food, than with the cloth mother. The infants behaved as though the latter provided a source of comfort and security and as though she had become an object of intense attachment – 'a finding completely contrary to any interpretation of derived drive in terms in which the mother-form becomes conditioned to hunger-thirst reduction' (Harlow, 1958). Again it was the perceptual contact with the object which determined social responsiveness – this time taking a tactile rather than a visual form.

3. Observations of human infants also fail to support the secondary drive hypothesis. Schaffer and Emerson (1964a) found that infants frequently formed strong attachments to such individuals as fathers, siblings and relatives who rarely or never participated in routine caretaking activities, and concluded: 'Satisfaction of physical needs does not appear to be a necessary precondition to the development of attachments, the latter taking place independently and without any obvious regard to the experiences that the child encounters in physical care situations.'

4. If emotional dependence arises from early physical gratification, a relationship should be present between the nature of such infantile experiences and the child's later dependency behaviour. This has not been demonstrated: the intensity of emotional dependence appears to bear no unanimously demonstrated relation to such experiences as

breast or bottle feeding, duration of feeding, rigidity of feeding schedule, age at weaning and severity of weaning (Sears, Maccoby and Levin, 1957; Sears, Whiting, Nowlis and Sears, 1953).

5. A number of studies of animal behaviour have experimentally demonstrated that parental punishment, far from discouraging the young animal's overtures to the parents, may actually enhance its approach behaviour. This was reported in chicks which had been shocked for following an imprinting model (Kovach and Hess, 1963), puppies punished for approaching a human caretaker during the critical socializing period (Scott, 1963), and infant monkeys administered painful airblasts by their mother-surrogate to which they subsequently clung all the more intensely (Harlow, 1962). Mothering, it appears, need not involve positive reinforcement to bring about an attachment.

6. Wolff (1965) reported that attention to external stimuli is lowest when an infant is hungry or otherwise viscerally excited. This hardly tallies with a view which suggests that the most meaningful forms of learning only take place when external stimuli mesh with a visceral drive state.

7. Even in the feeding situation, as Walters and Parke (1965) pointed out, the infant obtains not only oral gratification but also visual, auditory and tactile stimulation. During feeding the mother's face is generally at a distance of eight or nine inches from the infant's face, that is, at the distance optimal for clearest vision in the newborn. 'Consequently,' these authors conclude, 'in caretaking situations the infant has many opportunities for the development of social responsiveness on a purely perceptual basis.'

Examined empirically, the secondary drive hypothesis does not, therefore, appear tenable. It is contradicted by too much evidence of a direct or indirect nature. It is, moreover, based on a model of behavioural motivation that is no longer generally acceptable – a model, that is, which stipulates drive reduction as the foundation of all learning and development and which sees the infant bereft of any but somatically dictated interests. Explanations of early sociability, it seems, must take a different route.

Sociability based on perceptual interaction

Instead of searching for drives to explain the facts of social development, it is more profitable to conceive of sociability as being rooted in the infant's perceptual encounters with his environment. From birth, the infant is equipped with a species-specific cognitive structure which ensures that he is selectively attuned to certain types of environmental stimuli. Such stimuli tend to represent aspects of the infant's surroundings essential to survival and amongst these parental characteristics are particularly prominent. Thus, from the beginning other individuals will exercise an attention-compelling influence on the young that is unrivalled by any other single feature of the environment. As, in addition, parents are similarly attracted to the infant, prolonged and frequent encounters are likely to take place and the stage is, therefore, set for an enmeshing of parent–offspring interaction patterns.

Although initial attraction is determined by the infant's inherent cognitive structure, modifications of his responses are soon brought about as a result of his experience with other people. For one thing, he becomes capable of taking in increased quantities of information during his encounters with others: from being set to respond to quite simple, primitive stimulus configurations which are abstracted from the total sensory input he progresses to being capable of assimilating 'total' people. And for another, by being exposed mainly to just a few specific individuals, he comes to learn those characteristics which distinguish these individuals, to form internal representations of them and thus increasingly to behave discriminatively on the basis of his past experience. In this way the cognitive structure becomes progressively modified and more complex, making it possible in turn for more complex forms of interaction to take place in the future.

Social responsiveness is, therefore, primarily derived, on the one hand, from the infant's sensitivity to certain kinds of sensory input and, on the other hand, from the fact that other people, considered as stimulus objects, are structured in such a way that they are best able to provide these inputs. External drives need not be postulated, for motivation, as Hunt (1964) has argued, can be regarded as part of information processing itself and not superimposed on it. The infant does not merely see, but the more interesting visual experiences he encounters the more he wants to see; not only does he hear and feel but he actively strives to hear and feel. And human beings provide him with stimulation of a particularly interesting kind, as a result of which he comes to attach special significance to such encounters and attempts to prolong and repeat them.

Sensory abilities of infants

All this assumes that even the very young infant is already capable of taking in information from his environment. But is this assumption justified? For a long time it was believed that in the early weeks of life infants are perceptually incompetent to the point of functional blindness and deafness. Thus Preyer (1882), despite the many astute observations contained in the biographical study of his infant son, could nevertheless assert that 'all children immediately after birth are deaf' – a view which remained unchallenged for decades through want of techniques to disprove it. Then Bronshtein and Petrova (1952), observing that when a tone is presented to an infant he will stop sucking, used this observation as a basis for an experiment on sensory discrimination in neonates and in this way were able to demonstrate objectively that children in the neonatal period are not only able to hear but already have considerable capacity for stimulus differentiation.

It is largely due to the recent availability of techniques such as this that an increasingly clearer picture of infants' sensory abilities has emerged. Most attention has been given to the study of visual responsiveness. Many studies have demonstrated, for instance, that the newborn's pupils can react to light: indeed, that the pupillary reflex is functional well before birth. Even the very young infant can thus already adjust to difference in the intensity of visually presented stimuli. The ability to focus the eyes on an object is, however, initially somewhat limited: under the age of one month, infants' accommodative responses do not adjust to changes in target distance and remain locked at a focal distance of about eight inches – the distance, it may be pointed out, at which the mother's face is generally held during feeding. Images nearer or further are blurred. But from about the middle of the second month the range of flexible accommodation increases and performance comparable to that of adults is attained by the fourth month. The ability to sustain visual fixation also improves rapidly, for though it is not present at birth it appears within a few hours and reaches a peak in four or five weeks. Similarly ocular pursuit movements show rapid improvement with age. The two-week-old infant can follow a moving object only with difficulty, his eye movements being jerky, inefficient and brief. In the coming weeks, however, visual pursuit becomes smoother, tracking can be accomplished over a wider arc as the infant can now turn his head in order to keep the stimulus in sight, and by about three or four months this function has become so well established that most objects moving at moderate speeds, such as a person moving about the room, can be kept in sight and not, as earlier, be so easily lost from the visual field.

Other visual accomplishments also mature early on. The neonate's visual acuity, though poor in relation to that of the adult, is very much better than previously believed, having been determined at a little under one degree (compared with an adult standard of about one minute of arc) and improving to almost mature levels in the first six months. The blink response to approaching objects, while absent at first, is found from about the age of two months. There are also indications that quite early on the infant is already showing some degree of sensitivity to colour (demonstrated by the ability to follow a spot of light differing from the background only in wavelength). In brief, most of the visual apparatus of human beings is functioning from the neonatal period on and though considerable improvement in its effectiveness must take place in the following weeks, it appears that even the very young infant can already become aware of the major events that are likely to occur in his visual environment.

A similar conclusion emerges from studies of the auditory system which, functionally, is already developed to a quite high degree of complexity at birth. By the use of response indices derived from such behaviour patterns as sucking, activity, respiration and heart rate, it has been shown not only that neonates can respond to a wide range of auditory stimuli but also that there appear to be systematic relationships present between signal input and behavioural output that resemble in their formal characteristics those obtained for adults. Differential responses have been reliably obtained from neonates to stimuli varied along the dimensions of pitch, intensity and duration. Despite some initial inferiority, rapid improvement can be shown to occur in all these respects in the early weeks of life. Although most writers consider that localizing the source of a sound is not evident before the age of four months, there have been suggestions that even this ability may be present much earlier. In an experiment in which the orienting response was habituated through repeated presentations of the stimulus, response recovery was obtained in infants just two hours old when the sound was presented from another location. It seems that the auditory system, too, can process sensory information to a surprisingly efficient extent even in the earliest phases of development.

Pressure and touch sensitivity appear to be present from the beginning and have indeed been found in foetuses several months before birth. Tactile sensitivity varies according to body part, with the area around the mouth being particularly sensitive – as seen by the ease with which rooting and sucking reflexes are elicited. Response thresholds also vary according to age, the most rapid decreases to electrotactual stimuli taking place within the first week of life. Similarly, responsiveness to such noxious stimuli as the prick of a needle improve rapidly within days of birth. This also applies to the mechanisms of thermoregulation, which are not fully effective at first but, being essential for survival, quickly become so in the neonatal period. Changes in the amount of sucking of milk varying in temperature have been observed in newborns, though the extent of individual differences is surprisingly great.

Few studies have been done on smell and taste sensitivities, though once again a picture of rapid improvement to adult standards is indicated. Finally, studies of propreoceptive sensitivities indicate that neonates are responsive to shifts in posture and that, indeed, vestibular functioning, as indicated by observations of rotational nystagmus, appears to be similar to that of adults. Kinaesthetic receptors are functional well before birth and it is believed that much of the apparently random bodily activity of the young infant in fact results from the stimulation of these receptors.

We must conclude that the infant's sensory abilities have in the past been vastly underrated. Even the neonate is already responsive to a wide range of stimuli. His sensitivity may not be commensurate with that of later life, but all his sensory systems are already functioning at birth or shortly thereafter. To characterize him as senseless is to mistake the nature of the organism.

Knowledge of an individual's sensitivities enables us to specify those aspects of the environment which will have impact upon him. If the young infant were indeed deaf, his mother's call would not attract his attention nor a lullaby soothe him when restless. A detailed specification of the various sensory systems is necessary if we are to understand which experiences are likely to shape the course of development. Ideally one would also like to know in what way the different sensory systems are related; it would be of interest in particular to know whether there are differences in dominance among them, so that information conveyed through one modality can be said to have a more potent effect than information arriving by other means. Such knowledge we do not possess as yet: studies of infants' sensitivities have generally concerned themselves with only one system at a time and comparison between them is, therefore, not possible. Statements such as that infants are more responsive to tactile than to visual stimulation and, therefore, require to be handled rather than be provided with visual experience are at present not justified.

Perceptual organization in infancy

The specification of sensory competence alone is, however, not sufficient. We need to know not only whether an individual is sensitive to stimulation but also how he organizes and arranges the information that is available to him. If every stimulus in the environment were directly to impinge on the infant, if every new event were to elicit yet another orienting response, then the infant's world would indeed be a blooming, buzzing confusion. Steps must be taken to avoid overloading the information processing apparatus, particularly when, as in infancy, this apparatus is of only limited capacity. The adult avoids confusion because he selects from his environment those aspects considered for one reason or another worthy of attention; all else is rejected. Moreover, he is capable of reducing the load by his appreciation of constancies, i.e. he realizes that an object remains identical despite changes in orientation, distance and illumination; he can recognize a previously seen object after a passage of time and need not begin afresh familiarizing himself with it; and in addition he can make allowance for changes in appearance caused, for instance, by another person appearing in unfamiliar dress or hairstyle. Without such abilities an individual's experiences would be a bewildering, frightening flux of numerous unconnected, everchanging sensations, where every stimulus that he happens to encounter has him at its mercy. Is this what the world looks like to the infant?

A certain fragmentation does appear to exist in the early

months. Piaget (1955) has argued that up to the third quarter of the first year an infant is not yet capable of considering objects as permanent entities endowed with a continuous existence independently of experiencing them. Instead, he perceives series of fleeting sensations that remain unconnected and unintegrated, so that when an object leaves the perceptual field he behaves as though it has ceased to exist and makes no attempt to search for it. The discovery of a universe of independent objects of permanent existence and the ordering of such objects in a continuous space and time come only gradually towards the end of the first year. Until then the continuities which the adult takes for granted are not yet known to the infant.

At a more elementary level, however, organization of perceptual experience does exist. Bower (1966) has claimed that some indications of shape and size constancy are to be found from at least the second month on. By establishing a conditioned response to a cube of a particular size and placed at a given distance from the subject and by then testing for the occurrence of the response to variations in size and distance, Bower obtained data suggesting that the infants' behaviour was affected by real size and real distance, not by retinal size or by retinal distance cues. Similarly, by presenting a rectangle in various orientations, Bower demonstrated that infants could respond to real shape, not retinal shape. Constancy, in this sense, was present as an organizing principle from the early weeks on.

Selective perception in infancy

The most firmly established conclusion about early perceptual functioning stems from the finding that infants' attention, far from being haphazard, is of a highly discriminative nature and that even the neonate can already select from among the stimuli available to him. Both the finding itself and the technique for demonstrating it come largely from the work of Fantz (1961, 1966).

Fantz based his approach on the observation that the infant, though motorically immature, spends much of his time visually exploring his surroundings and apparently showing particular interest in certain aspects of his surroundings. By recording this behaviour under well-controlled conditions, it is possible to ascertain not only *what* an infant looks at but what he *prefers* to look at. Fantz achieved this with his 'visual preference technique', which involved placing infants inside a stimulus chamber, exposing them there to pairs of stimuli (usually visual patterns differing from one another in some specified respects) and then measuring the amount of visual fixation on each. If one pattern is looked at more than another, it is regarded as evidence of 'visual preference' (a rather unfortunate term, perhaps, in that it suggests an affective 'liking' which is not necessarily implied; what is involved, rather, is the differential attention-capturing quality of the two stimuli and it is in this sense that the method has been found a useful one).

By means of this technique Fantz has shown that there are systematic differences among visual stimuli in the extent to which they are able to provoke the attention of infants. From the age of one week on the relative attractiveness of stimuli appears to depend on the presence of strongly patterned characteristics, so that almost any patterned surface (such as horizontal stripes, concentric circles or a face-like stimulus) is looked at more than a plain (even brightly coloured) surface. Infants, Fantz concluded, can resolve, discriminate and differentially attend to visual patterns, preferring these to such stimulus characteristics as colour, brightness and size. Some degree of form perception thus appears to be innate and to be responsible for such early selective attention.

The infant does not, however, merely prefer patterned over unpatterned stimulation; there are also preferences among patterns, some of which tend to change with age. Much recent work has been devoted to attempts to isolate the stimulus attributes giving rise to such differential behaviour.

Complexity is the characteristic that has come under closest scrutiny of late. While some doubts have been expressed

about its precise meaning and its unitary nature, most definitions have treated it in terms of the total quantity of information transmitted by a stimulus or, putting it another way,
as the variety or diversity of distinguishable elements contained within the stimulus. Operationally, complexity has
mostly been investigated by equating it with amount of internal contour and manipulating it experimentally with the
use of checkerboards. These make it possible to divide a
fixed stimulus area into black and white squares of different
densities (four or sixteen or sixty-four squares, and so on),
thereby varying the amount of internal contour while keeping the black-white ratio and the brightness of the total
stimulus constant.

In this way a number of investigators (e.g. Berlyne, 1958;
Spears, 1964) have shown that infants tend to be most
attracted to complex rather than simple stimuli. Thus, given
the choice between two checkerboards of varying number of
squares, infants were generally said to pay most attention
to the more complex board. Investigators using other stimuli
ordered along the complexity dimension in rather less systematic fashion have come up with substantially the same
conclusion. However, this unanimity of opinion was broken
by a report by Hershenson (1964), who found that his infant subjects paid most attention to the *least* complex of
the various stimuli shown to them. At first sight this finding
seemed a flat contradiction of previous reports; in fact, it
has added a valuable point which was subsequently made
explicit in a study by Brennan, Ames and Moore (1966).
These investigators presented checkerboards of three different degrees of complexity to infants aged three, eight and
fourteen weeks and found that the degree of complexity
preferred depended on age: the youngest group paid most
attention to the least complex stimulus, the oldest to the most
complex and the middle group to the stimulus of intermediate degree of complexity. There is thus an interaction
between age and complexity preference, and in so far as
Hershenson had used newborns in his study and other investigators mostly rather older infants, it becomes possible

to reconcile the apparent divergence in their findings. This conclusion is reinforced by a study by Karmel (1969), in which the relationship between amount of visual fixation and amount of internal stimulus contour was investigated in infants aged thirteen and twenty weeks. For all subjects the relationship could be described by an inverted U-curve, i.e. intermediate degrees of the stimulus dimension elicited most attention. There was, however, a shift with age in the amount of 'peak-preference', so that the older the child, the greater the amount of contour required to stimulate maximum interest.

A progression is thus indicated with increasing age – or rather with increasing experience, for as the individual grows older and becomes more accustomed to dealing with stimulation, his perceptual apparatus also grows in complexity. This fits in well with the suggestion by Dember and Earl (1957) that it may be useful to think not only of stimuli but also of individuals as having a certain complexity value, expressing the individual's ability to process that particular class of information. Changes in an individual's preferences are brought about by being exposed to 'pacers', i.e. stimuli with a complexity value just beyond that of the subject's, and stimuli will, therefore, be attention-arousing to the extent to which they contain pacers. As we shall see, this model has considerable applicability to the development of social responsiveness, in that there is a similar progression in the nature of the effective stimuli required to elicit such responses as the smile. What we can conclude at present is that the work on complexity illustrates well how infant attention is elicited by particular stimulus dimensions which interact with the individual's cognitive structure.

A number of other stimulus properties have also been shown to have attention-provoking effects on young infants. *Movement*, for instance, is an alerting event in the neonatal period. Haith (1966) confronted infants aged three to five days with a series of closely spaced light bulbs which, when lit in rapid succession, gave the impression of a single light moving about. As the response measure, he used suppres-

sion of sucking and found that such suppression occurred
to a greater extent to the moving as compared with a stationary light. Movement, it seems, elicited a much greater
orientation response, as part of which the infants' ongoing
activity was inhibited. In a study by Ames and Silfen (1965),
using the visual preference technique, infants between seven
and twenty-four weeks old were shown moving belts painted
with a black-and-white checkerboard design, each being
paired with a stationary belt similarly painted. Greater
attention to the moving stimulus was evident at all ages,
though the discrimination between the two stimuli required
a much faster rate of movement in younger infants than in
older infants.

Two further characteristics for which there is some relevant evidence are *brightness* and *solidity*. In the case of the
former, Hershenson (1964) found an inverted-U relationship between degree of brightness and amount of visual
fixation in newborns, in that the intermediate value presented
by him was fixated more than the bright and the dim values.
As to solidity, Fantz (1966) observed that from the age of
two months on a consistently greater interest in three-
dimensional objects is shown when these are paired with
otherwise identical flat objects. The contour and shading of
the former apparently made them more distinctive to these
infants than two-dimensional surfaces.

It is quite apparent that from the very beginning of life
the infant is no passive recipient of stimulation, but can regulate his stimulus input by selective attention. Thus his
perceptual world does not consist of an undifferentiated
mosaic of confusion: given the choice, he will expose himself to those environmental stimuli to which, at his particular stage of development, he is maximally sensitive. While a
great deal of work still needs to be done on the nature of
attention-eliciting characteristics and on their possible
arrangement in a developmental hierarchy, it does seem
that the attributes which receive most attention early on are
those that are dependent on a high rate of change in the
physical parameters of stimuli, e.g. movement, high bright-

ness contrast, and internal patterning, making the stimulus distinctive both in terms of its internal composition and its figure-ground relationships. And the stimulus to which such a description is most applicable in the infant's environment is, of course, the social object.

The impact of the social object

Treated as stimulus objects, human beings have built into them a number of features that make them particularly prone to become objects of an infant's attentiveness (Rheingold, 1961). They are in almost constant movement, they emit a great deal of highly varied stimulation, they can appeal to a number of different sense modalities simultaneously, they are complex, possess a distinctive pattern and are, furthermore, often responsive to the infant's own behaviour so that a continuous and reciprocal sequence may thereby be initiated. In short, the social object has a very much higher perceptual impact value than any inanimate part of the environment and as a result of possessing such inherently attention-worthy characteristics it can achieve a very considerable salience in the infant's world. A human being is, of course, a much more complex system than the sort of stimuli usually studied by psychologists under laboratory conditions; it should, nevertheless, be possible to stipulate its constituent features, study their effect on infants of different ages and in this way determine what distinctive features are attended to in the course of development.

Face perception

Such an analysis has been started on that part of the human being with which an infant is likely to make his most frequent and most significant contacts – the maternal face (not, we may note, the maternal breast). Neonates only two to six days old, according to Fantz (1963), pay more attention to a disc with human features painted on it than to any other stimulus of similar shape and size. The face, it is clear, has a significance which it does not share with other stimuli.

But this does not mean, we must stress, that recognition of the human face *qua* face is built in from the beginning. Biologically this would at first sight seem a useful arrangement, for it would ensure that the infant is immediately drawn to the 'correct' object required for his survival and that species membership can be established at once.

Such, however, does not appear to be the case. A number of studies have investigated whether it is indeed the face as such which has such a compelling influence or whether the necessary eliciting stimulus takes a different, perhaps more primitive form. Fantz himself initially believed that a specific visual preference for faces could already be found in neonates. In a study (1961) involving infants aged from four days to six months, he presented three stimuli in which the arrangement of facial features was systematically varied. All were painted in black on pink and were the size and shape of a human head (Figure 1). One of the stimuli (the 'real' face) contained the correct arrangement of eyes, eyebrows, nose, mouth and hair. A second (the 'scrambled' face) also contained these features but arranged in a scrambled form, while the third (a control pattern) had a solid block of black at the top end with an area equal to that covered by all the features. The three stimuli were paired in all possible combinations and amount of visual fixation was measured to each.

As is evident from Figure 1, the control stimulus elicited least interest. As far as the other two stimuli were concerned, Fantz concluded that 'the degree of preference for the "real" face to the other ones was not large, but it was consistent among individual infants, especially the younger ones. The experiment suggested that there is an unlearned, primitive meaning in the form perception of infants. . . .'

This conclusion has, however, had to be modified. That the control stimulus is of less interest than the other two stimuli can be readily accepted and has not been questioned by other investigators. It is a less complex stimulus and, therefore, presumably more easily assimilated. The other two stimuli are equal in terms of complexity but differ in

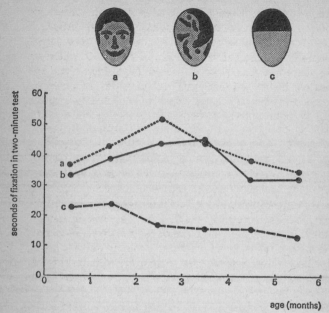

Figure 1 Average time scores of infants' visual fixation when presented with three face-shaped objects paired in all the possible combinations. (From Fantz, 1961)

the arrangement of the constituent parts, and if Fantz is correct one might have to conclude that an innate preference for face-like stimuli has been demonstrated. However, other investigators have not been able to find differential behaviour to regular and scrambled faces in the early weeks of life. Koopman and Ames (1968), for instance, constructed three face-shaped stimuli: a real and a scrambled face like those used by Fantz and, in addition, a 'symmetrical' face that also contained the features in a scrambled form but arranged symmetrically around the vertical axis. The stimuli were presented to ten-week-old infants in a paired-comparison procedure and visual fixation times were obtained. Neither this experiment nor a further one in which only the real and the scrambled faces were employed could demonstrate any difference in looking time: the unrealistic stimulus aroused as much interest as the more realistic one.

Fantz (1965) himself has subsequently also been forced to modify his original conclusions. In a study in which six face-shaped stimuli were shown to infants less than one week old it emerged that visual attention was primarily determined by complexity, i.e. the *number* of features, rather than by the particular pattern, i.e. the *arrangement* of the features. No difference was found here between the real and the scrambled face. On the other hand, there are indications that such a differentiation does develop subsequently and that the real face does come to assume a greater degree of attention-worthiness. The age when this preference emerges is still uncertain: in one study Fantz (1966) found it to increase up to the third month, while in another (Fantz and Nevis, 1967) a rather later age was indicated. The latter study was a longitudinal one, in which a group of home-reared infants was compared with an institutionalized group. The infants were seen at two-weekly intervals from two to twenty-four weeks of age and, among other stimuli, presented with a real and a scrambled facial pattern. The results (Figure 2) indicate that it is not until fairly late in the first half-year that the preference emerges and that, not surprisingly, it is found in rather more pronounced form in the home-reared group than in the institutionalized infants. As both Haaf and Bell (1967) and Lewis (1969) have found discrimination to occur rather earlier (at four months and three months respectively), it is most likely that the shift from responding to the face on the basis of its complexity value to responding to it on the basis of its 'faceness' occurs in the first quarter of the first year.

This interpretation is reinforced by a rather different line of investigation. In an attempt to trace the development of object orientation, i.e. the ability to conserve an object despite its lateral rotation, J. S. Watson (1966) presented infants aged eight to twenty-six weeks with two social stimuli, namely the mother's face and a stranger's face. Each was

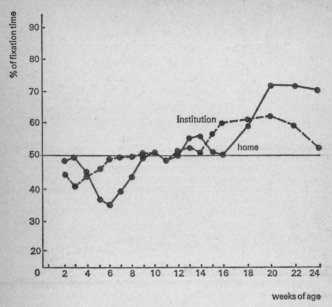

Figure 2 Age-preference curves for a schematic face over a scrambled face. (From Fantz and Nevis, 1967)

viewed in three orientations: a 0 degree orientation (i.e. 'normal' presentation, in which the adult's chin and eyes correspond to the infant's chin and eyes), a 90 degree orientation (in which the adult leaned over the infant from his left side), and a 180 degree orientation (involving an upside-down view). Figure 3 shows the results obtained. An analysis of the amount of smiling indicates that significantly more occurred to the 0 degree orientation than to the other two orientations, but that this was accounted for almost entirely by one of the four age groups, namely by those infants aged around fourteen weeks. This applied to both the mother's and the stranger's faces, but not to a non-social, complex stimulus consisting of a multi-coloured mask. In another experiment the same trend was observed for visual fixation times, though in a less marked form (possibly because two-dimensional representations were used rather than, as in the first experiment, real faces). Thus, with both

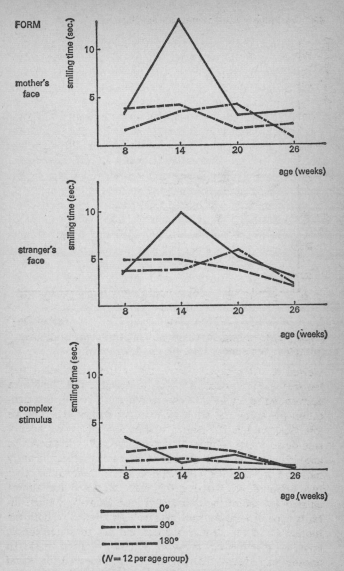

Figure 3 Curves showing age change in mean smiling time for the three orientations of mother's face, stranger's face, and non-social stimulus. (From Watson, 1966)

the number and the arrangement of the features held constant and only the relative position of the stimulus to the subject changed, infants in the fourteen-week age group showed maximal sensitivity to orientation change while neither younger nor older infants responded differentially. The most probable interpretation of these results is that the younger infants, for their part, responded to the face purely on the basis of its primitive, quantitative stimulus attributes and thus did not differentiate between its various orientations, while the oldest infants could conserve the face despite rotation and for this reason did not behave differentially.

In a report by McGurk (1970), however, no such clearcut age-related differences emerged. McGurk found the visual preference technique to be rather less sensitive than a familiarization technique. In the latter, infants aged six to twenty-six weeks were exposed for a number of trials to a stimulus in one orientation and then presented in a final trial with the same stimulus in a different orientation. During the initial series of trials, habituation of visual attention occurred to both a social (face-like) and a non-social (abstract) stimulus; on the final trial, however, a significant recovery of response took place which was not directly related to age.

So far we have discussed the face as a whole, including all of its features. A strong possibility exists, however, that initially an infant responds to only one part of this pattern, namely, the eyes. *A priori*, the eyes certainly seem the most attention-worthy, being shiny and moving independently from the face as a whole. For adults, moreover, they provide more information than any other single feature in their social partner's face. Their emerging importance in the early weeks has been demonstrated by studies of the smiling response; we shall refer to these in the next chapter. Fantz (1966) found that by three months of age a differentiation can be observed between a regular eye pattern of dots and an off-centre arrangement, and it may well be, therefore, that it is only the eye section which determines the nature of the infant's response to regular and scrambled faces. Investigations using scrambled faces but with the eyes left in their regular position should answer this question.

Most studies have used schematic representation of faces. Whether young infants are capable of recognizing such stimuli must remain questionable. Wilcox (1969) failed to obtain differences in response to real and scrambled pictures at any age between four and sixteen weeks; on the other hand, a preference did emerge at sixteen weeks for a photograph of a female face over a schematic representation. More realistic stimuli, such as those used by Kagan, Henker, Hen-Tov, Levine and Lewis (1966), would seem to be more appropriate for this type of problem. These latter investigators constructed three-dimensional, flesh-coloured heads with regular or irregular features and presented these to four-month-old infants. Their findings indicate, however, another source of variation, namely, the particular response index employed. Visual fixation scores showed no reliable differences between the two kinds of facial arrangement; on the other hand, more smiling was observed to occur to the realistic head and girls, but not boys, showed greater cardiac deceleration to this stimulus.

The suggestion that three-dimensionality enhances the attention value of social stimuli fits in, of course, with the work previously referred to on the effectiveness of solidity. Fantz (1966) investigated this variable by pairing a lifesize model of a female head with a similar flat form and found a strong preference for the former which developed suddenly in the second month of life. Similarly, the addition of movement to a social stimulus has been found to increase fixation times (Wilcox and Clayton, 1968): five-month-old infants who viewed motion pictures depicting a female adult showed considerably more attention when the adult nodded and bobbed her head than when she remained still. One can readily understand that attention is much less likely to habituate to a mobile than to a stationary stimulus; what is more, one can also expect that an irregularly, unpredictably moving stimulus will arouse greater attention than one moving with rhythmic regularity. Clearly the human face is of interest not only on account of its structural aspects but also because of its behavioural characteristics.

Auditory responsiveness to social stimulation

So far work in this area has been marked by its preoccupation with visual stimulation. It is, therefore, all the more interesting to find that a study of auditory responsiveness in neonates has brought to light findings very much in accordance with those reported above. Hutt, Hutt, Lenard, Bernuth and Muntjewerff (1968) obtained electromyographic responses from infants of three to eight days of age as a measure of responsiveness to pure (sine-wave) tones and patterned (square-wave) tones. They found that the patterned sounds elicited most responses and that within each of these categories tones with low frequency fundamentals were the most effective stimuli. Square-wave tones with low frequency fundamentals possess certain structural similarities to human speech sounds and as these were found to elicit more responses than the voice itself they may be regarded as 'supernormal' stimuli. The authors accordingly suggested that

the structure of the human auditory apparatus at birth ensures both that there is a limit of basilar membrane excitation beyond which defensive reflexes are evoked and that the voice at normal intensities is non-aversive and prepotent. The survival value of this differential responsivity may lie in the part it plays in the development of the affectional bond between parent and child.

Selective responsiveness to potentially meaningful stimuli appears, therefore, to exist in the auditory as well as the visual modality and to stem basically from the structure of the neonate's sensory apparatus. Such an interpretation is certainly more plausible than the view put forward by Salk (1962), according to whom the infant while still *in utero* becomes 'imprinted' on the maternal heart-beat. Salk continuously presented a noise similar to a heart-beat to newborn infants for four days and found that these subjects cried less and gained more weight than unstimulated controls –

a finding which inspired him to declare that the adult's interest in music and dance is the result of imprinting and is 'created and experienced by man in his attempt to remain in proximity with imprinted stimuli'. The pursuit of such interests would thus be an unconscious attempt to recapture sensory experiences similar to those received during prenatal life.

We are saved from the need to point to the folly of this argument by a number of studies which have failed to confirm Salk's original observation. Brackbill, Adams, Crowell and Gray (1966) presented four stimulus conditions to neonates: no sound, heartbeats, the beats of a metronome and a lullaby. Polygraph records were obtained for gross motor activity, respiration and heart rate, and an observer recorded the amount of crying in seconds. For none of these measures was a difference obtained between the heart-beat condition and the other sound conditions; the only difference that did emerge was between the absence of sound and its presence – in *any* form. Salk had failed to add the necessary control of other kinds of auditory stimulation and thus arrived at a misleading interpretation.

Conclusions

Instead of searching for drives to 'explain' social development it is more profitable to conceive of sociability as originating in the infant's perceptual encounters with other people.

From birth on the infant can respond to a wide range of stimuli; he can also already to some degree organize and structure his sensory impressions and select from those that are available to him. Given the choice, he is more likely to attend to some things than to others, and thus it becomes possible to determine pertinent stimulus characteristics. A number of these have now been isolated and though the evidence comes mainly from visual studies it appears that such characteristics tend to be found in their most marked form as inherent in social objects. The face in particular, treated as a stimulus object, possesses a number of qualities highly distinctive and interesting to the infant. Thus, on the one hand, infants are inherently structured in such a way that they are maximally sensitive to certain kinds of sensory input and, on the other hand, the source of the preferred stimulation that they are most likely to encounter is another human being. The child's caretakers have, therefore, a much higher perceptual impact than any inanimate part of the environment and can thereby achieve a considerable salience in the infant's world.

Biologically it is, of course, important that the newborn should be drawn towards other members of the species. Moreoever, the sooner the bond can be established the more quickly the survival of the helpless young can be ensured. One might, therefore, expect that a very specific mechanism of recognition would be genetically built into the newborn, enabling him to focus immediately on the socially correct object. Yet this is not so, either in the human infant or in the young of lower species. The perceptual characteristics to which the offspring is attracted are by no means confined to his parents, not even to his species. Thus the face is meaningful to the baby not because of its 'faceness' but because it possesses certain primitive stimulus attributes. In theory, non-social objects could become the principal foci of the infant's interests; in practice this is unlikely to occur (with the exception of such responses as sucking a dummy or cuddling a favourite blanket). For one thing, the human being has the advantage of combining all the various relevant stimulus attributes and thus being much more conspicuous than the majority of inanimate objects; and for another, he is by no means a passive recipient of the infant's attention but can initiate interaction as well as reciprocate the baby's overtures.

The advantage of being responsive to only simple stimulus configurations is that the infant thereby avoids the overloading of his immature information processing apparatus. Genetically he is programmed to respond to those aspects of his environment that are most likely to ensure his survival, i.e. other people. If his responsiveness were too specifically determined – if, for instance, it were confined to the particular woman who had given birth to him, difficulties would ensue in the comparatively large number of cases where a change in mother-figure has to take place subsequently. As it is, the infant has not only certain wide stimulus preferences but also a large learning capacity. He is, therefore, not only bound to come into frequent interaction with others but will also be able to become further acquainted with their more individual characteristics. The effects of this learning can be seen in the restriction that takes place in the nature of the effective stimulus required to elicit responsiveness: the scrambled face, for instance, ceases to be as interesting as the regular face, so that gradually the effective stimulus comes to resemble more and more the 'real' human being. Such learning becomes evident quite early on and will in due course give rise to differential behaviour to social as opposed to non-social objects. Categorization of experiences is essential if one is to make sense of the world and it does not seem unreasonable to conclude that the first general category established in infancy is that of 'human beings'.

3 Social Signalling Systems

It is apparent that in his interaction with the outside world an infant is far from passive. He does not merely lie in his cot waiting to be moulded by whatever environmental forces happen to impinge on him, stirred into activity only by strong internal stimuli denoting hunger or pain. Such a *tabula rasa* conception will not stand close examination. It is based on the infant's undisputed motor helplessness and neglects his competence in other areas.

There are, we have seen, certain kinds of stimuli emanating primarily from social objects to which the infant pays special attention. But the bond between parent and child is not only based on parental stimuli to which the infant responds; it is also based on stimuli which the infant offers and which exercise a compelling influence on his parents. They may be regarded as signalling devices, the function of which is to ensure proximity of caretakers and to bring about interaction.

Young children use a great many devices to draw the attention of other people to them: they call, they stretch out their arms, they tug at clothes, they climb up on the mother's lap, they hammer at doors and in this way are able to initiate social interaction. The comparative lack of motor abilities for the greater part of the first year which precludes the use of most of these patterns should not, however, blind one to the force of those devices with which the infant is equipped from the beginning. In particular, the baby's cry and the baby's smile are powerful means of affecting the people around him and of thus determining both the amount and the kind of stimulation to which he is exposed.

The crying response

Curiously, crying has been given far less systematic attention than has been paid to the smiling response. Yet the cry is present from birth, its physical characteristics are such that it can have a most arousing effect on the listener and while smiling can only take place when proximity to the other person has already been attained, the function of the cry is to bring about proximity in the first place. The information value of the cry is quite considerable and in its more extreme form the response may be regarded as a danger signal analagous to the distress vocalizations found in many animals (Scott, 1971).

The organization of the crying response

Crying is, in fact, a generic name that refers to a number of signals already differentiated from one another in the neonatal period. Wolff (1969), in one of the few intensive studies of this problem, was able to identify three distinct patterns by means of spectographic analysis:

1. A basic pattern, linked, amongst other factors, to hunger, which starts arythmically and at low intensity, but gradually becomes louder and more rhythmical.

2. The 'mad' or angry cry, characterized by the same temporal sequence as the basic pattern (namely cry rest–inspiration–rest) but distinguished from it by differences in the length of the various phase components.

3. The pain cry, which is sudden in onset, is loud from the start and is made up of a long cry, followed by a long silence (during which there is breath holding) and then by a series of short gasping inhalations.

Quite different information is carried by these patterns and Wolff found that mothers could fairly easily distinguish among them and react appropriately.

The crying response is an example of a response pattern that appears to be endogenously organized in terms of complex time sequences. Each sequence of expiratory cry, rest period, inspiratory whistle and rest period may be regarded is an instance of an intrinsically regulated high-frequency rhythmical pattern that appears already in neonates in remarkably stable serial order (Wolff, 1967). Mothers, to whom tape recordings of the pain cry were played, tended to respond with great concern; but when the time sequences of the same recorded cry were altered by removing most of the long silent period, mothers uniformly responded with less distress. The temporal arrangement apparently served as an important signalling function. When a masking noise was played into the infant's ear during crying the distortion of the feedback did not alter the basic pattern. This gives strength to the conclusion that neonatal vocalization rhythms are controlled by autonomous central mechanisms.

In normal neonates, according to Prechtl *et al.* (1969), the duration of cries and the intervals between them are characteristic for each infant – one of the earliest indications of individuality to be reported. Both the duration and the intervals tend to become shorter and less variable in the course of the first nine days of life. Neurologically abnormal infants, however, show large variation in crying parameters – as though the endogenous control mechanisms have been damaged and are not able to impose the same rhythmical regularity on crying. Thus, it is possible to use the characteristics of the cry response for the diagnosis of brain damage (Fisichelli and Karelitz, 1963): infants with known damage, given a standardized stimulus procedure (the snap of a rubber band), were less likely to respond to the first application of the stimulus than normal infants, showed longer latencies and did not sustain the cry for as long a period. The signalling capacity of such infants is thus disturbed from the beginning and mothering will, therefore, become a far more difficult task than with normal infants. If mutual adaptation is to take place between mother and child, the behaviour of each partner must be reasonably predictable to the other. This, it appears, is not the case with brain-damaged infants.

Eliciting and terminating conditions

Even in the first week, Wolff (1969) pointed out, the range of physical and physiological conditions that evoke crying is wider than has been commonly thought. Temperature, for instance, has a decisive influence, in that infants in a neo-natal crib kept at 78 degrees were found to cry considerably more than when the crib was kept at 88 degrees. Undress-ing, even when temperature changes were taken into account, also played a part, with both the elimination of skin contact and the release from the confinement of clothing apparently contributing to the provocation of cry-ing. Placing a blanket or a towel on the baby's body ter-minated distress, but plastic or a rubber sheet were far less effective in this respect.

Initially crying is mainly due to intense visceral activity, but with increasing age the eliciting and terminating con-ditions soon become much wider in range. Kessen and Mandler (1961), using the concept of 'specific inhibitor', identified such inhibitors of crying as non-nutritive sucking, physical contact, rocking and the sight of a human face. Wolff also found that sucking a pacifier tended to inhibit mass activity, thus reducing the inflow of self-stimulation and interrupting the self-arousing cycle of crying and limb thrashing. Anything, he concluded, which either reduces the total amount of proprioceptive feedback or renders the background of exteroceptive and proprioceptive stimula-tion constant or rhythmical will lower the general arousal state, inhibit crying and prepare the baby for sleep or quiet alertness. In addition, at later ages and with increasing pro-ficiency at visual pursuit, objects moved across the visual field, if of sufficient size and brightness and presented at the proper focal distance, also become efficient inhibitors.

A great deal of work requires to be done on all these various terminating conditions. That rocking, for example, is an effective means of reducing distress is a matter of com-mon knowledge among mothers, yet the properties of such stimulation and their precise effects on infants have received scant attention. Gordon and Foss (1965) were able to demonstrate the effectiveness of rocking by applying this form of stimulation to neonates and recording the incidence of subsequent crying. In comparison with non-stimulated controls, the amount of crying was considerably reduced. Not any kind of rocking will do, however. In a preliminary report, Ambrose (1969) has given details of a machine (a 'vestibulator') which enabled him to apply rhythmic vertical movement to a baby at various specified amplitudes and rates of oscillation – a kind of up-and-down stabilimeter. Using an amplitude of two and three-quarter inches, Ambrose has found a critical oscillation rate of approximately sixty per minute when babies invariably stop crying. They usually do so within fifteen seconds of reaching this rate and tend to remain quiet even when the machine is switched off. Simultaneously obtained polygraphic recordings of functions such as respiration and heart rate should lead eventually to greater understanding of the mechanism underlying this effect; in the meantime one may well wonder whether here, too, endogenously organized rhythms may not be operative and dictate the rate at which stimulation becomes effective. It is also tempting to speculate whether the self-initiated rocking movements observed mainly in deprived children might not have the same function: in the absence of human stimulation the infant supplies the required stimuli to himself at the appropriate rate and thus obtains the necessary comfort.

There is some evidence to indicate that constant stimulation has the same soothing effect as rhythmical stimulation. In an experiment on one-month-old infants, Brackbill (1971) applied continuous stimulation via one, two, three or four different sensory modalites (auditory, visual, proprioceptive-tactile and temperature). Indices of arousal level, including crying, heart rate, respiration and gross motor activity, were taken under the four experimental conditions as well as under a control condition of no extra stimulation. The results of this study indicate clearly the pacifying effects of continuously applied stimulation and, moreoever, show that the effect is not restricted to one modality but appears to be a general characteristic of sensory stimulation. It was also found that the drop in arousal increased with the number of modalities involved.

Inhibiting stimuli, it appears, are usually those that tend to be presented by other human beings: stimuli such as rocking, physical contact, interesting visual objects. At first these need not be specifically human; that is, any object meeting the necessary stimulus requirements will suffice. From about the fifth week on, however, Wolff found that crying was inhibited more effectively by human stimulation (voice or face) than by a non-social stimulus. Similarly, at this age crying began to be initiated more frequently by the disappearance of a social than a non-social object and though as yet no differentiation among social objects was shown, the restriction of the range of effective stimuli which is such a central theme in early development is well illustrated thereby.

The function of crying

At first crying is an expressive pattern, that is, it tends to be initiated more or less automatically by a set of stimuli – mainly of organic origin – which trigger off the response regardless of any likely consequences. Its signal function, though biologically adaptive, is not yet appreciated by the infant himself. Only as a result of repeatedly experiencing the effects of his actions will he come to learn that certain consequences tend to follow from them and in time the 'attention-please' type of cry will then appear. In infants as young as six to eight weeks Wolff found crying to occur when the child was left by an adult, but it was the act of disappearance with its resultant change in stimulation and not the absence of the person that evoked the distress – when a baby was allowed to continue to cry after being left he usually settled down again quite quickly. Another appearance and subsequent departure of the person would start the infant crying once again, and so on. Thus it was simply the sight of being left that triggered off the infant's protests, without any intentionality having to be invoked to explain this behaviour. Intentional signals, when the infant cries *in order* to summons the mother to his side, appear later. Crying is then no longer initiated by a change in stimulation to which the infant soon becomes adapted: it is object-oriented and is resorted to because the infant tends by this means to restore the mother.

An infant certainly has plenty of opportunity to learn the consequences of this response. Moss and Robson (1968) carried out six-hour observation sessions in infants' homes at the end of the first month of life and again at the end of the third month. During these sessions their fifty-four subjects provided 2461 crying episodes and of these 77 per cent were followed by a maternal response but only 6 per cent were preceded by contact with the mother. These figures, the authors believed, reflect the infant's influence on the mother: his crying draws the mother close, facilitates interaction with her and thus contributes to establishing conditions favourable to the development of an attachment.

One way in which this effect is brought about is illustrated in a study by Korner and Grobstein (1966). The authors had observed that when crying infants are picked up and put to the shoulder they not only quieten but also become visually alert and start scanning the environment. In order to explore this relationship more systematically the incidence of visual alertness of crying neonates was recorded for 30 seconds following the experimenter's intervention. This took the form of putting the infant either to the left shoulder or to the right shoulder or (as a control condition) of merely sitting him up. A further control condition in which the infant remained on his back without intervention by the experimenter was also added. It was found that infants generally quieted, alerted and scanned when put to the shoulder, whereas handling alone did not induce alertness significantly more often than the non-intervention condition. This, the authors suggested, may be one important pathway by which maternal ministrations may inadvertently provide visual experiences: by reducing the intensity of internal needs the organism can turn outward and attend to the external world. And the object to which they are then likely to give particular attention, one may add, is the mother herself.

The smiling response

The first observed occurrence of the smile is regarded by most mothers as a major landmark in their relationship with the child. It enhances the attractiveness of the infant, tends to lead to further responses on the part of the mother and thus starts a chain of interaction tying one partner to the other. Smiling, Darwin (1872) pointed out, has survival value, for it brings about and maintains the proximity of mother and child.

Eliciting stimuli

The smile is a peculiarly *social* response. Although it has been suggested that it may initially be triggered off merely by a change in brightness or contrast in the visual environment (Salzen, 1963) or, alternately, that it is a response to familiarity and thus a sign of recognition of any object, animate or inanimate (Piaget, 1953), it generally occurs in an interpersonal situation where it is mostly elicited by social stimuli, in particular the sight of the human face.

Nevertheless, a series of investigations (Ahrens, 1954; Kaila, 1932; Spitz and Wolf, 1946) have made it abundantly clear that in the early months the smile is evoked by a stimulus which, though inherent in human faces, is of a very much more primitive nature. This has been established by taking the face to pieces, as it were, and presenting its various features and characteristics one by one and in various combinations, either by covering up parts of an experimenter's face or by presenting cardboard masks. In this way it has become apparent that in the second and third months of life, i.e. following the first appearance of the smile, it does not require the whole human face to evoke the smile but merely certain quite simple stimulus configurations such as a pair of eyelike dots. A mask containing nothing but such dots will evoke the smile in the very young infant as surely as his mother's face. Movement of the stimulus object is a useful but not essential condition – presumably because it helps to keep the infant's attention on the stimulus. If the lower part of the experimenter's face is covered with a piece of white cardboard, the smiling response can be elicited as easily as without hiding the adult's mouth. If, however, the upper part of the face, including the eyes or even one of the eyes, is covered, the smile can no longer be evoked. If the adult turns his profile to the infant so that he can see only one eye, the response stops abruptly.

The eyes, in the first two months, thus represent the crucial eliciting stimulus. Again, however, we find that the necessary stimulus is of a simpler, more primitive form than is presented by the human being. Ahrens compared a number of dot arrangements, angles and a rectangular bar drawn on a piece of cardboard with a realistically portrayed face and found the dot patterns to be actually more effective than the face. The contour of the cardboard, oval or round, was of no significance – the infant's attention was centred entirely in the dots. Moreover, just as an egg-retrieval response in birds will occur in a much more intense and persistent form to eggs of an inordinately large size than to eggs of a natural size, so a mask with six dots will evoke more smiling in two-month-old infants than one with two dots. In both instances a supra-optimal stimulus is functioning more effectively than nature herself (Tinbergen, 1951). These considerations led Spitz (1965) to suggest that the Gestalt centred around the eyes constitutes a key stimulus to an innate releasing mechanism analogous to those described by ethologists for a wide range of species-specific responses in animals. In all these instances the animal is equipped with an inherently determined readiness to respond in a particular manner to certain quite specific stimuli: the pecking response of the young herring gull is released by the red dot which (normally) is found on the parent's beak; fly-catching behaviour in frogs is elicited by the movement of small objects within a certain range; chaffinches show mobbing responses to models portraying owl-like features. And the human infant, too, is structured in such a fashion that certain biologically important stimulus-response sequences – such as smiling to eye-like patterns – are part of his innate endowment, bringing him into contact with other human beings and thereby increasing his chances of care, protection and survival.

Developmental changes

Lower animals continue all their lives to respond in this more or less automatic fashion. The human infant, however, soon learns to respond to more differentiated and more individualized forms. Thus, with increasing age, the effectiveness of the various facial features changes: on the one hand, more and more of the face is required in order to elicit the smile and, on the other hand, the stimulus must resemble to an increasing extent real human beings rather than geometrical patterns, until eventually it comes to be evoked only by certain specific human beings.

Figure 4 illustrates the critical properties of the human face which elicit smiling at different ages. With increasing maturity the child comes to attend to features other than the eyes; his information-processing apparatus ceases to handle only those stimuli to which it is innately linked and takes account of their context as well; and as a result the necessary eliciting stimulus requires greater, more detailed specification. From three months on the infant attends not merely to the eyes but visually relates the various features to one another. Up to five months of age he responds alike to smiling, scowling or crying faces; thereafter he begins to differentiate among the various expressions. The movement of the mouth now matters: a wide-drawn, moving mouth elicits the smile more readily than a stationary, closed mouth. At six months two-dimensional models are no longer sufficient and solidity must be added to the requirements. And after seven months the most important change of all takes place, as from then on smiling is no longer indis-

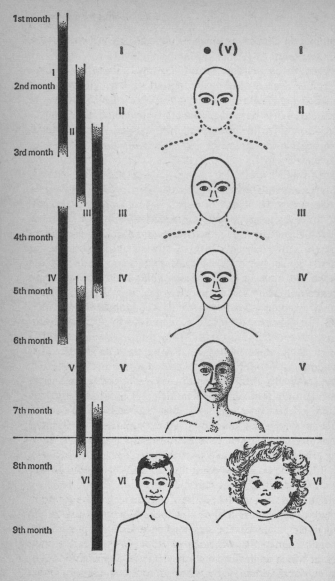

Figure 4 Necessary and sufficient conditions for evoking smiling in infants up to the ninth month. (From Ahrens, 1954)

criminately elicited by all faces but only by certain specific, familiar ones.

Even in its earliest stages, however, there is nothing mechanical about the occurrence of smiling. From a very detailed longitudinal investigation, Wolff (1963) concluded that the internal and external conditions eliciting the smile are of considerable complexity and that at no point should one regard the behaviour pattern as completely stereotyped. While others have stipulated the age on first appearance as being around six weeks, Wolff, employing a much more intensive method of observation than otherwise customary, found evidence of smiling already in the first week. At this stage, however, it takes the form of a spontaneous discharge pattern rather than of a response linked to particular external stimuli. These first become effective in the third week, in that a high-pitched voice began at this time to evoke clear-cut, broad smiles whenever the infants were awake and alert. Thus the discrepancy in findings about age of onset appears to be due, in the first place, to the fact that Wolff concerned himself not only with visual but also with auditory stimuli and, in the second place, to the attention which he paid to internal state as a determinant. Initially, the smile is found only under certain conditions of organismic state (drowsiness in the first week for spontaneous smiles, alert arousal subsequently) and it is not until the child reaches older age levels that the response achieves a greater degree of autonomy from variations in internal condition. At the same time the 'stimulus-boundness' of smiling gradually recedes and the infant smiles more selectively, as if he were no longer compelled to smile each time he was confronted with the relevant stimulus.

Thus certain orderly, progressive changes can be found in the development of smiling – changes which Gewirtz (1965) suggested could be encompassed in a three-stage developmental framework consisting of (a) a phase of reflex smiling in which smiles occur in the absence of readily indentifiable visual stimuli, (b) a phase of 'social' smiling, in which human faces in general represent the necessary stimuli, and

(c) a phase of 'selective' social smiling, when the infant no longer reacts indiscriminately to all social objects and only certain selected individuals continue to evoke the response.

How quickly and in what manner the child moves along this progression appears to be largely a function of the kind of social environment in which he is reared. Ambrose (1961), in a comparison of the development of the smiling response in institutionalized and family-reared infants, found that the form of the growth trend in the two samples was by and large similar but that the equivalent characteristics of each trend occurred significantly earlier in the family-reared sample. For these infants, for instance, smiling was first observed to occur in the experimental situation within the six- to ten-week range, compared to the nine- to fourteen-week range for the institution infants, and while the response-strength peak occurred between eleven and fourteen weeks for the former group, it was found in the range of sixteen to twenty weeks for the latter.

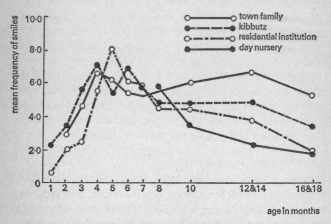

Figure 5 Age curves for mean frequency of smiles in two minutes for infants from four Israeli child-rearing environments, in the one- through eighteen-lunar-month range. (From Gewirtz, 1965)

Gewirtz (1965), too, observed differences according to method of rearing. In his study four groups of Israeli infants were examined, namely, infants reared respectively in a residential institution, a family, a kibbutz and a day nursery. Apart from quantitative differences in the rate of development, Gewirtz also noted differences in the form of the developmental trend. Not only did the curves of response strength for the family and the kibbutz infants rise to an earlier peak, but the amount of smiling to the experimenter declined less in these two groups than in the other two samples (Figure 5). This study illustrates well the use that can be made of existing nuances in child rearing. One can then proceed to search for the factors responsible for the differences observed – factors which, Gewirtz suggests, can be discussed in terms of the differential availability of stimuli that elicit and reinforce the smiling response in each case.

Individual differences in 'signalability'

The function of the crying response is to bring about proximity between mother and child; the function of the smile is to ensure that this proximity is maintained and that interaction takes place. Yet it is apparent that in some infants signal strength, or 'signalability', is greater and more intense than in others. By being capable of emitting more powerful signals their effect on the social environment and their ability to bring about and sustain interaction is superior. What may account for such differences?

Environmental determinants

Two kinds of factors need to be taken into consideration: environmental and organismic. As to the first, it is apparent from the studies by Ambrose and Gewirtz just referred to that in certain types of childrearing settings infants are given more encouragement to make use of signals than in others and that their responsiveness becomes consequently increased. This process may be demonstrated experimentally.

Brackbill (1958), using an operant-conditioning procedure, set out to investigate whether the smiling response in four-month-old infants can be brought under environmental control. A baseline rate for smiling was obtained while the experimenter stood motionless and expressionless over the infant. During the conditioning period reinforcement was given contingent upon the occurrence of a smile: the experimenter smiled in return, talked to the infant and briefly picked him up. Some infants were regularly reinforced, others intermittently. In this way Brackbill was able successfully to increase the rate of smiling during conditioning and also to show that the intermittent reinforcement schedule resulted in a slower rate of extinction than was found among the continuously reinforced infants. Amount of smiling is thus a function of the particular manner in which the infant's caretakers respond to him.

Brossard and Decarie (1968) attempted to refine this conclusion further by examining the effectiveness of various modes of responsiveness to the smile. They compared eight types of reinforcement, consisting of visual, auditory, tactile and kinaesthetic response patterns, used singly or in combination. Picking up the infant was found to be the most effective reinforcer, merely touching him the least. When the subjects whose reinforcement involved some kind of kinaesthetic stimulation were compared with the remainder, a significant difference in favour of the former emerged. This technique is clearly a promising one in attempts to isolate the particular stimulus conditions operative in influencing the development of early social behaviour; caution must, however, be exercised in generalizing results, as so frequently the subjects employed are drawn from institutions where normal reinforcement patterns are likely to be very different from those encountered by family-reared infants. How an infant responds to an experimental situation is most probably a function not only of the particular experimental conditions employed, but also of the norm established by his everyday experience. And for institutionalized infants there may be qualitative as well as quantitative differences in this respect.

Working with another social response, namely, vocalization, Rheingold, Gewirtz and Ross (1959) were also able to demonstrate a conditioning effect. In two parallel, identical experiments involving three-month-old infants, vocalizations were reinforced by three simultaneous actions on the part of the experimenter, i.e. a smile, a 'tsk' sound repeated three times and a light touch on the abdomen. As seen in Figure 6, the conditioning procedure raised the level of vocalizations from a mean of approximately fourteen during the baseline period to a peak of twenty-five. At the end of extinction the number had dropped once more to about fifteen. Vocal behaviour can thus be reinforced by a complex act on the part of the adult. Moreover, a subsequent experiment by Weisberg (1963) established that social as opposed to non-social stimulation (at least in the form used in this experiment) has a particularly potent effect in this respect. Comparing the rate of conditioning in a group of

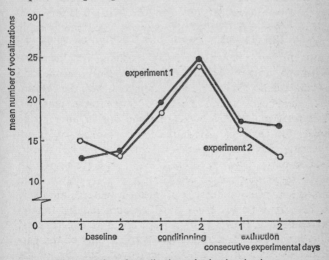

Figure 6 Mean number of vocalizations obtained under three experimental conditions from two parallel experiments. (From Rheingold, Gewirtz and Ross, 1959)

three-month-old infants treated as in the Rheingold, Gewirtz and Ross experiment with that in a group reinforced by the sound of a door chime, Weisberg found evidence of conditioning only in the socially reinforced infants. It was also shown that the mere presence of an adult, who stayed with a control group throughout the experimental session but remained immobile and unresponsive, did not act as a releaser for vocalization. The same applied to randomly administered stimulation: only the adult's contingent participation in an interaction sequence initiated by the infant's signals will, it must be concluded, affect signalability.

Organismic determinants

The powerful effect of experience should not, however, blind one to the existence of inherent individual differences. This point can be illustrated most clearly by reference to the extreme. In an attempt to obtain material about the early behaviour of children subsequently diagnosed as suffering from autism, the present writer interviewed the mothers of nine such children aged, at the time, between two and six years. While the retrospective and indirect nature of the data impose obvious limits on their reliability, certain fairly consistent conclusions do emerge from this material. In particular, it appears that the signalling ability of these children is severely impaired during the early months of life. The mothers usually described them as 'very good babies'; on closer inquiry it emerged that in all these cases being 'good' referred to an almost complete absence of the ability to cry in situations where this response could normally be expected to occur. Thus (with one exception) these infants never cried when hungry: it was left entirely to the mother to determine times for feeding and even if a feed had for some reason to be grossly delayed the infant still did not protest. Again, whereas the normal infant, at the end of his feed, would turn his head away or adopt some other means to indicate that he had had enough, these infants did nothing: they remained utterly passive and it was left entirely to the mother to decide when to terminate the feed. None of these children was reported as having ever cried for attention during infancy, even when left alone for lengthy periods of time, and the departure of an adult, whether the familiar mother or anyone else, never elicited protests. In most circumstances there was impaired responsiveness to pain and discomfort: dirty nappies, gastric upset and even sudden painful stimuli such as injections rarely called forth the protests one can usually expect under such circumstances. On the other hand, signalling ability in some sectors did appear to be present, in that all these infants were said to have smiled and vocalized, at any rate in the early months before their serious social disability emerged in a clear-cut form towards the end of the first year. Thus the disability referred primarily to a severe, pathological absence of the crying response and, being evident from the early weeks on, the condition may be assumed to be of inherent origin.

While such extremes are fortunately rare, they do indicate the possibility that 'signalability' may be constitutionally as well as environmentally determined and that individual differences in fussiness or ability to smile are not necessarily built into the infant by his environment, but that they represent a part of his make-up from the beginning. Direct evidence for this proposition is so far somewhat meagre. In a study primarily concerned with the genetic basis of early social behaviour, Freedman (1965) observed a group of eleven identical and nine fraternal twins at monthly intervals throughout the first year. The data obtained by him suggest that a trait labelled 'social orientation' appears to be under genetic control, in that a greater concordance of scores for amount of smiling and for visual fixation of a face was found for the identical than for the fraternal twins. Also suggestive are the findings from a further study by Freedman and Freedman (1969), in which American-born neonates of Chinese origin were compared with American-born neonates of European origin. A number of measures of temperament, sensory development, central nervous system maturity, motor development and social responsiveness were obtained. Of these it was only the scores for temperament that clearly differentiated the two groups: in particular, the Chinese neonates showed less lability of state, were more easily consoled when picked up after crying and stopped crying sooner even without soothing. Thus, although there were no differences in the actual amount of crying, there are indications that the Chinese are less changeable and less perturbable – even as babies.

The fact that both Gottesman (1966) and Scarr (1969) have isolated from their respective twin studies a genetically determined factor labelled 'person orientation' or 'sociability' provides further support for the proposition that individual differences in social behaviour are partly determined by heredity. This, as Scarr points out, is strengthened by the finding that several longitudinal studies have reported considerable stability over age in such differences. Nevertheless, studies in this area are still too few to enable us to discuss with confidence the factors that underlie signalability.

Conclusions

Crying and smiling illustrate well the spontaneous quality that characterizes so much of early social behaviour. They show that the infant himself can initiate social interactions and that these signalling devices may be used to regulate the required stimulation obtainable from other people.

Crying in particular has sometimes been attributed to 'stimulus hunger' – the infant, that is, who has been left to his own devices for a long period of time will summons in this way company and attention and so bring about a change of position and of scenery. It may, on the other hand, also stem from too much stimulation – whether the source is an overfull stomach or an over-solicitous mother. In either case it is a signal for intervention and is usually responded to as such by the child's caretakers. It thus serves an essential function, for whereas the adult has a great many mechanisms available whereby he can modulate his own level of stimulation, the infant initially needs an external agent to take the necessary steps on his behalf.

In the early weeks crying and smiling serve as signals only

in the sense that other people will almost invariably be impelled to react to them. They are not yet signals in the sense that the infant uses them purposely in order to summons help and attention. They tend to be triggered off by certain primitive stimuli, with no foresight involved on the part of the infant as to the likely consequences of his actions. The realization that these responses have quite predictable effects on others comes only with time and will depend on the learning opportunities that an infant encounters in his particular social environment. Thus the institutionalized infant whose cries generally remain unanswered and whose smiles produce only minimal effects is not likely to use these methods of social intercourse as much or as selectively as the infant brought up by a mother who responds in a sensitive and regular manner. All normal infants will in time graduate from the stage at which their inborn signalling patterns are elicited in a purely automatic fashion, but the speed with which they do so, the extent to which they use these devices and the situations in which they employ them depend entirely on their social experience.

Learning is also involved in the changes which can be found in the kinds of stimuli to which the infant responds with smiling and crying. Just as visual fixation is initially brought about by a number of simple stimulus properties that are inherent in the human face but not exclusive to it, so the infant's signals are at first associated with stimulus characteristics that are not necessarily of a specifically social nature. The smile will appear to any eye-like configuration and crying may be terminated as effectively by certain physical as by social stimuli. But just as the infant's visual fixation changes by becoming more selective in favour of social objects, so his signalling responses also gradually become restricted in the course of the first few months to the biologically 'correct' object. This developmental change, too, is a function of learning experience: born to respond to certain limited stimuli, the infant learns that these stimuli generally appear in a particular context and in time the context is also required as part of the eliciting stimulus. An increase in information processing capacity is thus indicated – the more an infant is exposed to complex stimuli like faces, the more of these stimuli is he able to assimilate. His inborn equipment provides him with the first step; experience must do the rest.

Let us finally note that the full range of signalling devices available to infants at different ages remains to be ascertained. Crying and smiling may be the most essential, but they are by no means the only ones even in the first half year. Babbling and cooing are certainly other 'come hither' signals, but in addition there appear also to be devices whereby infants can *terminate* interaction: devices like turning the head, shutting the eyes and even falling asleep. Detailed study of mother–infant interaction sequences should make it possible to identify such mechanisms, to specify the conditions under which they are brought into play and to assess their role in the developing relationship between mother and child.

4 The Familiarization Process

Other people are salient to an infant because, in the first place, they possess sensory qualities that attract his attention and, in the second place, because they respond to his signals and thereby make possible the establishment of reciprocal behaviour sequences. The more an individual is exposed to an object the greater are his opportunities to become acquainted with its specific characteristics, and it thus comes about that an infant will in due course learn not only the universal features of human beings but also the particular features which distinguish those with whom he comes into regular daily contact.

Initially the infant is 'pre-set' to respond only to a relatively limited number of universal features, such as eyes, and to neglect all individual characteristics. Some lower species will always remain at this stage: the apparently highly developed community life of ants rests entirely on undifferentiated groups within which all animals are responded to as alike and never become recognized as individuals, so that each member is interchangeable for any other. The human organism is of a more flexible nature: it is pre-set only to the extent that contact with other human beings is ensured, but once this has occurred it may then bring into play its additional capacity of learning also those features which differentiate one individual from another.

Such learning represents the second major accomplishment in the growth of early social behaviour. It is dependent on the storage of previously encountered experiences and the ability to compare present sensory input with retained past impressions. Its achievement means that the child can recognize people and classify them into the known and the unknown. The basis of responsiveness consequently changes: the child does not merely ask of the stimulus 'Is it interesting?' but also 'Have I seen it before?'

Discriminating the mother

Our knowledge about the beginnings of social discrimination is still extremely limited. Considering both the importance of this development and the amount of work that has been done on the growth of the ability to differentiate inanimate stimuli in terms of previous experience, it is surprising that we are still unable to supply answers to such fundamental problems as the age when infants first become capable of recognizing the mother, the range and determinants of individual differences in this respect and the conditions under which social differentiation takes place. At a purely descriptive level a lot more material is required before a fully adequate picture of this stage of social development can be presented.

Observational studies

Recognition of the mother is, without doubt, a very early achievement. On this point there is general agreement, though just how early is far less certain. Normative studies carried out in the course of developmental test construction generally refer to the second month as the time when infants can first be expected to show signs of visual recognition (Bayley, 1969; Griffiths, 1954). However, the criteria according to which recognition is judged to have occurred tend to be rather vague: Bayley instructed her testers to watch for 'any change of expression' that occurs when the child looks from stranger to mother, while Griffiths considered that a child can differentiate the mother if he greets her 'first with a lovely smile and afterwards with an intent expression attending to what she is saying'. The lyrical quality of such instructions cannot, unfortunately, obscure the lack of reliability of the procedures involved.

A number of observational studies have specifically concerned themselves with the problem of social differentiation. Yarrow (1967), in the course of a study on the effects of early maternal separation involving a change in mother-figure, obtained data on the growth of differential responsiveness in a sample of one hundred infants, of whom at least forty were available in any one age group. The infants were studied during one-and-a-half-hours observation sessions held in their own homes, in the course of which their responses to both the mother's face and voice and the observer's face and voice were recorded. Differential responsiveness was measured in terms of changes in activity, including both marked increases or decreases, changes in approach–withdrawal movements, changes in facial expression and changes in amount of vocalization. Latency, duration and intensity of responsiveness were noted. From his material (which, like his methodology, is unfortunately reported only briefly), Yarrow concluded that passive selective responsiveness, in which the infant concentrates on the mother and ignores the stranger, is shown by some infants as early as one month of age. By the end of the first month 38 per cent of the sample were showing varying degrees of positive affect and approach movements towards the mother (but not towards the stranger) and by three months eighty-one per cent showed definite signs of recognition of the mother. At five months of age this type of response was well established in all of the infants.

Yarrow studied a multiplicity of responses in order to obtain evidence for differential behaviour. Most other investigators, however, have concentrated on certain specific responses, of which the smile has been the most popular. In his investigation of this behaviour pattern, Ambrose (1961) found that peak response strength to the strange observer's face was reached at about thirteen weeks by home-reared infants. Before this age Ambrose believes that the faces of people other than the mother are hardly or not at all discriminated by the infant, so that the expectations he learns in relation to the one face are generalized to all other faces. The peak appears to mark the time at which such generalization ceases and discrimination begins. From then on the infant continues to smile as much at familiar individuals but shows a decline in response strength to strangers. This is confirmed by the findings of a longitudinal study of the responses of thirty-six infants to a standardized interaction sequence with a stranger (Schaffer, 1966a). Here, too, it was noted that in the initial weeks of life all infants showed automatic responsiveness, i.e. they smiled almost immediately at the stranger and gave no indication of any awareness of unfamiliarity. At ages varying from thirteen to nineteen weeks, however, a lag in the smile appeared and while the mother continued to elicit an immediate positive response the stranger was in all cases greeted with a 'sobering of the features'.

Ainsworth (1964, 1967) found somewhat earlier signs of differential behaviour in a longitudinal study of early social development. Her sample, however, was composed of African babies from Uganda who have been described as generally advanced in their early behavioural growth (Geber, 1958) and who cannot, therefore, be regarded as representative of non-African populations. Ainsworth noted that differential smiling occurred from about ten weeks of age, though her opportunities to observe it were limited due to the infrequency of face-to-face confrontations between mother and baby in this culture. Differential crying was first found at nine weeks, but as only one infant was observed before the age of eight weeks Ainsworth agreed it may well have been present even earlier. In any case, this index does not necessarily imply recognition: the fact that an infant cries when handled by a stranger but quietens when taken by the mother may merely be a reaction to more or less skilful methods of providing kinaesthetic stimulation. Finally, vocalization was also found to be an index of differential behaviour, in that infants tended to vocalize more readily and more frequently in interaction with the mother than with other people. This pattern did not, however, emerge till about twenty weeks of age.

It is highly likely that differential behaviour does not

appear in all response systems simultaneously, but that some are more sensitive to variations in familiarity than others. It is also possible that the various parameters used to describe any one response (such as the three parameters of latency, duration and intensity employed by Yarrow) show up differential behaviour to varying extent. It is certain that the nature of the particular observational techniques used to obtain the data will have a considerable influence on the conclusions reached by the individual investigator. Thus field studies, despite the richness of the available material, suffer from the limited extent to which the investigator can interfere with the situation and set up conditions for optimal observation of the relevant behaviour (e.g. by asking African mothers to adopt what to them is an unnatural method of face-to-face contact with their infants). The mere frequency of observation may be crucial in picking up the earliest occurrences of certain forms of behaviour. Wolff (1963), for example, found that by the fifth week of life the mother's voice was already more effective for eliciting vocalization than the voice of the observer. His observation procedure, however, involved five four-hourly and one ten-hourly session per week, so that the chances of noting a new developmental event were clearly considerably better than in studies employing a less intensive schedule of observation.

Merely to demonstrate differential responsiveness is, of course, not enough. If we wish to conclude that differential behaviour involves recognition, i.e. that it is the result of repeated exposure to one person and the lack of experience with another, it is necessary to demonstrate that initially no such differentiation existed and that it has come about as a result of experience. Otherwise the greater or more quickly mobilized responsiveness to the mother could be a function of her particular stimulating qualities, or of her greater awareness of the infant's requirements, or it might even reflect an inherently determined greater sensitivity to, say, a female voice than to a male voice. It is, therefore, essential to carry out longitudinal studies in order to demonstrate that stimuli that are initially equally effective in eliciting particular responses are no longer equal after varying amounts of exposure to them.

Experimental studies

Investigations carried out in the field tend to be suggestive rather than definitive. For the latter purpose laboratory-based studies supply the control and exactitude which an observational study often lacks. The few experimental studies that have concerned themselves with the problem of social differentiation have unfortunately not examined it longitudinally; nevertheless, the techniques used are of considerable interest and their results promising.

Fitzgerald (1968) measured the amount of pupillary dilation of infants aged one, two and four months to five visual stimuli, namely, the mother's face, a female stranger's face and three non-social stimuli (two checkerboards and a triangle). It was found that even at one month greater pupillary dilation occurred to the social stimuli. It was not till four months, however, that Fitzgerald found evidence for differentiation between the social stimuli, in that only infants of this age showed greater dilation to the mother than to the stranger. In evaluating these results it should be borne in mind that the stimuli were presented via a closed-circuit videotape television system and were thus two-dimensional, as well as being subject to the usual distorting effects of televised pictures. As the stimuli were, moreover, still photographs it seems likely that recognition was delayed and that a potentially very sensitive index failed to show the differentiation at earlier ages than one might otherwise have expected.

That such experimental parameters, as well as the particular response system investigated, can influence the results obtained is suggested by a study by Banks and Wolfson (1967). These investigators used cardiac rate as their measure of reactivity and found differential responding as early as six weeks of age. As mothers and strangers were presented in the flesh and as they did not remain immobile but interacted with the infants through vocalizing, a situation more closely resembling the infant's previous natural experience was used and presumably accounts to a large extent for the earlier age of differentiation.

A very different approach is found in a report by Wahler (1967). This study examined only three-month-old infants and, therefore, has nothing to say about the age when social differentiation *first* appears; on the other hand, it does offer a technique which could easily be used longitudinally in order to answer this question. It is based on the demonstration (referred to in the previous chapter) that infants' behaviour is subject to social reinforcement control, i.e. that the effect an infant's responses have on other people will either increase or decrease the likelihood that these responses will be repeated. Wahler's aim was to investigate whether three-month-old infants would be differentially responsive to the social reinforcers presented by familiar and unfamiliar adults, i.e. mothers and female strangers. After a baseline period during which the adult remained immobile and quiet, the reinforcement procedure, consisting of calling the child's name, smiling and lightly touching his chest, was applied on a continuous schedule immediately following the onset of each of the infant's smiles. In a final extinction period the adult once again remained unresponsive to smiling. As shown in Figure 7, the effectiveness of the adult as a source of reinforcement varied with his identity. On those occasions when infants were mother-reinforced, the baseline level of responding was raised to a considerably greater extent than when they were stranger-reinforced. Smiling to the mother was generally more likely to occur than smiling to the stranger, but under the mother-reinforcement condition more obvious changes took place between periods than under the stranger-reinforcement condition. Differential responsiveness to social reinforcers presented by familiar and unfamiliar adults is thus demonstrated.

Mixed observational and experimental designs have recently come to be increasingly used in infancy research. The focus of such studies is on the child's natural behaviour,

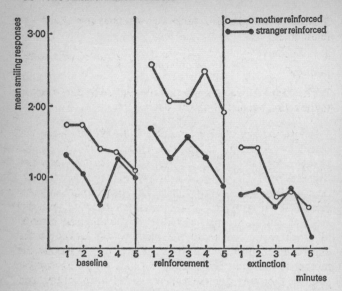

Figure 7 Mean number of smiling responses of thirteen infants reinforced by their mothers and by female strangers. (From Wahler, 1967)

but observed in situations specifically set up for this purpose and designed to highlight the phenomena of interest to the investigator. One such study was undertaken by Caldwell (1965), in which the differential visual behaviour of infants ranging in age from one to fifteen months was investigated. Caldwell set up seven consecutive situations in which the infants were observed:

1. Mother and stranger stood immobile and silent, one to each side of the infant.

2. The stranger, still immobile, smiled and talked to the infant.

3. Mother, still immobile, smiled and talked to the infant.

4. The stranger smiled and talked to the infant while walking back and forth.

5. Mother did likewise while the stranger was silent and immobile.

6. Mother left the room and the stranger moved over to her position.

7. The stranger picked up the infant and, on mother's return to the room, handed him over to her.

Before the age of three months, Caldwell was unable to detect any signs of differential behaviour in any of the episodes, amount of visual interest being about equally distributed between the two adults. After three months differential behaviour did occur, but took the form of a greater interest in the stranger. Even in episodes 3 and 5, when the stranger was silent and the mother stimulating, the infants, although looking more at the mother, still looked at the experimenter more frequently than they had looked at the mother in the equivalent episodes 2 and 4. Presumably the stranger exercised a novelty effect on the older infants and the greater amount of looking indicated the extent to which they were attempting to assimilate the strange experience.

There can be little doubt that by three months of age, and possibly even considerably earlier, an infant is able to recognize his mother and distinguish her from other people. But whatever the precise age, this development represents a considerable achievement for so young an organism, for it involves, in the first place, the ability to learn and retain information about the mother's particular appearance and thus, on subsequent encounters, to match sensory input with stored impression, and, in the second place, the ability to appreciate that the mother remains the same person despite the perceptual transformations that she undergoes almost continuously. These two processes refer respectively to perceptual learning and the development of perceptual constancies, both of which have received some attention from students of infant behaviour.

Perceptual learning

Traditionally, the topic of learning has been treated by psychologists in terms of two paradigms, namely classical (Pavlovian) conditioning and instrumental conditioning. Both these forms of learning involve the acquisition of particular motor responses in association with particular stimulus conditions and both are assumed to require reinforcement through reward or punishment.

Recently, however, it has become increasingly apparent that not all forms of learning can be forced into these two paradigms and that a great deal of learning takes place that requires neither conventional reinforcement nor the acquisition of specific stimulus–response bonds. For instance, rats brought up in cages in which geometrical shapes had been placed were subsequently found superior in discrimination learning involving such stimuli to rats brought up in bare cages – presumably because animals reared in perceptually 'rich' environments are able to register information that may later be applied to the solution of learning problems. Failure to have sufficient perceptual experience in early development, on the other hand, has repeatedly been shown to constitute a drawback to later adaptation. The concept of 'observational learning' (Bandura, 1965) likewise draws attention to the fact that an individual can acquire and retain information without the involvement of overt responses, having been used to indicate that mere exposure of a subject to a model may result in the acquisition of behaviour patterns without any practice of the relevant responses taking place.

Perceptual learning is thus the registration by the individual of his environment and occurs in the course of exposure to stimuli. He is thereby enabled to progress towards increasing stimulus differentiation, as manifested in the ability to respond to variables not previously responded to (Gibson, 1969). Perceptual learning is by no means a purely hypothetical, undemonstrable phenomenon; nevertheless, its most important consequences may be thought of in terms of central processes and, in particular, in the building up of inner structures variously referred to as central representations, cognitive maps, schemata or models.

The acquisition of central representations

The need for an individual to acquire an organized representation of his environment, i.e. a system of relations within which he himself can be located and which permits him to represent to himself those features of his surroundings that are regularly encountered, has been recognized by many writers (see Miller, Galanter and Pribram, 1960). The nature of central representations has been conceptualized in a number of different ways, but probably the most influential account is that offered by Sokolov (1963). This is based on the concept of *neuronal model*, which signifies an organization of neuronal cells in the cortex that processes and retains such information about a particular stimulus event as its intensity, duration and quality. A neuronal model is developed through repeated encounters with the same stimulus, each encounter further strengthening and elaborating the model. If the stimulus perceived by the organism is found to correspond with an existing model, some type of negative feedback occurs, resulting in the absence or attenuation of the orienting response. When, on the other hand, a novel stimulus is encountered for which there is no corresponding model available, an orienting reaction is elicited and the organism put in a state of readiness to deal with this new phenomenon. Repetition or persistence of the stimulus will, in time, result in the setting up of a further model, enabling the organism on future occasions to recognize the stimulus and to classify it as familiar. In the course of development, a considerable repertoire of such central representations will be built up and exposure to any stimulus situation will then inevitably result in an immediate search operation in order to ascertain whether the present sensory experience can be matched with any part of the memory store.

The acquisition of such models or representations is likely to be of greatest significance in the earliest period of development, when the infant first comes into perceptual contact with his environment. It is at this time that his basic orientations to the most frequently occurring aspects of his environment are established and it is naturally those objects with the greatest perceptual impact – such as other people – that are most likely to provide him with learning opportunities. The growth of social differentiation is thus intimately linked to the growth of perceptual learning abilities.

The development of these abilities in infancy has been most frequently studied by means of the habituation phenomenon. Habituation has been defined as the decrease in responsiveness that results from the repeated presentation of a stimulus (Harris, 1943) and is generally taken to imply that the central nervous system has retained the stimulus in some form. While the first experience with a novel stimulus will bring about maximum attention, subsequent encounters tend to elicit less interest, and growing familiarity thus results in response decrement. To check that such decrement is not due to receptor fatigue a novel stimulus of *less* intensity can be presented in order to observe whether dishabituation (i.e. recovery of attention) occurs. In this way it is possible to study developments in the ability to retain stimuli over varying gaps of time.

From such studies it has become apparent that habituation in the infant is primarily a function of age. In the early weeks of life, repeated stimulation produces no response decrement (other than that due to fatigue) and the ability to carry forward experiences across time gaps increases only gradually with age. Thus Fantz (1964), in a study of infants aged one to six months, used a simultaneous presentation technique in which ten pairs of magazine photographs were shown to the subjects. One photograph remained constant throughout the ten trials, while the other member of each pair was always a novel photograph. Figure 8 shows the changes in attention to the constant pat-

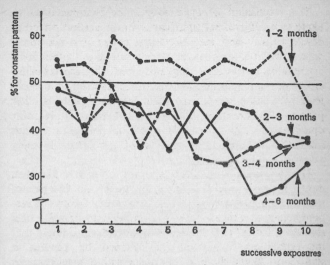

Figure 8 Change in amount of visual fixation of a repeatedly exposed (constant) pattern relative to a novel pattern on successive paired exposures. (From Fantz, 1964)

tern as a percentage of total attention. It is evident that, as a result of increasing familiarization, reduced interest in the repeatedly exposed pattern occurred in the oldest group, but that infants under two months of age showed no change in responsiveness. These younger infants behaved as though they were unable to differentiate between novel and familiar stimuli: even at the end of the series they distributed their attention equally among the two patterns, as though unaffected by their previous encounters with one of the stimuli. The older infants, on the other hand, were able to recognize the constantly appearing stimulus as familiar and, therefore, showed increasing interest in the novel pattern. The time gap between trials was thus successfully spanned by them – presumably because they had been able to form a central representation of the constantly appearing stimulus.

In a study using a successive rather than simultaneous

presentation technique and investigating a very much wider age range, Lewis (1969) also found evidence for the age-related nature of habituation rate. Infants aged between three and forty-four months were given four thirty-second trials, with thirty-second intervals, of a single blinking light. Habituation data, based on the decrement of amount of visual fixation from the first to the last trial, indicate that the rate of habituation is very closely related to age, with younger infants showing less response decrement than older infants. Thus habituation to a redundant signal follows a developmental pattern indicative of the organism's information processing efficiency: just as it has been shown that habituation is reduced in sleep and that it is affected by brain damage and intelligence (Thompson and Spencer, 1966), so it may also vary with age. The very young infant has as yet no capacity to store and carry forward information from one experience to another and as a result he responds to each repetition of a stimulus as though it were a completely new event. There have, admittedly, been a number of reports of habituation already occurring in neonates (Bartoshuk, 1962; Bridger, 1961), but these findings have not been corroborated by others (e.g. Haith, 1966) and may well have been a function, as Hutt, Bernuth, Lenard, Hutt and Prechtl (1968) suggest, of changes in the subjects' arousal state. The waking neonate, it seems, behaves like the sleeping or brain-damaged adult: none has a fully functioning capacity to be affected by previous experience.

Age is, of course, not the only condition to determine the extent to which information can be carried forward over time. This will also vary with the number of times the stimulus has been experienced, the lengths of such trials, the nature of the stimulus and, above all, the length of the time gap to be bridged. With regard to the latter variable, Bower (reported in Bruner, Olver and Greenfield, 1965) found that if a moving stimulus is passed behind a screen and emerges unchanged within a period of approximately one second, little change in the heart rate of two-month-old infants occurs. If, on the other hand, the moving stimulus disappears and then reappears in altered form, the re-appearance produces a marked cardiac deceleration – only, however, if the emergence occurs within the critical time limit of one second. Beyond this limit altered appearance has no effect: the infant (one may interpret) is no longer comparing the new with the old and is thus not surprised by the change.

In the absence of further parametric studies, one can at present only assume that the infant gradually becomes cap-able of spanning increasingly longer time intervals. The more frequently an object or person is perceived, the more easily will it be learned and subsequently recognized. On the other hand, the more complex a stimulus is, the more likely it will sustain interest and resist habituation. Caron and Caron (1968), for instance, showed checkerboards to infants aged three-and-a-half months and found that re-peated exposure leads to response decrement, but that the degree of decrement varies inversely with the complexity of the stimulus. Furthermore, Charlesworth (1966) found that the persistence of orienting and attending behaviour in infants aged five to nineteen months varies positively with the degree of stimulus uncertainty in a peek-a-boo game. When an infant could predict with certainty the locus in which a peek-a-boo face would appear he lost interest very much earlier than when the locus was varied randomly.

Novel or familiar?

The studies reviewed so far all suggest an inevitable preference for the novel. Given a choice (as in the experi-ment by Fantz) between a familiar and a novel stimulus, an infant finds the latter more attractive. Exposed re-peatedly to the same stimulus, his attention will decline.

Yet there are indications that this is not always so. Hunt (1964) has proposed that at about four months of age a phase begins in which the child comes gradually to try actively to retain situations or forms of input which he has encountered repeatedly in the past. He is now learning to recognize previously experienced stimuli, finds the confirmation of existing templates in his nervous system pleasant and strives to retain or regain them. Familiarity *per se* is what the infant desires at this stage and the pleasure of recognition is indicated by the smile evoked in encounters with familiar objects and people. But while at first emerging recognition is a source of pleasure and excitement, a further 'landmark of transition' occurs towards the end of the first year, when the infant becomes increasingly intrigued by what is novel and relatively unknown. The familiar has become too well known, it matches the central representation too closely and now merely brings about boredom. In this phase, therefore, the infant switches his interest from the familiar to the unfamiliar, curiosity emerges and to explore the unknown becomes one of the principal motives of the child.

While we need not take the ages stated in Hunt's proposal too literally (they are almost certainly grossly over-estimated), the notion of a two-stage developmental sequence, from an interest in the familiar to an interest in the novel, is appealing. So far, however, only meagre empirical evidence exists to back up such a proposal. The strongest data come from a study by Weizman, Cohen and Pratt (1971), in which infants were tested at six weeks and at eight weeks of age with a mobile which they had seen for thirty minutes daily since the age of four weeks. Visual fixation times at six weeks of age indicated more attention to the familiar than to a novel mobile presented simultaneously during the testing session; by eight weeks, however, fixation time to the novel had increased and the overall difference in attending to the two types of stimuli disappeared.

These findings contradict the common belief in the existence of a monotonic relationship between age and attention to novelty. It may be that in a generally bewildering world the familiar spells security to the young infant and that his 'preference' for it is really more an expression of a need to avoid the unfamiliar. On the other hand, it may indicate the challenge of a just emerging schema, of a newly familiar sight that has not yet been firmly assimilated and still requires repeated attention to confirm it. But whatever direction the infant's attention takes, whether towards the familiar or towards the novel, its dependence on past experience means that perceptual learning has occurred and that the infant is now capable of responding on the basis of his previous encounters with stimuli. And this, it appears, he can already do from a very early age.

Perceptually learning the social object

Social differentiation, we assume, depends on the same processes as those that enable an infant to distinguish the inanimate stimuli generally used in laboratory experiments in terms of his past experience of them. There is certainly no suggestion that long-term familiarization differs basically from short-term familiarization. A period of perceptual exposure to the mother must obviously take place before she can be recognized as different from other people, and on the basis of the resulting differential behaviour we may postulate that a central representation of her has been established. Such a representation is likely to take the form of a caricature rather than a photograph, but its existence means that the infant can now relate to the mother as something more than a bundle of external sensations and that she will begin to assume a significance different from that of unfamiliar individuals.

But what precisely happens during the initial period of perceptual exposure to the mother? What is it that the infant learns about her? Which features are included in the caricature and which left out?

Perceptual learning, as Gibson (1969) has stressed, involves the discovery of distinctive features, but what these are in the case of the infant's initial social learning we do not know. The end-result, namely, the ability to recognize the mother, can be described, but we are still ignorant as to how the infant achieves this. Almost certainly he will not be responding to her total appearance – some characteristics are likely to play a greater part in distinguishing her than others. Eyes, we have learned, assume an important role in the infant's responsiveness to social objects generally – are we to conclude that they are the first features which enable the infant to recognize specific individuals? Much has been written (albeit at a speculative level) about the crucial role of touch and the manner in which a mother holds her infant – are these the cues on which recognition is initially based? What part do voices play? Are olfactory stimuli of significance? A great deal of systematic research still needs to be done on these problems.

Perceptual constancy

One crucial difference between social objects and the laboratory stimuli used in the studies referred to above does exist. The latter generally appear in identical form from one trial to the next; the former are in a state of almost continuous change. Thus the infant must not only learn the characteristics which distinguish the mother from other people but he must also conserve her in the face of all the perceptual transformations likely to affect her appearance in different encounters. Sometimes she will be seen at a distance and sometimes close by; on some occasions she will appear full-face and on others in profile; she may have her curlers in and her teeth out, be with or without her spectacles, have or not have a hat, be wearing different clothes on different occasions and perhaps even different coloured hair – and yet must still be recognized as mother.

To be able to do so involves a considerable capacity for perceptual constancy. About the development of this ability in infancy not a great deal is as yet known. Is the capacity for object constancy innate or does it appear in the course of development? If the latter, when and under what conditions are the various constancies achieved? In a series of ingenious experiments Bower (1965, 1966) tested the development of size and shape constancy and found indications that these are already present in quite young infants. However, Gibson (1969), in a masterly review of work in this area, has suggested that what matters is not so much the development of constancy as such but rather the detection of invariants that characterize an object despite the transformations it undergoes. As she puts it: 'Constancy develops, I think, as the child has the opportunity to watch events. The face appears in the doorway and then looms towards him; after a bit, it recedes. The continuous transformation that the infant witnesses, of this object and of others, provides direct stimulus information for an invariant.'

A rich field of potential experimentation exists here. An infant of three months may be said to recognize the mother, but what constraints are there on such recognition? Is the mother with a hat still the same mother as without a hat? Must she always (as suggested by some of the studies of smiling) be seen full-face? In short, what changes are permissible at various ages that will still allow an infant to treat the mother as 'same'? Such information is vital if we are to understand the development of social differentiation.

The discrepancy hypothesis

To learn the familiar is one thing; to use it as a standard of reference for the comparison of other events is another. Thus, an infant not only learns the characteristics of the mother, but this knowledge becomes the means whereby other people are judged as unfamiliar. These two aspects are, however, not merely opposite sides of the same coin: as we shall see later, they represent different developments of varying degree of cognitive sophistication.

The relationship between attention and the difference between a familiar and a novel stimulus has been expressed by a number of writers in the form of the so-called discrepancy hypothesis (Hebb, 1949; Hunt, 1964; McClelland, Atkinson, Clark and Lowell, 1953). This states that stimuli which represent a moderate degree of discrepancy from an existing central representation, schema or adaptation level will elicit maximal attention, whereas those that are either very similar or extremely discrepant will elicit only minimal attention. If, therefore, several magnitudes of discrepancy are tested, the organism's response should yield a curve of an inverted-U shape.

This problem has been experimentally investigated by familiarizing infants on one stimulus and then presenting a new stimulus of a stated degree of difference from the standard. So far, unfortunately, the evidence for the discrepancy hypothesis is not very convincing. McCall and Kagan (1967) presented a standard stimulus and subsequently one of three graded discrepancies to four-month-old infants. They found the expected relationship for only one of their two indices (for cardiac rate, not for visual fixation), and even this was shown only by their female subjects. In a subsequent study McCall and Melson (1969) did obtain the hypothesized relationship with male infants, though once again only with cardiac and not with fixation measures. A small difference between the standard (S) and a discrepant stimulus (D) produced more attention to D than to S, whereas with larger differences D received less attention relative to S. However, as in another study by McCall and Kagan (1969), visual fixation rather than cardiac measures showed sensitivity to discrepancy and as only some infants provided evidence for the expected relationship to degree of discrepancy, our verdict of the hypothesis must be, at best, 'not proven'.

Nevertheless, the hypothesis has been used to account for some of the data on responses to normal and distorted faces. It has repeatedly been found that around four months of age responsiveness is greatest to regular faces, as represented by outline drawings and clay masks. Presumably, one may interpret, the infant has by now established a representation of his mother's face, and any generalized yet normal picture, being a moderate variation from this central standard, is of maximum interest. A scrambled drawing, however, represents too great a discrepancy and is thus disregarded. At subsequent ages, on the other hand, the central standard has itself become of so general a form that the infant assimilates slight deviations from real human faces without any difficulty and therefore without any great interest. It is now the greater discrepancies, as found in scrambled faces, that elicit the most interest.

Imprinting

The relevance of perceptual learning to early social development has been most clearly recognized by students of the imprinting phenomenon.

As originally formulated by Lorenz (1935), imprinting was regarded as a form of learning qualitatively distinct from other, associative types of learning. It was characterized by him as (a) occurring only during a brief critical period early on in the animal's life-cycle, (b) being irreversible, (c) constituting a supra-individual learning of species characteristics and (d) influencing behaviour systems that appear only at some subsequent stage, such as the selection of a sexual partner. Although other investigators had already described the tendency of newly hatched precocial birds to follow the first moving object that they encountered, Lorenz was the first to formalize this process, name it and put forward suggestions regarding the mechanisms underlying this phenomenon. Thanks to his efforts a considerably body of research on imprinting has now come into being.

As a result of these further studies, however, Lorenz's views have had to be drastically changed. None of the original four criteria has stood up to empirical testing in the form first put forward and imprinting is now no longer regarded by ethologists as an all-or-none phenomenon with irreversible effects, rigidly confined to one particular, sharply delimited, developmental period. Few now regard it as a distinct type of learning and increasingly it has come to be used merely as a generic name for the process whereby young animals acquire preferences for particular objects encountered in their environment (Bateson, 1966). Indeed, the term is no longer confined to the acquisition of social preferences, but has also been used to refer to the development of an animal's preference for a particular habitat or other feature of its physical surroundings.

Of particular relevance to the emergence of this new conception is the change of emphasis from motor processes to perceptual processes. Having originated in work with precocial animals, imprinting was initially thought of as *learning to follow*, so that the whole phenomenon was regarded virtually synonymous with the establishment of a particular motor response. More recently, however, it has been shown by a number of workers that imprinting can take place without the following response ever occurring. Moltz, Rosenblum and Stettner (1960), for instance, placed ducklings in a small enclosure which permitted an unobstructed view of the moving object but prevented any following, and found in subsequent tests that these animals were as strongly imprinted as ducklings that had been allowed to follow the object freely. As a result of similar findings, Baer and Gray (1960) concluded that 'imprinting is not a learning to follow, but a learning of the characteristics of the parent-object', and in similar vein Sluckin (1965) has drawn attention to the *exposure learning* that appears to be the essential process involved in imprinting. The main problem, it is now thought, is not why a particular response comes to be linked to a particular object, but rather how an animal familiarizes itself with the various features of its environment. As Hinde (1966) has put it,

imprinting during the sensitive period consists largely of the development of familiarity with the moving object. . . . If familiarity is the issue then imprinting would seem to have much in common with perceptual learning, for in both cases the responsiveness to a stimulus is influenced by previous experience of that stimulus independently of its association with any reward.

Such a formulation makes apparent that the various attempts to put forward a human equivalent of the following response are hardly appropriate. Gray (1958), for example, has proposed that the smiling response fulfils the functions in human development that following does in precocial animals, and in similar vein Brody and Axelrad (1971) have put forward the infant's visual following response as their candidate for this role. The learning involved, however, is not one which, like conditioning, is based entirely on one particular motor response. If imprinting is concerned with the formation of attachments, then a diversity of responses, even in lower animals, may mediate it. Attempts to explain it cannot, therefore, merely concern themselves with the eliciting of some specific behaviour pattern; instead, it is necessary to try to understand the familiarization process through which objects and individuals come to be learned and distinguished on the basis of previous encounters.

That such a process is an essential prerequisite to the formation of social attachments cannot, of course, be doubted. Some writers, however, have gone so far as to equate the two. Salzen (1966), for example, has put forward a 'neuronal model hypothesis' for imprinting, according to which an animal's primary tie is explained in terms of the establishment of central models referring to the previously encountered parent object. Subsequent encounters lead to a match between sensory input and central model, as a result of which the animal will approach and attempt to maintain the proximity of the familiar object. Deviations from the central standard will lead to distress and avoidance. We have already discussed the usefulness of conceptualizing the familiarization process in these terms; but to be able to differentiate the familiar from the novel need not imply the formation of an imprinted attachment to the former. A bond can obviously not be formed to the mother before she can be recognized but, as we shall see later, the formation of the bond requires more than just the process of familiarization. And similarly, fear of strangers does not automatically follow from the young organism's ability to recognize the stranger as different.

Conclusions

Exposure to a structured environment produces changes in the infant's cognitive apparatus. In particular, the amount of information that can be handled increases: at one month of age the infant attends primarily to the eyes; at six months he can assimilate the whole face. At the same time, the categories into which his experiences are sorted increase in number. Initially all people are treated alike, as only those features appearing in every human being are responded to; subsequently, as a result of experience, individuals are treated according to a familiarity-novelty dimension and thus responded to differentially.

The cognitive apparatus which mediates social behaviour does not develop in a vacuum; it requires the necessary experience so that the innately determined structures may accommodate themselves to the nuances of the environment. One would, therefore, expect individual differences in social differentiation to be related to the amount of mothering infants receive – a conclusion supported by Ambrose's (1961) finding that smiling to strangers declines at a later age in institutionalized infants than in family-reared infants. It is possible, however, that what is crucial is not so much the quantity of mothering as its consistency: where it is distributed over a number of different mother-figures an infant is more likely to respond to universal features and to develop less differentiated central representations than when a single mother provides him with a more precise, articulated standard.

The establishment of central representations through perceptual exposure means that a change takes place in the basis of an infant's responsiveness to his environment – a change, that is, from 'outer-directedness' to an increasing degree of 'inner-directedness'. The infant's attention is no longer solely determined by the sensory characteristics of the stimuli he encounters; now each experience can be related to the past and checked against the memory traces of previous experiences. Central as well as peripheral factors influence responsiveness.

This change is one of the main themes of early childhood. It is, of course, not confined to social experience nor is it tied to any particular age range. In a discrimination situation in which a conflict was generated between the attractions of the perceptual salience of stimuli, on the one hand, and of their novelty, on the other hand, infants of six months were found to choose on the basis of the sensory attributes of the stimuli while twelve-month-old infants chose on the basis of past experience (Schaffer, 1971). Thus, with increasing age and experience, the infant can begin to relate present to past and in this way become capable of differentiating among the objects and people around him.

Such developments in cognitive functioning are by no means to be regarded as affectless events divorced from all motivational striving. The activities involved in receiving, attending to and interpreting incoming stimulation may in themselves give rise to acute feelings and striving, and to postulate external drives to account for these becomes quite unnecessary. The phrase 'recognitive familiarity', for instance, is used by Hunt (1964) to suggest that the mere act of matching sensory input with central representation provides its own motivation either to investigate further or else to withdraw interest. It is the 'aha' reaction involved in this matching process that is responsible for the young infant's pleasure in catching sight of his mother's face and not the secondary reward value that this particular stimulus happens to have acquired through its association with the alleviation of bodily discomfort. And once a central representation has become firmly established it is the discrepancies in input that have motivating power. As Kagan (1967) has put it, interest is then most likely to be mobilized by those stimuli that 'require tiny, quiet, cognitive discoveries – a miniaturized version of Archimedes' Eureka'.

5 Formation of the Bond

Once an infant has learned to recognize his mother and to differentiate her from others, he is ready to take the third and final major step to the achievement of the primary social relationship. This is represented by two interrelated developments. One refers to the focusing of positive social responsiveness on just one or two specific individuals (in particular the mother), whose proximity the infant actively seeks to gain and maintain. The other involves the appearance of negative responsiveness shown to unfamiliar individuals who may come to be feared and avoided. Whereas previously the infant was content to remain with and receive attention from anyone, familiar or strange, he will now cease to regard people as interchangeable companions and become *object-oriented* instead. A meaningful bond with a mother-figure transcending separations of space and time can then emerge.

The concept of attachment

We have already seen that the secondary drive theory of early social development ('mother love is cupboard love') has run into a series of difficulties in its attempt to account for the child's bond to the mother. Emotional dependence, it appears, is not exclusively or even primarily based on physical dependence: the emerging relationship must be conceptualized in a different way. To mark this change of orientation Bowlby (1958) has suggested that the term 'dependence', with its particular theoretical connotation, should be dropped and replaced by the more neutral term 'attachment'. This suggestion has now been widely adopted and in the account below we, too, shall follow it.

Attachments are inferred from sets of responses designed to bring about affectional social interaction. An attachment may occur in individuals of all ages, vary in intensity over time, manifest itself to greater extent under some conditions than under others and appear overtly in a vast variety of ways. While both animate and inanimate objects can elicit attachment behaviour, the most intense attachments tend to be found in those cases where a reciprocal relationship occurs and will thus most likely involve a member of the same species who, in turn, can respond to and reinforce the behaviour directed at him.

To the adult mind the manifold emotions and sentiments implied by the term are so forceful that they may well be taken to constitute the whole phenomenon and to see it in its most basic form as it appears in infancy is by no means an easy task. In fact, attachment refers to one of the simplest yet most fundamental elements in social behaviour, namely *the tendency to seek the proximity of certain other members of the species*. Though expressed in many different ways, it represents a relatively clear-cut behaviour tendency occurring almost universally among animals as well as in man, the biological utility of which in a condition of infantile helplessness is obvious. A basic requirement of the young organism is represented thereby, to which powerful emotions are linked but to which, in the early stages of development, direct behavioural expression is generally given.

The behaviour patterns expressing this tendency are by no means unique to attachment. Each may appear in a variety of other contexts and be employed for many different purposes. What characterizes attachment behaviour and makes it possible to bring it together under the same heading is its aim, i.e. the seeking of proximity. Aim, as used here, is not a teleological concept; it refers simply to the question of what brings a behaviour pattern to an end. In this sense the terminating condition of overtly quite different responses – crying, following, stretching out arms, and so on – is the attainment of proximity to some particular individual. Once attained, these responses may lead to a variety of further consequences: the reduction of arousal level, the sensory experience of warmth, the provision of food or protection against danger. Most important, however, is that a whole host of mutually entwining patterns of behaviour between mother and child will thereby be set in motion, so that an interaction sequence can then take place in which each partner reinforces the behaviour of the other and thus increases the likelihood of more attachment responses.

Proximity seeking is one general component of early social behaviour; proximity avoidance is another. Biologically, this tendency, too, has important consequences, for it ensures that the young stays with its caretakers and that it will not seek the proximity of those who, for their part, have no motivation to respond positively and solicitously. The interplay of these two tendencies forms an important theme in early social development.

Patterns of attachment behaviour

Far more has been found out about the attachment behaviour of precocial birds and of rhesus monkeys than that of human infants. In the two lower species the proximity seeking tendency is largely expressed through one particular behaviour pattern – the following response in one case, the clinging response in the other. They are responses which, given the ecology and neuromuscular system of the animals, uniquely suited to ensure that the young remains in contact with the parent.

Accounts of human attachment formation were also at first based on the search for a limited number of such innate vehicles of sociability. The best known of these suggestions is that by Bowlby (1958), who submitted a list of five behaviour patterns that he regarded as constituting the 'component instinctual responses' of which attachment behaviour is made up, these being sucking, clinging, following, crying and smiling. Each of these is part of the infant's innate endowment and serves to bring him into contact with the mother. By being directed at a common object they come to constitute the total attachment system.

So far descriptive material on the manifestations of human attachments derived from empirical investigations is still meagre. One exception, however, is Ainsworth's (1967) investigation of early social development in Uganda, the data from which yield a useful picture of the great range of attachment behaviour to be found in the human infant.

From a mixture of interview and observational material gathered in the course of approximately fortnightly home visits during varying parts of the infants' first fifteen months, Ainsworth was able to distinguish the following sixteen patterns of attachment behaviour:

1. Differential crying: the infant cries when held by someone other than the mother and stops when taken by her.

2. Differential smiling: the infant smiles more readily and more frequently in interaction with his mother than in interaction with another person.

3. Differential vocalization: the infant vocalizes more readily and more frequently in interaction with his mother than in interaction with others.

4. Visual-motor orientation: the infant, when apart from his mother but able to see her, keeps his eyes more or less continuously oriented towards her.

5. Greeting responses: on the mother's return after an absence, the infant will smile and show general excitement.

6. Lifting arms in greeting: also seen on the mother's return after an absence, when the arms are lifted towards her.

7. Clapping hands in greeting: instead of lifting his arms, the infant will clap his hands together in a gesture of obvious delight.

8. Crying when the mother leaves: the infant protests when the mother departs from the visual field.

9. Scrambling over the mother: the infant climbs over his mother, exploring her person and clothes.

10. Following: the infant, once able to crawl, not only cries when the mother leaves the room but attempts to follow her.

11. Burying the face in the mother's lap: the infant, whether in the course of scrambling over the mother or having returned to her from a distance, buries his face in her lap.

12. Clinging: if already in the mother's arms the infant clings tightly to her when apprehensive.

13. Approach through locomotion: after the child is able to crawl, he generally terminates his greeting responses by crawling to the mother as quickly as he can.

14. Embracing, hugging, kissing: in response to the adult's affectionate advance, the infant returns the embrace or kiss.

15. Exploration from the mother as a secure base: once able to crawl, the infant makes little excursions away from the mother but returns to her from time to time.

16. Flight to the mother as a haven of safety: when faced by a fear-producing stimulus the infant immediately flees back to the mother.

These findings cannot, of course, be regarded as representative of infant behaviour in other settings; nevertheless, they do provide a striking indication of the great variety of responses through which attachments, even in the early months of life, may be expressed in the human infant. There is, moreover, no reason to believe that the number given has any kind of finality about it and that one may not add at will other patterns (what about differential listening, for instance, or stroking the mother's face or tugging at her clothes?). What does become apparent is that there is no small, limited set of response systems in the human infant, the specific purpose of which is to carry the whole burden of attachment formation. Despite its poor beginnings the behaviour repertoire of the human infant will eventually become far more extensive and flexible than that found in other species, and to bring about the aim of proximity attainment any response that happens to be available and that is appropriate to the particular situation may be used. It is the aim, not the nature, of certain response systems that provides identity to the attachment function.

Determinants of attachment behaviour

The great variety of means whereby attachments may be expressed does not, of course, imply that responses are resorted to in a purely haphazard fashion. At any one time in any one individual only certain patterns will be observed. What, then, are the factors that determine the choice of response?

Five kinds of determinants can be discerned, namely those associated with an individual's species, his age, and with social learning variables, individual difference factors and situational determinants.

Species

Each species, given its particular sensorimotor apparatus, its habitat and mode of living, may employ some responses rather than others to ensure proximity to the caretaker. Thus the rhesus monkey lives in the main an arboreal life and the following response would under these circumstances be of little use to the infant in keeping up with the parent. The combination of an innate clinging reflex and the mother's possession of a hairy coat, however, ensure that proximity can be maintained and the infant is in no danger of losing contact. The chimpanzee, on the other hand, is not equipped with a clinging response strong enough to support its weight in the early months and a different behaviour pattern, namely, distress vocalization, must therefore be resorted to in order to bring about proximity to the parent.

In the human infant neither following nor clinging become effective until the end of the first year – some time after attachments have already been formed. The danger of extrapolating from one species to another is thus well illustrated: other means are more appropriate in early human development to bring the child into contact with the parent. These, as both Rheingold (1961) and Walters and Parke (1965) have pointed out, are more concerned with the child's distance receptors than with near receptors, for though the young infant may have little motor competence to bring about physical contact, his sensory apparatus is already sufficiently well developed in the early weeks of life to enable him to remain in visual contact with the mother. Perceptual rather than more active locomotor means, together with signalling devices, are thus the primary human vehicle for ensuring interaction with the parent.

Age

Just as there are species-specific responses, so it is possible to distinguish age-specific patterns. Age exerts its influence primarily through sensorimotor maturation: following can only occur when a child becomes able to walk or at least crawl and lifting arms towards a person is impossible until the capacity for directed reaching has made its appearance. Thus the range of available means of expression is at first limited, becomes wider with growing motor competence and increases considerably once linguistic skills can be drawn into the service of the attachment function.

Social learning variables

Sooner or later the nature of a child's particular experience will begin to shape the expression of its attachments. This is well illustrated by Ainsworth's observation that among her Ugandan sample embracing, hugging and kissing were virtually absent. Clapping hands, on the other hand, was prevalent there to an extent rarely found in Western children. In each culture certain patterns are reinforced and others discouraged; moreoever, within cultures there are differences in that each set of parents will have certain preferences that will demarcate attachment behaviour. Thus, the social learning opportunities encountered from infancy on will shape the child's behaviour towards others and produce a diversity of expression not found in other species.

Individual difference factors

Not all diversity is, however, a product of experience. There are, in addition, a number of organismic factors which channel the infant's behaviour in certain directions rather than others. Blind infants, for example, cannot use visual means to build up the attachment bond; similarly, infants suffering from motor handicaps may be prevented from stretching out their arms, holding on to the mother or following her when she goes out of sight. Yet what little evidence there is suggests that attachments under such circumstances need not be seriously impaired: blind infants will rely more on auditory and tactual cues in responding to others (Freedman, 1964), and in an investigation of thalidomide children Decarie (1969) found that the absence of the usual forms of following and clinging did not affect the possibility of forming a relationship.

Less obvious, though more common, individual difference factors are also operative. One such factor became evident in a longitudinal investigation (Schaffer and Emerson, 1964b), in the course of which it was found that a number of infants actively resisted and protested at such forms of physical contact as being embraced, hugged and held tight. In so far as these 'non-cuddlers' differed from other infants ('cuddlers') in being generally more restless and in disliking physical constraints such as encountered during dressing and being tucked into bed, it was concluded that basically the two groups differed from one another in activity pattern and that, in consequence, the total amount of physical contact received by the non-cuddlers was very much less than that of more cuddly infants. The nature of the interaction with the mother was thus affected, yet it also emerged that the development of attachments in the non-cuddlers was by no means seriously impaired thereby. They were somewhat later at forming attachments and these were initially rather more shallow, yet by eighteen months of age they had caught up with the cuddlers and no longer differed from them in this respect. The non-cuddlers, it was found, simply used other means of making contact with the mother: when apprehensive, for instance, they made visual contact with her by looking away from the frightening object and turning towards her, or else they established a much less close physical contact such as holding onto the mother's skirt or hiding their face against her knee. Once again the considerable flexibility of human behaviour is indicated: when one avenue of expression is blocked others may be used.

Situational determinants

Biologically it is clearly useful to have considerable interchangeability among response patterns. The human infant is distinguished by the fact that he has access to a larger behaviour repertoire than other animals and that these responses are less rigidly arranged in a hierarchical order of availability. He can, therefore, more easily select the responses appropriate to each situation: when the mother leaves the room he may crawl or run after her as long as the door is open; if it is shut or if he is not yet able to follow he may call, shout or cry in an increasing crescendo of urgency. The means of bringing about the desired end are manifold.

Developmental sequence in attachment formation

When does the child first become capable of forming an attachment to a specific individual? That this is based on a long and continuous process going back to the infant's first encounters with human beings should be apparent by now; nevertheless, a lengthy preparation does not preclude a relatively sudden emergence. We may, therefore, inquire whether it is possible to assign an age to this development.

Operational criteria for attachments

However adept an infant may be in recognizing his mother, he cannot be said to have formed an attachment to her if he remains as content in the proximity of a stranger as in his mother's proximity and if the two individuals are thus responded to as essentially interchangeable. Some of Ainsworth's attachment patterns, such as differential smiling or visual-motor orientation, cannot, therefore, on their own be regarded as evidence of the existence of an attachment, for they need signify nothing more than that a perceptual differentiation has taken place. A more stringent criterion is required.

This is provided most clearly in those situations in which the infant's contact with the mother is terminated and he is prevented from seeking her proximity. If an attachment involves the direction of proximity seeking behaviour towards a particular individual, then the frustration of this tendency should lead to protest, emotional upset and vigorous attempts to regain the loved person. This will be highlighted particularly in those situations in which the child is provided with substitute mother-figures, as then the interchangeability of one person for another may be tested. It is now well known that the child in his preschool years generally reacts with violent protests when separated from his mother (through hospitalization, for instance), that he will cry for prolonged periods during her absence, cling to her on her reappearance, and avoid and resist all advances from substitute caretakers. The need for the mother's presence, as opposed to wanting attention and stimulation generally, is thereby indicated. As Bowlby (1960) has put it, the separation response is 'the inescapable corollary of attachment behaviour – the other side of the coin'. It therefore provides the criterion whereby we may test for the formation of attachments to particular individuals.

Age at onset of attachments

In a study of the effects of short-term hospitalization (Schaffer, 1958; Schaffer and Callender, 1959) a sample of seventy-six infants aged between three and fifty-one weeks was observed in order to ascertain at what age separation responses first become evident. When various indices of separation upset, such as amount of crying and of activity and degree of responsiveness to mother (during her visits) and to nurses, were plotted over age, a break was found to occur around seven months of age. In those above this age a pattern of behaviour emerged which took the form of the classic separation picture as described by Bowlby (1960) for preschool children: protest during the initial period of hospitalization, negativism to the staff, intervals of subdued behaviour and withdrawal and after return home a period of readjustment during which a great deal of insecurity centering around the presence of the mother was shown. In those below seven months, on the other hand, separation from the mother elicited no protest, strangers were accepted as mother-substitutes without change in the usual level of responsiveness, and though on return home a rather dramatic if brief upset occurred in most of these infants, its form differed from that of the older group, consisting of an intense preoccupation with the infant's surroundings and thus relating to the total change of environment rather than to the person of the mother.

These findings suggest that separation from the mother becomes a meaningful event only at the beginning of the second half-year. At this time a crucial milestone is reached as a result of which a change in mother-figure is no longer tolerated. What is more, it was found that the intensity of upset at seven months was every bit as great as that found at later ages, thus suggesting a step-wise development in the behavioural manifestation of specific attachments rather than a gradual onset.

We have already seen from studies of the smiling response that in this respect, too, a change occurs after the age of six months, for from then on a child will no longer smile at all individuals but restrict this response to certain persons only. Further confirmatory evidence comes from a longitudinal study by Schaffer and Emerson (1964a), in which a sample of sixty infants was followed up at four-weekly intervals from the early months to the end of the first year and then seen once more at eighteen months of age. The attachment criterion was again based on the infants' separation responses, though relating this time to a number of everyday separation situations, such as being left alone in a room, left in the company of other people and put down after being held by an adult. The data were obtained from maternal reports, but reliability checks based on direct observations were built into the study.

The investigation was principally concerned with three parameters of the attachment function: age at onset, intensity and breadth (i.e. number of individuals at which it is directed). At this point we are only concerned with the first of these. It was found that crying or some other form of protest on termination of contact with an adult was apparent from the early months on. However, the crucial characteristic of this early behaviour lay in its *indiscriminate* nature: in the first half-year infants were found to cry for attention from anyone, familiar or strange, and though responsiveness to strangers tended to become somewhat less immediate and less intense than to the mother, both could quieten the infant and the departure of both could re-evoke protest. At the age of approximately seven months, however, a change took place. The infants still protested in the same situations, but now their protests were directed solely at certain *specific* individuals. The departure of these alone elicited crying and only their renewed attention terminated the infants' distress. Strangers, quite on the contrary, upset the infant by *approaching* him. This development, in other words, is not marked by the appearance of a new behaviour pattern comparable, say, to the onset of talking or to the first smile; it is marked, rather, by the restriction of an already available response to certain individuals only.

Thus, from quite early on infants protest when isolated. But at this early stage the infant is more concerned with the stimulation as such than with the source from which it emanates. Not until the third quarter of the first year will he cease to treat people as interchangeable companions and to accept anyone's attention with positive responsiveness. From this point on an infant can remain oriented towards an absent person; he can hold the departed mother in mind, as it were, and direct his proximity seeking towards her despite her absence. The process of 'object acquisition' has thus been completed and the capacity for forming specific attachments comes into being.

Conditions determining age at onset

The age of seven months which we have quoted as the time of onset represents an average which conceals the existence of considerable individual differences. In the Schaffer and Emerson (1964a) study, a range of twenty-two weeks to fifteen months was found and, similarly, Ainsworth's (1967) data indicated that specific attachments (using the separation protest criterion) appeared at widely different ages in different members of her African sample. Most of these infants reached this milestone comparatively early; indeed the lower limit of Ainsworth's sample was only fifteen weeks. It is conceivable that this difference between the two samples is a reflection of the far greater amount of attention that African babies receive from their mothers and that age at onset is thus a direct function of the amount of exposure to the parent. That this relationship may not be so straightforward is indicated by Schaffer and Emerson's failure to find any correlation between age at onset, on the one hand, and any of various measures employed to examine the amount, nature and intensity of maternal stimulation, on the other – a finding which led to the conclusion that the differences observed may well have been related more closely to inherent than to environmental variables.

This does not mean, of course, that environmental influences do not play a part in determining when specific attachments appear. It seems, rather, that in the sample investigated, conditions even in the least stimulating families were sufficient to ensure that this development took place at an age determined by other factors. Under more extreme conditions, however, where the necessary minimal requirements are not met, it is likely that the ability to form specific attachments can be seriously impaired. This is most probable in an institutional setting where imper-

sonal methods of child rearing afford little opportunity for
the development of attachment behaviour. In an effort to
ascertain how far a temporary period of institutionalization would affect the capacity for attachment formation,
Schaffer (1963) investigated two groups of infants, both of
whom had spent a period of several months away from
home and who were at least thirty weeks old at the time
of reunion. One group (the 'hospital group') was obtained
from a children's hospital, where the total amount of stimulation received by the infants was extremely limited. The
other group (the 'baby home group') came from a residential nursery where the staff-child ratio was very much
more favourable than in the hospital and where consequently a far greater amount of social interaction prevailed.
For all infants the time lag between return home and the
appearance of the first sign of a specific attachment was ascertained. It was found that the baby home group established attachments (generally directed at the mother) very
quickly: five of the nine infants showed the first sign of
such behaviour within five days of returning home, while
two others did so within the second week after reunion. In
the hospital group all but one of the eleven infants took at
least four weeks to develop any attachment behaviour and
in a number of instances it was several months before the
bond with the mother was at last established.

It appears that the total amount of social stimulation,
irrespective of source, does influence age at onset of specific
attachments. Naturally, a suitable object in the form of
a principal mother-figure must first be made available for
this purpose and this was not experienced by either of these
two groups until they returned home. Yet the readiness to
make use of this opportunity appears to be a function of
the quantity of an infant's interaction with others in the
preceding period: when this is inadequate the cognitive
structure is unable to develop to the point where fully differentiated social behaviour emerges and proximity seeking
becomes focused on just one individual.

The critical period concept

The oldest infant in the above study at the time of reunion was fifty-two weeks of age. What we do not know is how much longer one could have delayed the restoration of the mother before the capacity to form an attachment became permanently impaired. Follow-up studies of deprived children subsequently adopted or fostered, such as those described by Goldfarb (1943, 1945), are generally of little help because of the vagueness of the criteria employed for assessment of social competence. In many animal species, on the other hand, quite sharply defined limits have been claimed for the occurrence of socialization, so that failure to be exposed to the biologically correct object during this time leaves the animal a permanent social cripple. The concept of critical periods was therefore advanced in order to draw attention to the existence of maturationally determined, age-linked stages of development during which an animal is maximally susceptible to certain environmental influences but beyond which it can no longer be thus affected.

More recently, however, students of animal behaviour have become dissatisfied with the rigid formulation of this concept (e.g. Sluckin, 1965), for the all-or-nothing effect implied thereby has not stood up to empirical investigation. Imprinting, it is true, is more likely to succeed at certain periods than at others, but the time limits of these periods can be artificially extended (Moltz, 1963) and are more probably a function of environmental as well as innate variables. The view advanced by Hinde (1963), that we are merely concerned with changing probabilities of certain forms of learning and that periods of maximum probability may be surrounded by periods of reduced probability, seems to do justice to the general feeling now current among ethologists and explains why the term 'sensitive period' has come to be preferred to the term 'critical period'.

In relation to human development the critical period concept is even less helpful. Caldwell (1962) has made the useful distinction between a 'during' and a 'beyond' sense in which the term 'critical period' is used. The former refers to the notion that during certain developmental phases an organism is more sensitive to certain influences than at other times – a statement which one can hardly contradict but which is also of only limited use, in that it is of a purely descriptive nature and does not explain *why* changes in sensitivity occur. According to the latter sense, critical periods are those beyond which an organism can no longer be affected at all, so that, for instance, a child who has failed to come into contact with a mother-figure during this time will subsequently no longer be in a position to benefit from such an experience. As we have already seen, no evidence exists for such a view. If there are limits, they are likely to be so wide and affected by such a multiplicity of variables that the concept of a critical period becomes meaningless. In any case, it might be argued that every stage in the development of social relations is 'critical' in some way: the early weeks in building up social responsiveness in general, the following months in bringing about discriminations between people, the third quarter of the first year in that specific attachments must be allowed to emerge, the subsequent months and years in strengthening the attachment, and so on. To assert merely, as Gray (1958) has done, that the first six months represent *the* critical period for the development of social bonds is of little help. The task is rather to ascertain what environmental requirements should be supplied to the individual at different stages of development for the adaptive functioning of various processes of growth. As it stands, the concept of critical periods is merely a *deus ex machina*.

Onset of fear of strangers

Not only does an infant cease to show positive responsiveness towards unfamiliar people in the second half-year, but he also now begins to react to them with fear.

Fear of strangers is as widespread a phenomenon in the animal world as attachment (Bronson, 1968). It has been described as bringing to an end the critical period during which attachments can be formed, in that the animal will no longer approach an unfamiliar object and cannot, therefore, become imprinted upon it (Scott, 1963). Certainly the two functions, attachment and fear, are closely interrelated and jointly provide early social behaviour with its selective character. Some writers have indeed considered them to be different facets of the same developmental process, so that the one may be taken as an indication of the existence of the other. More recent research, however, has suggested that different processes are represented by these phenomena: for one thing, their ages of onset do not necessarily coincide in all individuals, for another the conditions determining their respective intensities may vary and, finally, it is possible for one to occur without the other (as seen, for instance, in deprived infants who do show fear of strangers).

Most investigators have found fear of strangers first to occur around the age of eight months – hence Spitz's (1950) reference to it as 'eight-months' anxiety.' The range of individual differences in age at onset is, however, considerable. In the Schaffer and Emerson (1964a) study, the mean age at onset was indeed eight months, but the youngest infant in the sample to show this phenomenon was only twenty-five weeks at the time, whereas, at the other extreme, three infants were already well on into their second year before any evidence of fear was noted. It was also found that these ages diverged somewhat from the ages when specific attachments were first observed, the latter generally preceding the former by about one month.

More often than not the onset of fear of strangers is sudden and dramatic. In describing the responses of thirty-six infants to a stranger in the course of a longitudinal study, Schaffer (1966a) found that at one of the four-weekly contacts there would be no evidence of negative responses, while at the next the fear response was present in its full intensity. Reports by the mothers of these infants corroborated this finding, in that they were usually able to point to a particular episode when the infant for the first time quite suddenly showed fear towards a particular stranger.

This study also suggested, however, that such apparent suddenness of onset is misleading, in that indiscriminate responsiveness to strangers does not all at once switch over to avoidance behaviour. Only in the early weeks of life did these infants show automatic responsiveness towards the unfamiliar person, i.e. they smiled almost immediately and gave no indication of any awareness of strangeness. From about three months on, however, a lag in the smile appeared at first contact, during which time the infant stared at the stranger but without showing any sign of avoidance. With increasing age the lag grew longer, until in the weeks just before the onset of fear a period of complete unresponsiveness occurred in some of the sample, when neither fear not positive responses were observed and the infant remained 'frozen'. It is thus apparent that, as in the case of specific attachments, the sudden onset of a behaviour tendency does not preclude a long preparatory period leading up to its emergence.

Cognitive mechanisms in social selectiveness

The third quarter of the first year can now be regarded with confidence as the period during which selective social behaviour emerges. What we do not yet know are the precise mechanisms which make such a development possible at this point. In so far as it is marked by the restriction of positive responsiveness to familiar individuals and by the onset of fear of unknown individuals, the influence of stored experience on approach–avoidance behaviour is evidently implicated. Some guidelines to help us understand this process are now becoming available.

Selective approach–avoidance behaviour

Studies of precocial birds have given the impression that imprinted attachments and fear of the strange emerge as soon as the animal can categorize stimuli as known or unknown. In such animals sensory and motor functions appear contemporaneously and early learned discriminations can thus be expressed immediately in overt approach–avoidance behaviour; the ability to make the perceptual differentiation is, therefore, taken as the sufficient cause of the onset of selective motor behaviour.

In early human development, however, a disjunction is generally to be found in the appearance of receptive and productive functions. Speech can be understood before it is pronounced; designs are discriminated before they can be copied. In infancy the perceptual apparatus is already well developed before any degree of motor competence emerges, so that for a time it is possible for information to be acquired and processed and yet not be directly acted upon.

One area in which the effects of this disjunction can be observed is the study of infants' approach–avoidance responses to stimuli varied along a familiarity–unfamiliarity continuum. In an investigation by Schaffer and Parry (1969) six- and twelve-month-old infants were familiarized on a nonsense object in a series of seven half-minute exposure periods, separated by half-minute intervals. On the eighth trial a novel object was introduced and on the ninth trial the former object was brought back once again. On the basis of systematic changes with familiarity in *visual* responsiveness (see Figure 9), it was concluded that the younger group was as competent as the older group in perceptually classifying the stimuli in terms of their familiarity, i.e. of recognizing them. *Manipulative* measures, on the other hand, yielded a different picture. When one examines latency before contact is made with the object (Figure 10), it emerges that the older group behaved discriminatively in this respect, too: on the first trial there was prolonged hesitation before the strange stimulus was touched, sometimes accompanied by marked avoidance responses, and only with increasing familiarity did these infants become less wary at the beginning of each trial. The younger group, on the other hand, did not behave differentially in this respect, for from the very first trial on they showed an indiscriminate, almost reflex-like approach response to the stimulus as soon as it appeared each time. At this age, therefore, discrimination could be observed in the visual yet not in the manipula-

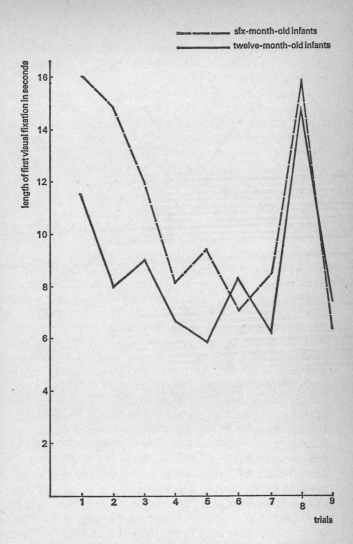

six-month-old infants
twelve-month-old infants

Figure 9 Length of first visual fixation per trial for six-month-old and twelve-month-old infants. (From Schaffer and Parry, 1969)

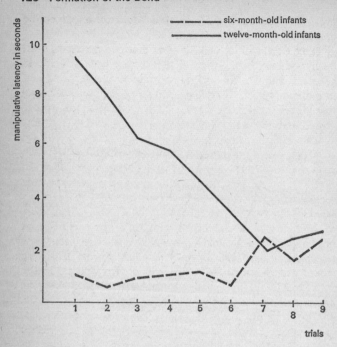

Figure 10   Manipulative latency per trial for six-month-old and twelve-month-old infants. (From Schaffer and Parry, 1969)

tive system – the ability to register information in terms of familiarity–unfamiliarity was not accomplished by selective approach–avoidance behaviour, the integration between the two apparently occurring only some time in the second half of the first year.

This conclusion was reinforced by a subsequent study (Schaffer and Parry, 1970), employing a simultaneous rather than a successive discrimination task. Again the disjunctive effect was observed: the ability to discriminate visually between simultaneously presented pairs of familiar and novel stimuli was evident even in the youngest of the age groups investigated (five to seven months); only after this age, however, was the perceptual discrimination accompanied by manipulative discrimination.

These observations make it clear that two processes must be hypothesized, the onset of which may well coincide in precocial animals but which in human development appear in sequential order. The first involves a *perceptual learning mechanism*, which is based on the acquisition of central representations and enables the organism to recognize stimuli in terms of its previous experience. This, as we have seen, can already be detected in the early months of human development. The second process refers to a *response selection mechanism*, which does not become evident until the second half-year. Up to this point indiscriminate approach responses are elicited by all objects – even those recognized as unfamiliar. Subsequently the infant becomes capable of holding in check such behaviour; responses are now selected on the basis of an appraisal process involving stored experience as well as present sensory events. Under some conditions the ensuing behaviour will then take the form of avoidance; under other conditions it may, on the contrary, involve approach and exploration. In either case, however, the nature of the response is now under the central guidance exerted by the infant's awareness of previous encounters. Two quite separate problems for explanation are thus involved, referring respectively to the development of the ability to hold in check primary approach responses and to the form which the consequent action takes.

Perceptual-motor integration can, of course, take place at several levels. The very fact that an infant from about four months on can reach toward a visually presented object indicates one such integration. Even in a simultaneous discrimination situation an infant of this age is capable of selective manipulative behaviour if the two stimuli differ in terms of their perceptual salience (Schaffer, 1971). Manipulative as well as visual attention will then be directed to the more distinctive stimulus; visual guidance of motor responses, that is, takes place on the basis of a comparison of sensory impressions only. When, on the other hand, the perceptual-motor integration involves the mediating role of memory, only infants later on in the first year are capable of selective action.

An initial period during which approach behaviour is shown indiscriminately to all other members of the species has been found in the early social development of many animals. The subsequent restriction of responsiveness is clearly dependent on the ability to categorize others in terms of their familiarity, but the disjunctive nature of human development makes it apparent that this is not the only mechanism involved. An infant may be capable of establishing central representations of external events and individuals quite early on, yet initially these contribute a self-contained system that does not yet exert control over productive behaviour. A stranger is recognized as unfamiliar but is still responded to positively. A further change in cognitive functioning is required, whereby an infant becomes capable of selecting his responses on the basis of his previous experience of that particular individual.

The construction of the social object

The changing relationship between memory and action is also found to underlie the development of object permanence. In the early months, according to Piaget (1955), the infant is not yet capable of conceiving of an object as a permanent entity, i.e. as a substance with an existence independent of his own perception of it. An object can be recognized when it is encountered repeatedly, but once out of sight the infant behaves as though it has ceased to exist. His world is thus composed of fleeting images that have no existence apart from his own activity. Only in the fourth sensorimotor stage (beginning in the third quarter of the first year) can one first find evidence of object conservation; only then can the infant initiate activities directed at the *representation* of an object (as shown by his ability to search for it after its disappearance) and not just at the object itself.

It is no coincidence that the criterion adopted by us for

the appearance of specific attachments, namely separation upset, also involves an orientation towards a missing
object. It represents the final step in the construction of the
social object, that is, the realization that the other person
exists in his own right independent of the child's perception of him and that it is, therefore, possible to remain
oriented towards him over gaps of time and space. Yet
it is evident, as we have seen, that a central representation
of the mother is established at a very early age – evident, that
is, whenever the mother is actually present. In her absence
there is no sign of awareness of her existence in the first
half-year; the infant appears not to miss her nor to use
her representation as a standard of comparison in his
encounters with strangers. In short, such an infant is
capable of *recognition*; he is not yet capable of *recall*. It
is as though the representation can function only when he
is confronted by the corresponding sensory input: however
much each encounter with the mother excites him, the representation remains dormant in the intervening periods.
Recognition, therefore, develops before recall; the spontaneous access to the memory store implied by the latter process does not appear until seven or eight months.

The recognition–recall distinction has been neglected by
those theories which relate the onset of fear of the strange
to perceived incongruity between sensory input and a central
standard (Hebb, 1946; Hunt, 1964). In so far as it is implied
that the ability to distinguish perceptually the familiar from
the unfamiliar is all that is required to explain the onset of
fear, incongruity theories adopt one-process explanations
and are, therefore, inadequate. The perception of incongruity, however, involves an active comparison with a standard: a stranger must be seen not only as unknown but also
as different from the mother. It is, therefore, necessary to
retrieve the maternal representation from memory in the
absence of the mother herself and this, it appears, is a relatively complex cognitive operation which does not become
possible until the third quarter of the first year. The differential behaviour to strangers that one sees initially (such as,

for instance, prolonged visual fixation) need not imply any realization that such an individual is different in relation to a familiar standard. A more economical interpretation is that the infant finds it impossible to assimilate the stranger to his existing schemata and that the signs of differential behaviour are thus merely due to the puzzling nature of the stimulus. To compare a present stimulus with a centrally stored representation requires spontaneous retrieval of the latter, i.e. action in the absence of the corresponding stimulus itself. This is too difficult a task for the infant in the first half-year.

On the other hand, there are some indications, albeit of a tentative nature, that one can make the infant's task easier by providing him with both the strange stimulus and the standard of comparison simultaneously in the perceptual field (Schaffer, 1971). For example, fear of a stranger may be found rather earlier than normally if the mother is present *at the same time* as the stranger. Infants have been observed to look to and fro as though comparing one with the other, and only then to show signs of fear. If, on the other hand, the mother was not present the infants merely stared at the stranger without upset.

Fear of strangers thus evolves as the infant becomes capable of increasingly sophisticated cognitive operations. In particular, the *spontaneous* access to central representations is implicated. This also applies to separation upset: Wolff (1969) found that infants as young as two months could already protest at the disappearance of a person, but their protests ceased the moment he had gone. Their response was to the change in ongoing stimulation, i.e. to the act of being left, whereas an infant later on in the first year is able to remain oriented towards an absent person for hours or even days after his departure. Wolff's infants, moreover, protested at being left by anyone; the older infant, in contrast, will reject the attention of substitute caretakers and thus show that his attachment responses are now under the control of clearly formulated representations of certain quite specific individuals. The internalized mother, that is, is now able to influence the infant's behaviour and it is in this sense that we can regard the construction of the social object as completed.

Conclusions

Proximity seeking responses can be found from an early age, but it is not until the third quarter of the first year that they become focused. Positive responsiveness is then restricted to certain familiar individuals while avoidance responses appear to other, unfamiliar individuals. The combined effect of these two developments is to ensure that people are no longer interchangeable: social relations have become differentiated and the process of object acquisition is thus complete. This represents the third major achievement of early social development.

In trying to understand these changes it is useful to view them as part of the overall developments that occur in the nature of cognitive functioning at this time. Previously the infant's central representations laid down by past encounters could be evoked only by the corresponding sensory experience and remained dormant otherwise; now, however, there are indications that the infant can spontaneously retrieve them, i.e. that he is capable of recall as well as of recognition. This greater mobility of representations means that the infant can relate to absent objects and initiate planned actions towards them and not merely be dependent on present sensory stimulation in setting response sequences in motion. Mother, that is, is not just a complex of sensory experiences but has become an internalized object that can be remembered over gaps of time, to which the infant can remain oriented while venturing forth to explore his surroundings and that can serve as a basis of comparison in encounters with other people.

6 The Nature of the First Relationship

Once attachments to specific individuals have come into being, the child's social behaviour changes radically. A great deal of emotion and feeling come to be invested in the primary relationship, separation becomes a meaningful and threatening event, and the complex social learning processes subsumed under the term 'identification' can now begin to take place. Socialization, the process whereby the individual adapts his behaviour to the requirements of the particular social group of which he is a member, can hardly proceed until the individual has defined his group and no longer regards all people as equivalent. The reinforcement that impels social learning is more efficacious if it stems from individuals with whom the child has formed a love relationship and whose rewards and punishment therefore have a greater impact than if a neutrally toned relationship is involved. Attachments thus provide the context within which socialization can develop.

Attachments are, of course, not static in their nature. They change in form and character as the child grows older and assume different meanings at different developmental periods. There are short-term changes, even moment-to-moment fluctuations in the intensity with which the mother's proximity is sought. With the ever-widening range of objects and situations which become familiar to the child and with his growing sensorimotor competence in apprehending and responding to them, the mother's presence will be required for different purposes and be used in different ways, and as the range of social encounters also increases changes may well occur in both the number of attachments and their hierarchical arrangement. The nature of all such changes must be described and the conditions responsible for their occurrence isolated.

Object choice

In the past, discussions of early social development have generally confined themselves to the child's relationship with the mother. The prevalent view was that the infant, once he becomes capable of establishing focused relationships, will form his initial attachment to only one person, that this person, under normal conditions of child rearing, will always be his mother, that other attachments are formed only gradually after the first relationship has become firmly established and that these other attachments are always subsidiary in intensity compared with that to the mother. Empirical evidence however, suggests a rather more complex picture.

Number and identity of attachment objects

In their longitudinal investigation of attachment formation, Schaffer and Emerson (1964a) found that a majority of infants in their sample did, indeed, form their intial attachment to one person only; nevertheless, as many as 29 per cent directed their first specific attachments at several individuals. The concept of 'monotropy', suggested by Bowlby (1958) and expressing his belief that a child has an inherent tendency to attach himself initially to one person only, is thus not borne out by the facts. That such single initial attachments occur more often than not is not contested: Ainsworth (1967) noted this tendency for her sample and it is also found frequently in the descriptions of the early social behaviour of the higher animal species. Scott (1958), however, has drawn attention to the fact that in dogs primary attachments are often multiple, in that the mother, just at the beginning of the socialization period, tends to leave the nest and that the puppy's first social bonds are, therefore, formed to its littermates. Similarly among bonnet macaques, where polymatric rearing is the rule, attachments take a multiple form (Rosenblum, 1971). The nature of the social setting thus determines the breadth of the attachment function: in those human families where the child's care is in the hands of a number of people and where his opportunities for social interaction are considerable, attachments are likely to be formed to several individuals from the beginning. In any case, breadth very quickly increases with age: three months after onset of specific attachments only 41 per cent of Schaffer and Emerson's sample had only the one attachment object and by eighteen months of age this percentage had decreased to 13. In this way, as Margaret Mead (1962) has pointed out, a child has at least some insurance against loss of parents – a state of affairs that is, of course, especially important in primitive societies.

As far as the identity of objects is concerned, the traditional view must also be challenged. The mother was certainly by far the most frequently chosen object in the Schaffer and Emerson study: only three out of fifty-eight infants did not initially focus their primary attachments on her. Yet what was particularly striking in this analysis was the frequency with which father was also chosen as an attachment object. Even in the first month after onset 27 per cent selected him and by eighteen months 75 per cent of infants had formed an attachment with him. Grandparents, aunts, neighbours and even young siblings were also frequently found to elicit attachment behaviour.

Factors determining choice

On what basis are objects chosen? And why are attachments to some individuals more intense than to others? Schaffer and Emerson found that attachment objects are generally arranged in a hierarchy. In the majority of cases the principal object was the mother, yet with increasing age there was a tendency for other people (mostly the father) to take on this position, so that by eighteen months nearly a third of the sample directed their most intense attachment behaviour at some individual other than the mother.

As long as attachments were regarded as growing out of the child's physical dependence, the question of object choice could be answered without hesitation. The child loves those who feed him and as the mother is generally responsible for his physical care it is she who naturally becomes the primary object. As we saw in chapter 2, this view is no longer tenable. No less than one-fifth of the persons selected by Schaffer and Emerson's infants as principal objects did not participate to even a minor degree in any aspect of the child's physical care. Instead, the characteristics that determined most clearly the choice of object were, in the first place, the individual's responsiveness to the infant's signals for attention and, in the second place, the amount of interaction which the adult spontaneously initiated with the infant. The amount of time spent together (at least above a certain level) appeared to play little part. In as many as 39 per cent of infants the principal object at eighteen months of age was someone other than the most available individual – generally the father, despite his absence for all but a brief part of the day. 'Strong attachments', it was concluded,

can clearly be formed to individuals who are available for comparatively limited periods, as long as these individuals are prepared to interact fairly intensely with the infant on such occasions. When, furthermore, the most available person (generally the mother) does not show a great deal of responsiveness and is not prepared to interact much with the infant, the latter is more likely to search for another object towards whom he can direct his most intense attachment behaviour. ... Thus, when a relatively unstimulating mother is found in conjunction with, say, an extremely attentive father, the latter is more likely to head the infant's hierarchy of attachment objects, despite the mother's greater availability.

The adult's overall value as a 'stimulator' emerges, therefore, as a more important determinant than his primary drive-reducing powers.

It is apparent that to isolate the mother–child relationship from the rest of the child's interactive behaviour and to concentrate on this alone is an artificial and misleading procedure. The mother, being the most available person, has of course the best opportunity to provide the child with the required stimulation and is thus the most likely person to become his principal object. Yet not every mother will avail herself of this opportunity: personality factors and practical considerations may prevent her and thus allow others to assume this role.

The intensity of attachments

Not only are there differences in the intensity of attachments shown by any one infant to different people, but infants may also differ among each other in their usual level of intensity. Furthermore, changes may occur in this respect from one developmental stage to another, generally in the direction of a decrease in intensity with age.

Individual differences in intensity

It is a matter of common experience that children of the same age and observed under the same circumstances differ in the extent to which they require the mother's presence. Some children have great difficulty in letting the mother out of sight for even short periods, cling to her a great deal whenever possible and make constant demands for her attention. Others, on the contrary, show little concern for her whereabouts, tolerate separations relatively easily and interact with her to only a limited extent. What is less obvious is the reason for such differences.

Schaffer and Emerson (1964a) investigated a number of variables for their possible association with degree of attachment intensity. No relationship was found with sex, birth order or socio-economic status, nor with such socializing variables as the rigidity of feeding schedules, the age and length of weaning and the severity of toilet training. Once again, the secondary drive hypothesis receives no support from these data. However, maternal responsiveness to the infant's demands and the amount of maternal interaction with the baby did show such an association. Though these two variables were not related to one another, each indicated that highly attached infants differed from low-attached infants with respect to maternal stimulation. What we do not know from this correlation is the direction of the cause-and-effect sequence. Do infants develop intense attachments because they have mothers who enjoy and foster this type of behaviour? Or do infants force the mothers to respond in certain ways by the urgency of their demands? The former view is probably more acceptable to those who believe that parental behaviour is the primary force responsible for moulding and directing a child's personality growth; yet to accept it in its entirety would be to subscribe to the *tabula rasa* conception of the infant. It is also possible that there are inherent components to a child's sociability, as a result of which parental behaviour may well be determined by child characteristics.

Support for such a conclusion comes from several sources. In a study of same-sex twins, Gottesman (1966) isolated a factor which he called 'person orientation' which contained the trait of 'sociability' and which appeared to be largely genetically determined, as indicated by the scores on a personality test obtained by the identical and fraternal twin pairs in the sample. A similar finding emerges from a study by Scarr (1965), based on personality ratings of identical and fraternal twin girls aged six to ten years. Individual differences in 'sociability' (conceived as a dimension extending from 'shyness to extraverted engagement with the interpersonal environment') were found to be highly heritable – a conclusion which Scarr believes may account for the finding of a number of longitudinal studies that sociability is among the most stable of personal traits. Even more directly relevant is Freedman's (1965) claim that a genetic component in social behaviour is already evident in infancy: the concordance in the age at which such aspects of early sociability as visual orientation to others, smiling and fear of strangers appear was found by him to be greater among identical than among fraternal twins.

Whatever the child's contribution may be, that of his environment cannot be doubted. The nature of the social setting in which he is reared, as defined by such variables as the number of his caretakers, the amount and quality of interaction, and the stability of caretaking arrangements, is likely to be a particularly potent influence. Few studies as yet exist which define the relationship of such variables to attachment behaviour. Stevens (1971) examined infants raised in an institutional polymatric setting and found that the ages at onset of specific attachments and of fear of strangers differed little from those reported for family-reared infants. Caldwell and Hersher (1964) compared infants raised in monomatric and polymatric families and found that monomatrically reared infants at the age of twelve months were more dependent on the mother for need gratification, protested more when left alone, responded more favourably to nurturant maternal behaviour and took action more frequently to attain the mother's proximity. They also tended to be more emotional in their interaction with the mother than was the case in polymatrically reared infants. Various aspects of the attachment function may, therefore, be affected by the structural characteristics of the infant's social environment, and it should thus become possible to establish links between the nature of the family setting in which a child spends his early years and the particular form which his interpersonal behaviour comes to assume.

Detachment

There are indications that specific attachments are at their most intense immediately after their first appearance (Schaffer and Emerson, 1964a). Far from gradually gaining in strength as a result of experience – as is generally the case with learned functions such as skills – the future history of attachment behaviour following its step-wise onset indicates a decrease in the extent to which proximity is sought. As he gets older, the child becomes less concerned to remain near his mother and increasingly able to tolerate minor separations. More and more frequently will he spontaneously leave his mother's side and each time he does so he stays away longer and travels further. The child, that is, has begun to detach himself.

Detachment has been studied far less than attachment; yet, as Rheingold and Eckerman (1971) have pointed out, it is well-nigh universal throughout the higher reaches of the animal kingdom and is certainly a marked feature of mammalian development. Studies of various species of monkeys, for instance, have provided data describing the manner and timing of detachment and have highlighted the extent to which behaviour systems other than attachment, such as exploration and peer relationships, come to play an increasingly important part. They have also shown that the mother is by no means a passive participant in this process. Initially she will restrain the infant monkey from departing and retrieve him if he does leave; subsequently, however, restraint and retrieval will decrease in frequency. This may be a response to the infant's growing desire to explore his environment, but there are also indications that the mother actively encourages this separation and, indeed, comes eventually to punish and reject her offspring for making approach movements.

Rheingold and Eckerman (1970) furnish one of the few descriptive studies available on human detachment. Children between twelve and sixty months of age were placed at one end of an unfenced lawn, leaving them at their mother's knee but free to roam. Observers traced the child's path on a map of the lawn. The mean furthest distance travelled from the mother by one year olds was 6.9 metres, by two year olds 15·1 metres, by three year olds 17·3 metres and by four year olds 20·6 metres. Variability after the second year was considerable; for example, one three-and-a-half-year-old boy went 31·5 metres, whereas another only went 8·5 metres. Much depends, of course, on the particular setting of such a study – on the attractiveness of the surroundings, on the possibility of keeping mother in sight and on the presence of other people. All such variables will influence the distance travelled; nevertheless, the age-ordered data can hardly be explained in terms of the child's growing motor competence and must be regarded as a sign of the loosening of the bond.

Such a situation lends itself well to experimental manipulation and to the exploration of individual differences. Rheingold (1969) has reported data from a study in which ten-month-old infants were observed in a setting in which the subjects were left with the mother in one room but able to see and obtain access to another, larger room. In some conditions the larger room was left bare, in others it contained toys. Observers behind one-way windows recorded how long each infant took to enter the second room, how long he stayed there, how far he went, what he contacted and manipulated, how often he returned to the mother and how much time he spent in contact with her. It was found that all twenty-four infants left their mothers and without distress crept out of the room to enter the larger one, whether it was empty or contained a toy. How quickly they left, how far they went and how long they stayed away from the mother were all controlled by the number and location of stimulating objects, as well as by whether the objects were part of the new environment from the beginning or were added later. Most infants kept returning to the mother and alternating between her and the second room – one infant doing so thirteen times in the ten-minute experiment. The fact that these infants spontaneously left their mothers without distress and freely explored the unfamiliar environment contrasts sharply with the marked distress and almost complete inhibition of locomotion which Rheingold found when infants were *placed* alone in the same environment and left there.

Why does detachment occur? Everyday observations do not suggest that maternal rejection is primarily responsible for its occurrence in human development. It seems more probable that the infant takes the initiative and that sensitive mothers tolerate the loosening of the bond – in the sense, that is, of permitting the infant to leave their proximity to an increasing extent. To the child the widening of his horizon is clearly beneficial, for it provides him with new learning opportunities and brings him into contact with an ever-increasing range of novel objects and situations. But does detachment in fact mean the lessening of attachment? If attachment is defined solely in terms of proximity seeking, the answer is obviously yes. If, on the other hand, attachments imply internal representations of the object and if it is conceded that a child becomes increasingly able to relate to such representations and regulate his behaviour accordingly, then it becomes possible to see that attachment and detachment need not be regarded as polar opposites. The frequent returns of the one year old to base reflect his need to confirm the central representation by checking it against sensory input. The older child no longer needs such constant confirmations: he can carry forward the image over much longer time gaps and can, moreover, make allowance for the independent movement of the mother, so that her departure from the spot where she was last seen is not experienced as the traumatic loss felt by the younger child.

Attachment and exploration

Ainsworth (1969) has suggested that a distinction may usefully be made between attachments and attachment behaviour. The former, she suggests, are based on intra-organismic structures which provide the person with a continuing propensity to direct his proximity-seeking behaviour towards certain individuals; they are durable, even under the impact of adverse conditions and can thus bridge gaps in space and time. Attachment behaviour, on the other hand, may vary from moment to moment: its intensity will be heightened or dampened in response to situational factors, in that the degree of proximity required will vary from one setting to another. At times a child may show little concern for his mother's whereabouts, playing happily on his own and, if mobile, spontaneously leaving her for extended periods. At other times, however, he will cling to her side, show little tolerance for loss of her presence and attempt everything in his power to prevent her leaving his side.

There are two kinds of conditions which can intensify attachment behaviour in this fashion: organismic and environmental. Examples of organismic conditions are illness and fatigue, as a result of both of which considerable demands may be made on the mother's comforting presence and attention. These are matters of common observation, but for environmental conditions the results of a number of experiments are also available. These studies (Ainsworth and Wittig, 1969; Cox and Campbell, 1968; Rheingold, 1969) have investigated the fluctuations of attachment intensity that may occur when an infant encounters strangeness – either in the environment as a whole or in the form of strange people or novel objects. That novelty *per se* has considerable attraction and can instigate curiosity and exploratory activities has frequently been demonstrated. However, an individual can only master a certain amount of novelty if he is not to be overwhelmed by unassimilable impressions, and the security of a familiar base is thus essential. The provision of such a base is one of the most essential aspects of mothering: having familiarized himself with her, the infant may then venture forth to explore new facets of his environment, knowing he can return whenever the load of novelty becomes too great. A delicate balance between attachment and exploration, between holding on to the old and seeking the new, can thus be found – a balance, moreover, that is continuously changing as the child's circumstances alter.

This is well seen in an experiment by Ainsworth and Wittig (1969). One-year-old infants were observed in a strange situation, the experimental manipulation consisting of a series of episodes to which they were successively introduced. In some of the episodes the infants were with their mothers, in others with a stranger as well as the mother, or with the stranger alone or they were left entirely on their own. The different episodes produced marked changes in a number of measures of exploratory behaviour. As long as

the mother was present, a considerable amount of exploration of the strange room and the toys therein took place: the
infant would merely glance up from time to time to establish visual contact with the mother and then, reassured by
her continuing presence, resume his play. Even when a
stranger entered the room the amount of exploration and
motility did not decrease appreciably. As soon as the mother
left the room, however, exploratory behaviour virtually
ceased and signs of distress and attempts to regain the
mother were shown instead. After the mother's return there
was approach behaviour and clinging, which was particularly intense after a second separation episode, when all
attempts to sever physical contact with the mother were
greeted with protest and struggling. Exploratory behaviour
thus fluctuated according to the infant's confidence in the
mother's availability. In just the same way, Harlow (1961) has
demonstrated that rhesus monkeys will use the mother as a
'haven of safety' to which they rush back whenever confronted by a frightening object but from which otherwise
they will depart in ever-widening circles in order to familiar-
ize themselves with the features of their surroundings.

In her experiments with ten-month-old infants, Rheingold
(1969) also noted the depressant effect on exploratory behaviour of an unfamiliar environment that did not contain
the mother. Thus infants left alone in an unfamiliar room
tended to remain inactive, moved hardly at all from the spot
in which they had been left and showed a degree of distress
which increased on subsequent trials. A control group
placed in the same environment but with the mother present
did not hesitate to explore it and, instead of crying, produced many non-protest vocalizations. However, when the
control infants were subsequently left by the mother, an
immediate decrease in exploratory behaviour took place,
though the total amount was still greater than found in
those infants who had been without the mother all along.
Presumably the familiarity with the surroundings, gained
while the mother was still present, served to reduce the fear

that being alone tends to induce. In further experiments the presence of toys and of an unfamiliar adult were studied. Toys were found not to distract the infants: distress and lack of exploratory activity were still observed when the subjects found themselves to be alone in the room. The presence of a female stranger had similar effects: the infants generally remained inactive and cried. In all these studies the mother had been instructed to remain passive in the infant's presence and not to encourage him to explore or to attract his attention to features of the environment; it was thus merely the awareness of her presence that provided the infants with the required security to approach and investigate the unfamiliar environment. In her presence novelty was attractive; in her absence novelty became transformed into strangeness.

Control-systems as models of attachment behaviour

It is apparent that the nature and intensity of a child's requirements for his mother's presence show considerable fluctuations of both a short-term and a long-term kind. Attachments are dynamic, i.e. they do not constitute an unvarying set of responses rigidly linked to a particular stimulus situation, but manifest themselves in a constantly changing form influenced by the infant's internal state, his appraisal of the environment, his perception of his mother's actions and whereabouts, and his knowledge of his own ability to attain her proximity speedily should the need arise.

A model of the attachment function which pays particular attention to this dynamic aspect of early sociability has been advanced by Bowlby (1969). Just as Frank (1966) found it useful to approach infant behaviour in terms of systems engineering, so Bowlby regarded a 'control-system' theory of attachments as fruitful both for understanding known phenomena and for stimulating further research. A control-system is a man-made device which simulates purposive behaviour, mainly because it has a 'goal' built into it and because it is provided with a feedback mechanism which enables it to achieve its goal. A well-known example is an anti-aircraft missile, which is set to seek out a particular goal – an aircraft – and intercept and destroy it despite its evasive tactics. Every change in the aircraft's position is monitored back to the missile which in turn modifies its own course accordingly. A predetermined goal is thus achieved by versatile means.

Human beings, in Bowlby's view, are equipped with a number of systems of varying complexity that show similar characteristics, and of these the attachment system is one. Attachment behaviour is regarded by Bowlby as a form of instinctive behaviour, the biological function of which is to protect the young organism from predators. For this purpose it is essential that the infant remains within the proximity of the mother and it is this requirement which Bowlby describes as the 'set-goal' of the attachment function. The system comes into play whenever the infant's sense organs inform him that the distance between him and the mother has increased beyond a certain maximum tolerable under present circumstances or whenever a frightening object is introduced. As soon as the child becomes aware of deviations in the distance specified by the set-goal, whether brought about by his own actions or those of the mother, steps are taken to restore the specified distance. Thus there is a continuous monitoring of the child's position in relation to the mother's position; just like the missile seeking its target, so the infant is equipped with an internal setting stipulating the aim of the system and with a feedback mechanism whereby he becomes aware of discrepancies between instruction and performance, as a result of which he can adjust his behaviour accordingly.

The attachment system is, however, balanced by other systems, such as exploration, that may have a contrary effect on the child, as a result of which oscillation of behaviour occurs as one or the other system gains ascendancy. In any given situation there is a dynamic equilibrium between proximity-seeking behaviour and behaviour patterns not geared towards proximity. Similarly the reciprocal maternal behaviour (to which Bowlby refers to as 'retrieving'), the biological function of which is to protect the infant from danger, has proximity as its set-goal, but must also compete with other goals of the mother relating to such activities as housekeeping, caring for other children and outside interests. The child's set-goal itself may change under conditions of fear, fatigue or illness, when a much closer distance will be required than normally. Thus the set-goal may vary – at least within certain limits – and any one of a variety of techniques for implementing it may be selected.

Bowlby's model is primarily concerned with the nature of attachments once they have come into being. He does, however, also suggest that the goal-corrected characteristic of attachment behaviour can emerge only towards the end of the first year, when the child's cognitive structure has evolved to the point where it is possible for him to formulate *plans*. Initially, attachment behaviour consists only of reflexive patterns and tracking movements. The child may cry at loss of proximity, but his crying is purely reactive. Towards the end of the first year, however, he becomes capable of formulating simple plans, the goal-corrected behaviour adopted for this purpose being variable and taking different forms to attain its end. Only then can the child be described as truly seeking the proximity of his attachment object.

Developmental trends in the fear-of-strangers syndrome

Proximity seeking evolves and changes its form as the child becomes cognitively more capable of handling his environment. Proximity avoidance is also by no means a static function: it, too, changes in the course of the child's environmental encounters with a diversity of individuals and objects.

Determinants of age at onset

Although it is generally agreed that fear of strangers first appears in the third quarter of the first year, the range of individual differences in age at onset is considerable. Schaffer (1966a) attempted to relate these differences to a number of variables expressing the nature of the child's past social interactions. Some of these variables (such as the amount of time the mother habitually spent with her child, her responsiveness to his crying and the extent to which she initiated interaction) may be regarded as defining the extent to which the child had been given the opportunity to learn the familiar person who would act as the standard of comparison; others (such as the number of his caretakers, the number of children in the family and the total number of people with whom he had come into contact in the course of one representative week) indicate the diversity of the child's social relationships and hence the degree to which a stranger can be experienced as different. According to the Hebb–Hunt incongruity hypothesis, these sets of experiences should determine how soon an infant becomes capable of first showing fear. In fact, age at onset was found to be significantly related to only two variables, namely, number of children in the family and number of people contacted, and even these leave a large part of the variance unaccounted for. As, moreover, both Ainsworth (1967) and Dennis (1940), in the case of the Ganda of East Africa and Hopi Indians respectively, have found fear of strangers to occur at the usual time despite the prevalence of child-rearing practices appreciably different from those of Western countries, it seems that environment alone does not account for individual differences in age at onset of fear.

The possibility that such differences may be a function of genetic factors is indicated by Freedman's (1965) study, in which a greater concordance in the timing and also the intensity of fear of strangers was found in identical twins when compared with fraternal twins. Bronson (1971), investigating sex differences in early social behaviour, has also argued for the influence of genetically based variables. Care must, of course, be taken not to postulate genetic factors merely because of the failure of environmental factors to show significant relationships; nevertheless, it does seem plausible that in those cases where at least minimal social learning opportunities exist, the rate at which new developmental events occur is closely related to an individual's genetic endowment.

Methodological considerations

Some disagreement exists as to the subsequent course of fear of strangers. Spitz (1950) and Tennes and Lampl (1964) found fear responses to be at their greatest intensity immediately after their first appearance and to decline thereafter. Other writers, however, have not been able to confirm this: Escalona (1953), Morgan and Ricciuti (1969), and Scarr and Salapatek (1970) all noted an increase in the intensity of fear with age, suggesting that the sight of a stranger is more likely to give rise to distress in the second than in the first year.

Such divergence of findings, both on this issue and on others concerning the developmental course of fear, is largely a function of the way in which investigators have dealt with two methodological problems, namely, the criteria used for defining fear and the techniques employed for eliciting them. As to the first, if fear is to be thought of in terms of proximity avoidance the simplest criterion would appear to be movement away from the stimulus. However, even in mobile animals the phenomenon of 'freezing' serves as a caution against adopting such an operational definition, which in any case is of little avail when it comes to the study of a pre-motor being like the human infant in the first year. The infant can manifest fear in many different forms and investigators have generally played safe by taking into account as wide a range as possible. Thus Brody and Axelrad (1971) considered stranger anxiety to be visible in prolonged stillness or soberness, or in prolonged restlessness, or in turning away or clinging, or audible in whimpering, crying or screaming. Morgan and Ricciutti (1969) tied their definition to an infant's score on three scales, referring respectively to facial expression (ranging from a broad, clear smile to marked puckering or wrinkling), vocalization (ranging from laugh or giggle to cry or scream) and visual and gross motor activity (ranging from reaching for or approaching the stranger to withdrawing or escaping). Bronson (1971) likewise took into account several possible indices and defined fear in terms of a long delay before smiling, inhibition of movement, and crying. Schaffer (1966a), however, did not consider mere failure to respond positively to the stranger as a justifiable index of fear. As has already been described, an infant's response to a stranger develops gradually in the course of the first half-year from immediate positive responsiveness through increasing delay in such responsiveness to its complete inhibition, before eventually negative responsiveness appears. If the function of fear responses is to terminate contact with the stimulus, mere lack of positive responsiveness can hardly be regarded as a sign of fear. A more pronounced indication of the infant's determination to be rid of the stimulus is required and for this reason Schaffer specified as the behavioural signs of fear such responses as looking or turning away, drawing back, running or crawling away, hiding face, whimpering, crying, lip trembling and screwed-up face. Solemn staring without smiling or vocalizing was disregarded. Such differences in operational definition must clearly be borne in mind when considering differences in results obtained.

This also applies to the other methodological problem referring to the variety of techniques that have been employed to elicit fear. It is now known that this phenomenon is highly sensitive to a variety of situational parameters, such as the sex of the stranger, the speed at which he impinges upon the infant, the distance between him and the child, the manner in which he attempts to interact with him, the mother's presence and her nearness to the child and the familiarity of the environment. Parameters defining the child's state and activity at the time are also likely to play a part. A number of these conditions were systematically explored in Morgan and Ricciuti's (1969) study. Each infant was tested both in his mother's lap and about four feet away from her; he was confronted sequentially both by a male and a female stranger; and interaction took the form of a standardized sequence of episodes varying both the distance and the behaviour of the stranger. The results show clearly that with increasing age infants are more likely to be distressed when apart from the mother than when close to her. Younger infants tended to become increasingly positive as the stranger approached, whereas older infants (i.e. those above eight-and-a-half months) became more negative. A slight but significant tendency for the reaction to the female stranger to be more positive than the reaction to the male stranger was noted, though the authors warn that the difference may well have been due to personal characteristics rather than to the sex difference.

A great deal still requires to be done in order to identify the precise stimulus conditions that give rise to fear. The notion that merely apprehending a stranger immediately triggers off a fear response can certainly not be upheld. By using a procedure consisting of a series of six steps involving progressively greater proximity, Schaffer (1966a) found that the first step (confrontation of the infant with a silent and immobile adult) hardly ever elicited fear. Contrary to what one might expect, the sight of a solemn, unsmiling stranger looking at the infant did not appear to be a fear-provoking situation. It was rather the active impinging of the stranger on the infant, particularly through physical interaction, that called forth fear responses. Thus, the very type of stimulation which, when administered by familiar people, will give rise to positive social responses, resulted in proximity-avoidance behaviour when offered by unfamiliar individuals. Presumably a stationary adult can be assimilated more easily than one whose active interaction provides the infant with a far greater stimulus load to process. As Hunt (1963) has pointed out: 'Not only degree of incongruity but also abruptness or rate at which incoming information appears to demand reorganization of information in the storage will be factors determining the degree of emotional arousal.' This may well account for the fact that strange objects tend to arouse less fear than strange people – with the former the child can himself regulate the speed and manner of stimulation to which he is exposed, and under these conditions exploration and approach may eventually occur rather than fear and avoidance.

Yet even active impingement on the part of the stranger does not inevitably result in fear. In Schaffer's sample between 30 and 50 per cent of infants at any given point of the follow-up period failed to evince any sign of fear; in three cases fear appeared to a marked degree at one point around eight months of age but was not observed again on any subsequent occasion; and in most other cases inexplicable variations took place from month to month, in that the infant sometimes showed fear and sometimes not. Thus, even with procedural variables held constant, fluctuations may occur.

Conclusions

Explaining the onset of attachments constitutes one set of problems, explaining their nature, manifestation and developmental course once they are in being, another. Whether a child's first relationship is in any way the prototype of all future relationships we do not as yet know; the clinical material bearing on this point is hardly convincing. What is certain is that a child's security and psychological well-being at the time are very much bound up with the nature of this relationship and that, however antithetical attachment and exploration may be in terms of the opposing attractions of mother and environment, a child can hardly be expected to deal adequately with a strange environment unless he is assured of the existence of a haven of safety to which he can fall back at times of stress. Paradoxically, it is one of the principal functions of mothering to free the child from the mother.

What eventually enables the child to leave the mother (or other attachment object) we do not as yet know. It seems likely, however, that this is dependent on his growing ability to represent the other person to himself in her absence, so that the internalized image provides him with the security which formerly only her physical presence provided. The more soundly the internal representation is established and the more easily the child can evoke it, the greater are the gaps of time for which he can be away to venture forth into unknown territory. In the course of such explorations he will encounter ever more novel objects and unfamiliar people, and as a result of increasing familiarization with these the intensity of his fear of strangeness is likely to become attenuated. Thus both proximity seeking and proximity avoidance will in due course lose the dramatically intense quality which characterizes the behaviour of the one year old.

7 Stimulation and Deprivation

Development does not take place in a vacuum; an orderly environment is required to bring about psychological growth. Cognitive structure needs environmental structure: an individual's ability to deal with the world around him can only develop on the basis of a history of exposure to forms of stimulation that enable him to acquire the information-processing skills necessary to encompass such stimulation.

Particularly in the early months of life, at a time of relative motor helplessness, stimulation comes to an infant primarily via his mother. Not only is she the social object most likely to capture his attention and become entwined in his ongoing behaviour, but exposure to other sources of stimulation is largely brought about by means of her activities. It is the mother who brings him toys and utensils, who picks him up and carries him around, who decides whether other people should interact with him and what environments outside the home he should be taken to. Stressing the importance of mothering is not new; but what is mothering?

Quantity of stimulation

One way of studying the mothering process is to examine unmothered infants. Are children brought up in this way different from family-reared children and, if so, to what aspects of upbringing can one attribute such differences?

Maternal deprivation

The literature on the effects of institutional rearing is large (Yarrow, 1961); it is also by no means unambiguous in its conclusions, for the complexity of such an experience is considerable and its outcome dependent on a great many variables. Nevertheless, it does appear that impersonally reared children are prone to develop certain pathological features. Two in particular have been singled out for attention: a general developmental retardation and a deficiency in social relationships. Thus Spitz (1945), in a series of reports on a syndrome named by him 'hospitalism', described the progressive deterioration in developmental test scores of infants brought up in a highly unstimulating orphanage; similarly Dennis and Najarian (1957) found infants living in a very depriving institution in the Lebanon to have developed at such a grossly inadequate rate that by the end of the first year they were functioning at mental deficiency level; and in a subsequent report Dennis (1960) showed that such retardation could remain evident through-our early childhood and affect a wide range of perceptual-motor functions. Social deficiencies are rather less easily demonstrated, for in the absence of tests the criteria employed by investigators are often vague and ambiguous. However, Spitz (1945) has provided some descriptive material on the grossly abnormal responses to other people of the deprived infants studied by him; Provence and Lipton (1962), in their study of institutionalized babies, mentioned such symptoms as diminished vocalization to others, failure to develop discriminatory behaviour, lack of any sign of either attachment behaviour or of fear of strangers, and absence of playful activity and social games; and both Bowlby (1951) and Goldfarb (1943) have commented on the superficiality of interpersonal relationships in the deprived.

Many of these studies have, justifiably, been criticized on methodological grounds. Nevertheless, there can be little doubt that in combination they do indicate the existence of a pathogenic element in the environment of institutionally reared infants. A lot more doubt exists as to the nature of this element. Spitz (1945) believed that all deficiencies observed by him could be ascribed to the absence of a mother-figure and that it was the lack of 'emotional interchange with a love object' that accounted for the symptoms of hospitalism. This conclusion must be questioned. For one thing, a love object is not acquired until after the middle of the first year; yet, as Spitz himself showed, retardation sets in well before this point. Moreover, as Pinneau (1955) has pointed out, the decline in developmental status in Spitz's sample generally began before the infants were actually separated from their mothers. In addition, a number of studies have shown that institutionalization *per se* need not result in retardation and that infants brought up without personalized mother love can remain well within the normal range of scores on developmental and intellectual tests (Klackenberg, 1956; Rheingold, 1956; Schaffer, 1965). On the other hand, it has also been found that children may develop all the symptoms of hospitalism without ever leaving home and that mother-reared children can be just as deprived as institutionally reared children (Provence and Coleman, 1957; Prugh and Harlow, 1962).

Perceptual deprivation

If the presence or absence of a mother-figure cannot adequately account for the data, we must search elsewhere for the pathogenic element. A number of writers (especially Casler, 1961) have suggested that what is crucial in the early months of life is the total *amount* of stimulation that is available to an infant and institutionalized infants, therefore, suffer not from maternal deprivation but from perceptual deprivation. That an adequate level of stimulation is essential for normal psychological functioning has been repeatedly demonstrated (e.g. by observing the effects of sensory deprivation); what is particularly relevant are the many studies, mainly inspired by Hebb's (1949) developmental theory, that have shown a relationship to exist in a wide variety of animal species between early stimulation and subsequent behavioural development. Perceptual deprivation, on the one hand, leads to poverty of problem-solving skills, inappropriate emotional reactivity and deviant social behaviour; perceptual enrichment, on the other hand, can bring about superior performance in these areas.

There can be little doubt that in human development, too, the level of psychological functioning varies with the amount of stimulation available. Dennis and Sayeg (1965), working with institutionalized infants suffering from gross retardation, obtained a significant increase in developmental test scores as a result of providing a daily session of extra stimulation over a period of three weeks. In an investigation of two groups of infants, both institutionalized but under different conditions of perceptual stimulation, Schaffer (1965) found that the developmental quotients (D Qs) of the relatively more deprived group were significantly lower than those of the other group during the period of institutionalization. On return home, however, while the scores of the non-deprived group remained constant, those of the deprived group showed an immediate increase, suggesting that they were now able to function at normal levels once again. And in a further test of the proposition that scores on developmental tests vary according to the level of current stimulus input, Schaffer and Emerson (1968) administered tests to a group of five-month-old infants on three successive days under indentical conditions, preceded, however, by a brief period of isolation on the first day and a period of social interaction on the second and third days. A significant rise in D Q occurred on the second and third days over the initially obtained score, whereas the D Qs of a control group, to whom the isolation condition was given on all three days, did not significantly change from one test to the next.

It may, therefore, be argued that one of the essential functions of mothering is the administration of an adequate amount of stimulation. Having only limited resources for self-stimulation, the young infant is dependent on others for this task. Only then can he perform at a level appropriate to his abilities. This applies to his social behaviour too. Thus Rheingold (1956) demonstrated that extra mothering provided by an experimenter for a group of six-month-old institutionalized infants over a period of eight weeks brought about an increase in the subjects' social responsiveness to the experimenter that was greater than for unstimulated controls (see Figure 11). The responsiveness to a stranger (the 'examiner') also increased, though not to the same extent; an increase in social responsiveness was thus brought about which was not evident in the control subjects.

On the assumption that maternal attentiveness is the chief source of stimulation for home-reared infants, Rubenstein (1967) investigated the relationship between degree of maternal attentiveness and various aspects of exploratory activity of six-month-old infants. Measures for maternal attentiveness were derived from home observations by means of a time-sampling procedure, attentiveness being defined as the number of times a mother looked at, touched, held or talked to her baby. Two indices of exploratory

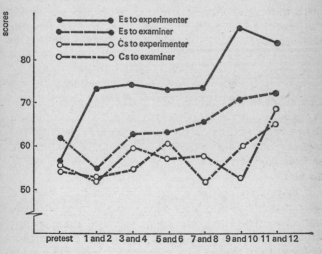

Figure 11 Means of Social Test for experimental and control groups in response to experimenter and examiner. (From Rheingold, 1956)

behaviour were used, namely, the total amount of attention (visual, tactile, oral and vocal) paid by the infant to a novel object presented for a period of ten minutes and the relative amount of attention paid to novel stimuli in preference to simultaneously presented familiar stimuli. The results indicate a positive relationship between the amount of sensory-social stimulation received by the infants and their exploratory behaviour: infants with highly attentive mothers paid more attention to the novel stimulus and preferred it to a greater extent over the familiar stimulus than infants with non-attentive mothers.

Yet another study to investigate the relationship between developmental status and amount of mother–infant interaction is that by Lewis and Goldberg (1969). Arguing that the amount of response decrement to a redundant signal may be taken as an index of cognitive capacity, Lewis and Goldberg repeatedly presented a visual stimulus to twelve-week-old infants and related the degree of habituation found for each individual to a time-sampling measure of the mother's stimulation of her baby during a half-hour waiting period before the experiment. Results indicate that response decrement correlated with the amount of touching, holding, looking and smiling by the mother. The amount of time spent reading magazines during the waiting period was negatively correlated with habituation rate.

Modulating arousal level

The supply of an adequate amount of stimulation appears to be an important aspect of the mothering process in infancy. Yet to identify maternal effectiveness with sheer quantity of stimulation is hardly satisfactory. Mothering involves a warding off of stimulation as well as an increase, a protection against excessive dosages as well as the supply of extra stimuli. The mother must, that is, help to modulate the infant's general arousal level.

In early development this level can fluctuate considerably, changing fairly rapidly from deep sleep to intense excitement, and unlike the adult an infant has relatively few mechanisms available whereby he himself can bring about changes in arousal. He is dependent in this respect on others, and a mother will accordingly supply particular types of stimulation in keeping with the infant's state: bouncing on knee, swinging through the air, or laughing and tickling in order to induce upward changes of arousal; and physical contact, cradling or dummies in order to induce downward changes. Indeed some writers, such as Scott (1962), have suggested that emotional arousal is a crucial part of being in contact with others and that the formation of social attachments is dependent on the extent to which it is experienced in the course of particular relationships.

A complex yet predictable interrelationship exists between arousal level and various behaviour patterns. Mason (1965) has described this relationship for chimpanzees, showing how a given level of arousal will predispose the infant to certain social activities and how these in turn will influence arousal. An animal at a low level of arousal, for instance, is likely to engage in particular play activities, thereby raising the level. Should this reach too great a height, the animal will retreat and, instead of exploring whatever novel objects are present in its surroundings, avoid these and cling to the familiar mother. Where no mother is available, the animal will engage in huddling and self-clasping or show intense vocal and escape activities. Thus play and exploration have arousal-producing properties, whereas clinging is arousal-reducing. Mason suggested, moreover, that variations in arousal level may be reinforcing and that a mechanism is, therefore, indicated whereby attachments are formed to individuals who are habitually associated with such variations. Both lowering and raising excitement in the infant can be pleasurable if they involve return to an optimal level, and if these changes always necessitate the presence of the mother the infant in time will learn to seek her out as the agent of arousal-production or reduction.

Walters and Parke (1965) have drawn attention to the

many studies which have established an association between arousal and attention, showing that changes in arousal level can influence cue utilization and perceptual organization. It may well be that the relationship between class differences in maternal behaviour and infant performance, as described by Kagan and Tulkin (1971), can be interpreted in this light. Middle-class mothers, these authors found, spent more time in face-to-face contact with their infants, talked more to them and also more distinctively and entertained them more with objects than lower-class mothers. But in addition to using such arousal-producing devices, the middle-class mothers were also more prone to resorting to arousal-reducing methods, for they responded more quickly to the infants' crying and thus made possible a quick return to normal levels of functioning. In short, they were more attuned to their infants' needs to be aroused at certain times by various forms of personal or non-personal stimulation and to be quietened at other times by soothing ministrations. By ensuring that their infants were not overwhelmed by excessive internal stimulation and yet provided with sufficient external stimulation, the middle-class mothers helped these babies to attend effectively to their surroundings and to profit from available learning opportunities. This became evident in a subsequently administered laboratory test, in which the middle-class infants were found to be superior to lower-class infants in such tasks as differentiating between the mother's and a stranger's voice and between meaningful and non-meaningful speech. Lowering as well as raising arousal level can thus result from maternal attention and produce a more effective learning situation. Similarly the finding by Korner and Grobstein (1966), that visual alerting and scanning behaviour occur when neonates are picked up and put to the shoulder, is interpreted by these authors as due to a reduction in arousal. A pathway is thus indicated whereby maternal ministrations may inadvertently provide visual experience, and it is the lack of this facility that might well constitute one of the earliest causes of the developmental deficit of institutionalized infants.

Variety of stimulation

So far we have been concerned with quantitative aspects of stimulation and according to some writers these are the only ones that play a part in infancy. Moltz (1963), for example, has pointed out that there is much evidence to suggest that in the earliest ontogenetic stages of development, behaviour is largely determined by stimulus intensity rather than stimulus quality. This statement receives its strongest support from the studies by Levine (1960), according to which handling by an experimenter and the administration of electric shock have equivalent beneficial effects on a wide variety of behavioural and physiological functions in the rat, whereas unstimulated animals are greatly inferior in these functions. Similarly, the various studies referred to in chapter 2 which show that maternal punitiveness produces attachment behaviour in animals as effectively as maternal nurturance indicate that early on in development the qualitative features of stimulation appear to be of little consequence.

Whether such findings can be extrapolated to human development remains doubtful. Little empirical work exists that is directly relevant; what does exist suggests that for the human infant parameters of stimulation other than quantitative ones are crucial. Two in particular may be mentioned, namely, variety and timing. As to the former, it is of interest that Dennis (1960), writing of the severe retardation found by him in some institutions, considered the basic cause for such a condition to lie in the homogeneity of the stimulation provided. A nursery containing ten or twenty babies is by no means a quiet place and the total number of attendants moving in and out will certainly exceed the number of caretakers a home-reared child encounters. On the other hand, when an infant hardly ever leaves that one noisy room and when all the attendants are identically dressed and trained to perform identical activities, the stimulation impinging on the infant in such an environment is characterized above all by its monotony. A stimulus constantly repeated produces habituation of attentional responses – variation is required to maintain interest. Too much variation is, of course, also harmful: an environment that is in constant flux will overload the child's processing capacity and evoke defensive responses. The stimulation provided by the mother will, therefore, need to meet a 'happy mean', exposing the infant to carefully graded amounts of novel experience against a background of familiarity.

The timing of stimulation
Contingency relationships

No less important than the variety of stimulation is its timing – the timing, that is, in relation to the infant's own responses. One of the advantages of the learning theory analysis of early social behaviour presented by Bijou and Baer (1965) and by Gewirtz (1968) is its stress on the contingency relationship that must exist between stimulus and response if the latter is to become part of the infant's behaviour repertoire. The extent to which the mother acts as a source of reinforcement depends on her ability to respond *contingently* to her baby, namely, to administer stimulation that is appropriate in relation to the ongoing activity of the infant. The previously mentioned studies of infant conditioning by Brackbill (1958) and by Rheingold, Gewirtz and Ross (1959) show very well the powerful reinforcing effects of contingently administered stimulation. When, on the other hand, stimulation is randomly administered it fails to bring about acquisition of behaviour. For example, Weisberg (1963), in his extension of the Rheingold, Gewirtz and Ross study, compared the effects of contingent and non-contingent social stimulation on the frequency of vocalization by three-month-old infants. The non-contingent stimulation was administered according to a prearranged schedule irrespective of the infant's activity at the time, whereas in the contingent condition the stimulation followed each of the infant's vocal responses. Weisberg's results show clearly that only the contingent stimulation was able to influence the frequency of response emission. Thus maternal behaviour, if it is to be reinforcing, must be timed in such a manner that the infant can become aware of the consequences of his actions.

According to Lewis and Goldberg (1969), contingent reinforcement does not merely bring about the acquisition of specific responses, but also enables the child to develop a general motive which is the basis for all future learning. This is the *effectance motive* (White, 1959), characterized by the individual's belief that his actions successfully affect his environment. Lewis and Goldberg suggested that such a motive is developed primarily through the interaction with the mother, for it is mainly in this context that the infant can learn about the consequences of his behaviour. If the mother reinforces the infant consistently and with short latencies (i.e. within the limits of his memory span), she can create a *generalized* expectancy in the infant regarding his effectiveness in obtaining rewards through his own actions. Behaviour patterns other than those specifically reinforced will thereby also benefit. Institutionalized children, who tend to be treated in a much more routine and arbitrary manner, do not have the chance of learning such an expectancy and are, therefore, more likely to develop a general feeling of helplessness regarding their ability to affect the environment.

Phasing and the establishment of reciprocity

The precise nature of the timing relationship requires a great deal of further examination. A most promising beginning has been made by Richards (1971) with the use of frame-by-frame analysis of films depicting interaction sequences of mothers and babies. A mother, holding her infant on her lap, typically begins such an interaction sequence by smiling and vocalizing to the baby, at the same time moving her head rhythmically towards and away from his face. The infant first responds by rapt attention, with a widening of his eyes and a stilling of his body movements.

Gradually his excitement increases, he may vocalize and finally a smile appears and spreads over his face. At this point he turns away and the cycle begins once again. Throughout this sequence the mother's actions are carefully phased with those of the infant. Thus, during the initial attention phase, her behaviour is restrained; as the infant's excitement increases, however, she starts to vocalize more rapidly until he reaches the point where he is about to smile – then her movements are suddenly reduced, as if she was allowing the infant time to reply. But not all mothers, Richards reported, behave in this way. Some are unable to adopt such sensitive timing and instead subject the infant to a barrage of constant and unphased stimulation. The infant is given no time to reply and will soon be reduced to crying and turning away from the mother's face.

This example illustrates well the reciprocal nature of the mother–infant relationship. On the mother's part, stimulation must be paced to ongoing activities in the infant – a very different conception from that based on stimulation arbitrarily imposed on a passive organism. As Rheingold (1968) put it, it is not only the mother who socializes the infant: the infant also socializes the mother. It is, therefore, not surprising that investigations of the relationship between maternal characteristics and infant behaviour (e.g. by Ainsworth, Bell and Stayton, 1971) have found the degree of a mother's sensitivity to her child to exercise an all-pervasive influence and to be clearly associated with a wide range of infant characteristics.

Sensitivity involves the ability to adapt one's behaviour to the specific requirements of the other person. Mothers, that is, must be able to take into account the individuality of their infants. They must also, however, be able to change their practices over time as the growing infant develops new skills and modes of interaction. Moss (1967) found that of sixteen maternal variables only seven remained constant between infant ages of three weeks and three months – a reflection of the relative instability of the mother–infant system at that early stage of life. Those variables which showed stability referred mainly to affectionate-social responses (such as amount of smiling and of verbal interaction), suggesting that these may well be more sensitive indicators of enduring maternal attitudes than absolute time spent on such activities as feeding and physical contact. Obviously some characteristics of a mother remain stable, particularly those which reflect the 'formal' aspects of her personality such as rigidity and emotionality. These will be evident at all stages of the child's development, yet at a phenotypic level even these will change in accordance with the mother's perception of the child's ability to assimilate her behaviour.

There are many ways in which the developmental aspect of the mother–infant relationship can be conceptualized. One of the most interesting schemes recently put forward is that by Sander (1969), who viewed the relationship as a sequence of adaptations common to all mother–infant pairs but acted out in somewhat different ways by each. On the basis of detailed longitudinal observations, Sander has put forward a sequence of five levels of adjustment that can be isolated and defined in the first eighteen months of life. Each of these is associated with certain prominent infant behaviour patterns which must become coordinated with maternal activities at that time. For instance, the initial issue to be settled in the first three months is concerned with the achievement of stability in such basic biological processes as feeding, sleeping and elimination and with stimulus needs for quietening and arousal. In particular, the regulation of the infant's rhythm must receive attention at this stage. At one level of analysis this involves microrhythms, such as those observed in sucking and smiling; at another level macro-rhythms, such as the day–night oscillation of crying and activity, are implicated. Stabilization comes through environmental transactions, the nature of which will do much to regularize or disorganize the rhythm.

For example, twenty-four-hour cumulative motility and crying counts were obtained over a ten-hour period by Sander and Julia (1966) from a group of six infants kept in a neonatal nursery and a group of three infants who 'roomed-in' (i.e. received individual care from their mothers) in a maternity hospital. As seen in Figure 12, the difference in motility is relatively slight at first. From the third day on, however, the two groups (with the exception of one nursery infant) become sharply differentiated: restlessness for the

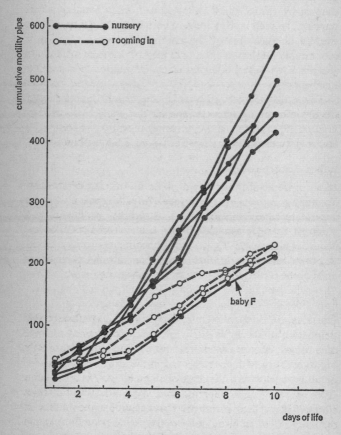

Figure 12 Cumulative frequencies of motility scores for six nursery babies and three rooming-in babies for the first ten days of life. (From Sander and Julia, 1966)

nursery infants remains at a high level, while that of the other group decreases. The same tendency is also reflected in the crying records of the two samples. The rooming-in infants, moreover, showed not only a general decrease in motility and crying but also a shift in the twenty-four-hour pattern of these activities: their behaviour was marked, that is, by the gradual emergence of a preponderance of daytime activity and crying, whereas the nursery infants showed no such shift. It seems that regulatory stability is more easily established in an environment where infants are given individualized care and where (as records of caretaker interventions showed) the time of delay between infants' signals and adult attention is relatively brief. In this way the initially disparate organizations of functions in mother and child proceed, through interaction, to modify one another, until harmony of coordination is established.

Infant characteristics

It is apparent that the amount, kind and timing of stimulation must be adapted to the individual infant if it is to produce a predictable outcome. The effects produced by a stimulus depend as much on the characteristics of the receiver as those of the signal and it, therefore, becomes essential to define more precisely the nature of the responding infant if one is to understand the ensuing behaviour.

The concept of state

One line of investigation that has served to emphasize this point is centred on the study of state. Considered as level of arousal, this concept has been used to differentiate between degrees of sleep and wakefulness and has been defined in behavioural and physiological terms by Prechtl (1965) along a scale referring to five quantitatively distinct states. The cyclical variations that occur between states in the daily life of an infant may well provide another example of an inherently determined rhythm within the central nervous system.

An infant's state will affect both the nature and the intensity of his responsiveness to stimulation. In each state, as Brown (1964) has put it, 'there are characteristic ways of responding to external stimuli in regard to how soon the baby's response occurs, how long it is maintained, whether it is specific or generalized, what type of response occurs and the amount of suppression of responding that is present'. This means that a mother's decision as to the timing and nature of stimulation offered by her should optimally depend on her reading of the child's present condition. An example is presented by Levy (1958), who observed the behaviour of mothers when their infants were brought to them for feeding during their stay in a maternity hospital and found that a mother's behaviour tended to vary considerably in this one situation as a function of her awareness of the baby's state. How she greeted him, her method of handling and the speed with which she offered the breast could all be related to her perception of the infant's readiness for these forms of stimulation. Maternal sensitivity to the infant's state at the time of interaction is thus an important determinant of the appropriateness of the stimulation offered.

Patterns of individuality

State has been studied primarily as an intra-individual variable. In addition, however, attention has also been given to a number of variables that define rather more stable characteristics of infants and that mediate the effects of stimulation according to particular patterns of individuality. Thomas, Chess, Birch, Hertzig and Korn (1964) compiled a list of nine such intrinsic reaction patterns (e.g. activity level, threshold of responsiveness, distractibility, and attention span), some of which have been studied in detail by other writers.

Of these, *perceptual sensitivity* has been considered as a constitutionally determined dimension in several investigations. In a clinically oriented article, Bergman and Escalona (1949) suggested that some children may well be born with a hypersensitivity to stimulation, as a result of which they are insufficiently protected against external forces and, therefore, more liable to develop a variety of psychopathological conditions. Differences in sensitivity, Escalona (1969) pointed out, may mean that the same maternal treatment meted out to different infants can have quite different effects or, conversely, that different maternal treatments may bring about the same effect in different infants. Thus, one mother may interact frequently and intensely with her baby and be generally energetic in her dealings with him; another mother may handle her infant gently and relatively infrequently. Yet these two very different forms of stimulation can generate similar experiences if applied, respectively, to an insensitive and to a sensitive infant. Whether it is justified to talk, as Escalona did, in terms of a global sensitivity or whether there are differences according to modality remains to be established. What is more certain is that there are marked individual differences in behavioural and autonomic reactivity to stimulation, that these can be already detected in neonates and that there is at least some short-term consistency in such differences (e.g. Birns, 1965; Bridger, 1962; Richmond and Lustman, 1955).

Another characteristic in which consistent individual differences have been demonstrated to occur in early infancy is *activity level* (Kessen, Williams and Williams 1961). Such differences, it has been suggested (Thomas *et al.*, 1964), remain stable over lengthy periods of time and are relatively independent of maternal and other environmental influences (Schaefer and Bayley, 1963). Activity level, too, it appears, can modify the impact of external stimulation. Escalona (1963), in a comparative study of two hyperactive and two hypoactive infants, observed that the latter showed their developmentally most advanced behaviour only when in interaction with other people, whereas the active infants performed best when left unstimulated. 'The same maternal interventions', Escalona suggested, 'which for some infants encourage the activation of developmentally important behaviour patterns may make no difference or even be a hindrance for other infants', and concluded: 'The hypothesis arises that at this age social stimulation is a necessary condition for the emergence of relatively mature behavior in motorically inactive children, whereas this is not the case for markedly active ones.'

Two studies provide findings relevant to this point of view. In one, Schaffer (1966b) investigated the hypothesis that under conditions of deprivation inactive infants are more likely to be adversely affected than active infants. By examining the drop in developmental quotient that had taken place during a period of institutionalization and relating it to activity level, confirmation for the hypothesized association was obtained. The more active infant, one may assume, is more likely to effect changes in position and hence encounter new environmental stimuli, thus avoiding the perceptual monotony that is the lot of the inactive infant. In addition, the feedback effects of the activity will induce a state of alertness, which in turn will increase the responsiveness of cortical areas to afferent stimuli in general (Gellhorn, 1957). A hyperactive infant is thus alerted not only by his own considerable activity but also by increased responsiveness to external sources.

The other relevant study is a further investigation by Escalona (1969), based on a longitudinal and very detailed examination of a group of thirty-two infants between the ages of four and thirty-two weeks. By dividing her sample into active and inactive infants and contrasting their behaviour in a wide range of situations, Escalona noted that tactile and visual exploration tended to be more prominent among inactive infants, that hunger led to more intense excitation in active than in inactive infants, that object stimulation greatly alerted the behaviour of inactive subjects while active babies showed little change and that active infants responded prominently to minimal social stimulation (the mere sight of a person) whereas inactive infants required very much more intense social stimulation (such as handling) before they showed similar signs of responsiveness. Stimulation, it can be concluded, plays a different role in the experience of active and inactive infants, and the same maternal practices, therefore, result in widely divergent patterns of mother–child interaction when applied to infants of different primary reaction patterns.

Some organismic response patterns appear to be of a *sex-linked* nature. There is now a substantial body of evidence to indicate the existence of differences between boys and girls in the rate of early behavioural development. These differences, it is true, cannot be detected in the results of global developmental assessment as given by infant scales (Bayley, 1965); they emerge, rather, from an examination of various more specific cognitive functions. Kagan and Lewis (1965), for example, found that girls display more sustained attention to visual stimuli and show a greater preference for novel auditory patterns than boys at both six and thirteen months of age. If sustained attention and a preference for stimuli that deviate from the accustomed can be regarded as mature response patterns, it appears that from at least six months on girls are developmentally more advanced in these respects. When confronted with familiar stimuli (faces), Kagan *et al.* (1966) found girls to respond with shorter fixation times than boys at the age of four months – a finding interpreted by these authors as indicative of a maturational difference in favour of the girls, in that the more mature child can be expected to assimilate the stimulus faster and habituate more quickly. From studies of social behaviour a similar sex difference has been reported: both Gewirtz (1965) and Laroche and Tcheng (1963) have found that boys tend to lag behind girls in the decline of indiscriminate smiling, and Schaffer (1966a) observed that age at onset of the fear-of-strangers syndrome was reached somewhat earlier by girls than by boys.

Sex differences will affect a mother's perception of her child and accordingly her behaviour and attitudes. In an observational study, Moss (1967) noted that at the age of one month the amount of contact that mothers had with their infants was positively related to the babies' fussing and crying. At this age the relationship held for both males and females; at three months, however, a sex difference was evident. For the males (who were generally more irritable) the correlation between amount of crying and maternal contact was negative whereas among females the relationship remained positive. Moss concluded that, while the females could respond to maternal ministrations, the failure of the males to become pacified had actually led to a reduction in the mother's responsiveness to their crying.

The examples given above refer to only a few aspects of an infant's inherent make-up; many others, no doubt, remain to be isolated. They suffice to illustrate, however, that the effects of stimulation must be understood not only in terms of the stimulus itself but also in terms of the stimulated organism. The ability to assimilate and mediate encounters with the environment tends to vary with age; at any one age, as we have seen, considerable individual difference factors may also be operative. All these must be taken into account if one is to predict the outcome of specific experiences.

Conclusions

The basic characteristic of all interpersonal behaviour is reciprocity. Reciprocity involves the building up of chains of coordinated interaction sequences, during which each partner participates in a process of stimulus interchange, the nature of which is affected both by the signals received and by the structural characteristics of the receiver. Thus, an infant may initiate such a sequence by emitting a particular signal for attention, to which his mother will then respond in a characteristic fashion that will, in turn, affect not only his ongoing activity but also his tendency to respond on future occasions under similar circumstances. The relationship is, therefore, an ever-changing one, in that the behaviour of each partner gives rise to an increasingly complex response organization in the other partner; the mutual entwining of interaction sequences thus takes place at progressively higher levels. This will occur as long as the stimulation is *relevant* – relevant, that is, to the individual's existing cognitive structure. The explanation of social development is thus essentially a matter of accounting for the nature of cognitive structure at different developmental levels and of explaining the relevance of stimulation at each.

Where reciprocity is not found, the possibility of psychological growth is limited. As Escalona (1969) pointed out, it is the lack of this element which distinguishes the child's play with inanimate objects from his play with the mother:

Object stimulation provided by a social partner is specifically attuned to the infant's momentary state and movement pattern; it is appropriately varied in tempo and intensity; it is embedded in a back-and-forth flow of social interaction; and thus it facilitates novel behaviour adaptations in a manner that even sophisticated programmed automatic stimulation cannot be expected to approximate.

Such devices as mobiles, taped music or televised pictures can supply stimulation, but they cannot adjust the nature, timing and intensity of stimulation to the child's requirements as efficiently as a sensitive mother. Hence the defects that ensue from being reared in an impersonal environment, even one where the overall level of stimulation is high. Hence also the pathological outcome for Harlow's (1962) monkeys, whose early experience with contact-giving surrogate mothers did not include the element of reciprocity and who, therefore, did not develop the skills necessary for real interpersonal relationships in adulthood.

Methodologically, psychologists have in the past found it easier to study only one of a pair of interacting individuals at a time, isolating him from the total context and considering stimulation as flowing in only one direction. Masks or human faces are presented to infants and their readiness to smile is observed; the taped recordings of infants' cries are played back to mothers and their responsiveness is noted.

The traditional stimulus–response paradigm of experimental psychology is thus preserved; yet each of these S–R sequences is only one artificially isolated element in a chain of interactions and the flavour of the relationship can only be obtained through study of the chain as a whole. There are few investigations that have been attempted along these lines and those of human adult–infant relationships have only too often become bogged down in masses of clinically descriptive data. Among students of animal behaviour the use of this approach has been somewhat more conspicuous. Schneirla, Rosenblatt and Tobach (1963), for example, have employed it in order to understand the establishment and maintenance of 'behavioural synchrony' (Rosenblatt, 1965) in the mother–offspring relationship of cats and rats. In this way it has become possible for these authors to describe the processes that, from birth on, set in motion a course of interrelated changes in the behaviour of both young and mother – changes that are the products of reciprocal stimulative interaction and that eventually lead, on the one hand, to independent functioning of the offspring and, on the other hand, to a gradual decline of the female's maternal behaviour towards her litter.

Despite the scarcity of comparable data for human development, it is now increasingly appreciated that justice must be done to the two-way nature of early social behaviour. To do so, the stimulative and responsive characteristics of both partners need first to be defined at each developmental level. It will then become possible to understand the characteristics of the other to which each partner is differentially responsive; it will then also become possible to trace the continuity of change from level to level. In this way it has already become evident that maternal behaviour in just its quantitative sense is insufficient to account for the facts of developmental progress. Infants, we have learned, are not empty vessels to be filled with as much experience as we can cram into them; they are active partners in even the earliest social encounters and a much finer analysis of stimulation is, therefore, required – an analysis that will take into consideration not only the nature of stimuli offered by the mother but also the infant's own characteristics and what these, in turn, evoke in maternal responsiveness.

References

AHRENS, R. (1954), 'Beitrag zur Entwicklung der Physiognomie-und Mimikerkennes', *Z. exp. angew. Psychol.*, vol. 2, pp. 412–54.

AINSWORTH, M. D. S. (1964), 'Patterns of attachment behavior shown by the infant in interaction with his mother', *Merrill–Palmer Q.*, vol. 10, pp. 51–9.

AINSWORTH, M. D. S. 1967), *Infancy in Uganda*, Johns Hopkins Press.

AINSWORTH, M. D. S. (1969), 'Object relations, dependency and attachment: a theoretical review of the infant–mother relationship', *Child Devel.*, vol. 40, pp. 969–1025.

AINSWORTH, M. D. S., and WITTIG, B. A. (1969), 'Attachment and exploratory behaviour of one-year-olds in a strange situation', in B. M. Foss (ed.), *Determinants of Infant Behaviour*, vol. 4, Methuen.

AINSWORTH, M. D. S., BELL, S. M. V., and STAYTON, D. J. (1971), 'Individual differences in strange-situation behavior of one-year-olds', in H. R. Schaffer (ed.), *The Origins of Human Social Relations*, Academic Press.

AMBROSE, J. A. (1961), 'The development of the smiling response in early infancy', in B. M. Foss (ed.), *Determinants of Infant Behaviour*, Methuen.

AMBROSE, J. A. (1969), Discussion contribution in J. A. Ambrose (ed.), *Stimulation in Early Infancy*, Academic Press.

AMES, E. W., and SILFEN, C. K. (1965), 'Methodological issues in the study of age differences in infants' attention to stimuli varying in movement and complexity', paper to the Society for Research in Child Development, Minneapolis.

BAER, D. M., and GRAY, P. H. (1960), 'Imprinting to a different species without overt following', *Percept. mot. Skills*, vol. 10, pp. 171–4.

BALDWIN, A. L. (1968) 'Cognitive theory and socialization', in D. Goslin (ed.), *Handbook of Socialization*, Rand McNally.

BANDURA, A. (1965), 'Vicarious processes: a case of no-trial learning', in L. Berkowitz (ed.), *Advances in Experimental Social Psychology*, vol. 2, Academic Press.

BANKS, J. H., and WOLFSON, J. H. (1967), 'Differential cardiac response of infants to mother and stranger', paper to the Eastern Psychological Association, Philadelphia.

BARTOSHUK, A. K. (1962), 'Response decrement with repeated elicitation of human neonatal cardiac acceleration to sound', *J. comp. physiol. Psychol.*, vol. 55, pp. 9–13.

BATESON, P. P. G. (1966), 'The characteristics and context of imprinting', *Biol. Rev.*, vol. 41, pp. 177–220.

BAYLEY, N. (1965), 'Comparisons of mental and motor test scores for ages 1–15 months by sex, birth order, race, geographical location and education of parents', *Child Devel.*, vol. 36, pp. 379–411.

BAYLEY, N. (1969), *Bayley's Scales of Infant Development*, Psychological Corporation.

BERGMAN, P., and ESCALONA, S. (1949), 'Unusual sensitivities in very young children', *Psychoanal. Study Child*, vol. 3, pp. 333–52.

BERLYNE, D. E. (1958), 'The influence of the albedo and complexity of stimuli on visual fixation in the human infant', *Brit. J. Psychol.*, vol. 49, pp. 315–18.

BIJOU, S. W., and BAER, D. M. (1965), *Child Development: II. Universal Stage of Infancy*, Appleton-Century-Crofts.

BIRNS, B. (1965), 'Individual differences in human neonates' responses to stimulation', *Child Devel.*, vol. 36, pp. 249–56.

BOWER, T. G. R. (1965), 'Stimulus variables determining space perception in infants', *Science*, vol. 149, pp. 88–9.

BOWER, T. G. R. (1966), 'The visual world of infants', *Sci. Amer.*, vol. 215, pp. 80–97.

BOWLBY, J. (1951), *Maternal Care and Mental Health*, World Health Organization.

BOWLBY, J. (1958), 'The nature of the child's tie to his mother', *Int. J. Psychoanal.*, vol. 39, pp. 350–73.

BOWLBY, J. (1960), 'Separation anxiety', *Int. J. Psychoanal.*, vol. 41, pp. 1–25.

BOWLBY, J. (1969), *Attachment and Loss: I. Attachment*, Hogarth Press.

BRACKBILL, Y. (1958), 'Extinction of the smiling response in infants as a function of reinforcement schedule', *Child Devel.*, vol. 29, pp. 115–24.

BRACKBILL, Y. (1971), 'The cumulative effect of continuous stimulation on arousal level in infants', *Child Devel.*, vol. 42, pp. 17–26.

BRACKBILL, Y., ADAMS, G., CROWELL, D. H. and GRAY, M. L. (1966), 'Arousal level in neonates and preschool children under continuous auditory stimulation', *J. exp. child Psychol.*, vol. 4, pp. 178–88.

BRENNAN, W. M., AMES, E. W., and MOORE, R. W. (1966), 'Age differences in infants' attention to patterns of different complexities', *Science*, vol. 151, pp. 354–5.

BRIDGER, W. H. (1961), 'Sensory discrimination and automatic the human neonate', *Amer. J. Psychiat.*, vol. 117, pp. 991–6.

BRIDGER, W. H. (1962), 'Sensory discrimination and autonomic function in the newborn', *J. Amer. Acad. Child Psychiat.*, vol. 1, pp. 67–82.

BRIDGES, K. M. B. (1931), *The Social and Emotional Development of the Pre-School Child*, Routledge & Kegan Paul.

BRODY, S., and AXELRAD, S. (1971), 'Maternal stimulation and the social responsiveness of infants', in H. R. Schaffer (ed.), *The Origins of Human Social Relations*, Academic Press.

BRONSHTEIN, A. I., and PETROVA, E. P. (1952), 'An investigation of the auditory analyzer in neonates and young infants', *Zh. vyssh. nerv. Deiatel.*, vol. 2, pp. 333–43.

BRONSON, G. W. (1968), 'The development of fear in man and other animals', *Child Devel.*, vol. 39, pp. 409–31.

BRONSON, G. W. (1971), 'Fear of the unfamiliar in human infants', in H. R. Schaffer (ed.), *The Origins of Human Social Relations*, Academic Press.

BROSSARD, L. M., and DECARIE, T. G. (1968), 'Comparative reinforcing effects of eight stimulations on the smiling responses of infants', *J. child Psychol. Psychiat.*, vol. 9, pp. 51–60.

BROWN, J. L. (1964), 'States in newborn infants', *Merrill–Palmer Q.*, vol. 10, 313–27.

BRUNER, J. S., OLVER, R. R., and GREENFIELD, P. M. (1965), *Studies in Cognitive Growth*, Wiley.

CALDWELL, B. M. (1962), 'The usefulness of the critical period hypothesis in the study of filiative behavior', *Merrill–Palmer Q.*, vol. 8, pp. 229–42.

CALDWELL, B. M. (1964), 'The effects of infant care', in M. L. Hoffman and L. W. Hoffman (eds.), *Review of Child Development Research*, vol. 1, Russell Sage Foundation.

CALDWELL, B. M. (1965), 'Visual and emotional reactions of an infant to his mother and other adult females', paper to the Tavistock Study Group on Mother–Infant Interaction, London.

CALDWELL, B. M., and HERSHER, L. (1964), 'Mother–infant interaction during the first year of life', *Merrill–Palmer Q.*, vol. 10, pp. 119–28.

CARON, R. F., and CARON, A. J. (1968), 'The effects of repeated exposure and stimulus complexity on visual fixation in infants', *Psychonom. Sci.*, vol. 10, pp. 207–8.

CASLER, L. (1961), 'Maternal deprivation: a critical review of the literature', *Monogr. Soc. Res. Child Devel.*, vol. 26, no. 2 (whole no. 80).

CHARLESWORTH, W. R. (1966), 'Persistence of orienting and attending behavior in infants as a function of stimulus locus uncertainty', *Child Devel.*, vol. 37, pp. 473–92.

COX, F. N., and CAMPBELL, D. (1968), 'Young children in a new situation with and without their mothers', *Child Devel.*, vol. 39, pp. 123–31.

DARWIN, C. (1872), *The Expression of the Emotions in Man and Animals*, Philosophical Library.

DARWIN, C. (1877), 'A biographical sketch of an infant', *Mind*, no. 7, pp. 285–94.

DECARIE, T. G. (1969), 'A study of the mental and emotional development of the thalidomide child', in B. M. Foss (ed.), *Determinants of Infant Behaviour*, vol. 4, Methuen.

DEMBER, W. N., and EARL, R. (1957), 'Analysis of exploratory, manipulatory and curiosity behaviors', *Psychol. Rev.*, vol. 64, pp. 91–96.

DENNIS, W. (1940), 'Does culture appreciably affect patterns of infant behavior?', *J. soc. Psychol.*, vol. 12, pp. 305–17.

DENNIS, W. (1960), 'Causes of retardation among institutional children: Iran', *J. genet. Psychol.*, vol. 96, pp. 47–59.

DENNIS, W., and NAJARIAN, P. (1957), 'Infant development under environmental handicap', *Psychol. Monogr.*, vol. 71, no. 7, pp. 1–13.

DENNIS, W., and SAYEG, Y. (1965) 'The effects of supplementary experiences upon the behavioral development of infants in institutions', *Child Devel.*, vol. 36, pp. 81–90.

DOLLARD, J., and MILLER, N. E. (1950), *Personality and Pyschotherapy*, McGraw-Hill.

ESCALONA, S. K. (1953), 'Emotional development in the first year of life', in M. Senn (ed.), *Problems of Infancy and Childhood*, Josiah Macey Foundation.

ESCALONA, S. K. (1963), 'Patterns of infantile experience and the developmental process', *Psychoanal. Study Child*, vol. 18, pp. 197–244.

ESCALONA, S. K. (1969), *The Roots of Individuality*, Tavistock.

FANTZ, R. L. (1961), 'The origin of form perception', *Sci. Amer.*, vol. 204, pp. 66–72.

FANTZ, R. L. (1963), 'Pattern vision in newborn infants', *Science*, vol. 140, pp. 296–7.

FANTZ, R. L. (1964), 'Visual experience in infants: decreased attention to familiar patterns relative to novel ones', *Science*, vol. 146, pp. 668–70.

FANTZ, R. L. (1965), 'Visual perception from birth as shown by pattern selectivity', *Ann. New York Acad. Sci.*, vol. 118, pp. 793–814.

FANTZ, R. L. (1966), 'Pattern discrimination and selective attention as determinants of perceptual development from birth', in A. H. Kidd and J. L. Rivoire (eds.), *Perceptual Development in Children*, International Universities Press.

FANTZ, R. L., and NEVIS, S. (1967), 'Pattern preferences and perceptual-cognitive development in early infancy', *Merrill–Palmer Q.*, vol. 13, pp. 77–108.

FISICHELLI, V. R., and KARELITZ, S. (1963, 'The cry latencies of normal infants and those with brain damage', *J. Pediat.*, vol. 62, pp. 724–34.

FITZGERALD, H. E. (1968), 'Automatic pupillary reflex activity during early infancy and its relation to social and non-social visual stimuli', *J. exp. child Psychol.*, vol. 6, pp. 470–82.

FRANK, L. K. (1966), *On the Importance of Infancy*, Random House.

FREEDMAN, D. A. (1964), 'Smiling in blind infants and the issue of innate *v.* acquired', *J. child Psychol. Psychiat.*, vol. 5, pp. 171–84.

FREEDMAN, D. A. (1965) 'Hereditary control of early social behaviour', in B. M. Foss (ed.), *Determinants of Infant Behaviour*, vol. 3, Methuen.

FREEDMAN, D. A., and FREEDMAN, N. (1969), 'Behavioural differences between Chinese–American and European–American newborns', *Nature*, vol. 224, p. 1227.

GEBER, M. (1958), 'The psycho-motor development of African children in the first year, and the influence of maternal behavior', *J. soc. Psychol.*, vol. 47, pp. 185–95.

GELLHORN, E. (1957), *Automatic Imbalance and the Hypothalamus*, University of Minnesota Press.

GESELL, A. L. (1928), *Infancy and Human Growth*, Macmillan.

GEWIRTZ, J. L. (1965), 'The course of infant smiling in four child-rearing environments in Israel', in B. M. Foss (ed.), *Determinants of Infant Behaviour*, vol. 3, Methuen.

GEWIRTZ, J. L. (1968), 'Mechanisms of social learning: some roles of stimulation and behavior in early development', in D. A. Goslin (ed.), *Handbook of Socialization Theory and Research*, Rand McNally.

GIBSON, E. J. (1969), *Principles of Perceptual Learning and Development*, Appleton-Century-Crofts.

GOLDFARB, W. (1943), 'Effects of early institution care on adolescent personality', *J. exp. Educ.*, vol. 12, pp. 106–29.

GOLDFARB, W. (1945), 'Effects of psychological deprivation in infancy and subsequent stimulation', *Amer. J. Psychiat.*, vol. 102, pp. 18–33.

GORDON, T., and FOSS, B. M. (1965), 'The role of stimulation in the delay of onset of crying in the newborn infant', *Q. J. exp. Psychol.*, vol. 18, pp. 79–81.

GOTTESMAN, I. I. (1966), 'Genetic variation in adaptive personality tests', *J. child Psychol. Psychiat.*, vol. 7, pp. 199–208.

GRAY, P. H (1958), 'Theory and evidence of imprinting in human infants', *J. Psychol.*, vol. 46, pp. 155–66.

GRIFFITHS, R. (1954), *The Abilities of Babies*, University of London Press.

HAAF, R. A., and BELL, R. Q. (1967), 'A facial dimension in visual discrimination by human infants', *Child Devel.*, vol. 38, pp. 893–9.

HAITH, M. M. (1966), 'The response of the human newborn to visual movement', *J. exp. child Psychol.*, vol. 3, pp. 235–43.

HARLOW, H. F. (1958), 'The nature of love', *Amer. Psychol.*, vol. 13, pp. 673–85.

HARLOW, H. F. (1961), 'The development of affectional patterns in infant monkeys', in B. M. FOSS (ed.), *Determinants of Infant Behaviour*, Methuen.

HARLOW, H. F. (1962), 'The heterosexual affectional system in monkeys', *Amer. Psychol.*, vol. 17, pp. 1–7.

HARRIS, J. D. (1943), 'Habituation response decrement in the intact organism', *Psychol. Bull.*, vol. 40, pp. 385–422.

HEBB, D. O. (1946), 'On the nature of fear', *Psychol. Rev.*, vol. 53, pp. 250–75.

HEBB, D. O. (1949), *The Organization of Behavior*, Wiley.

HERSHENSON, M. (1964), 'Visual discrimination in the human newborn', *J. comp. physiol. Psychol.*, vol. 58, pp. 270–76.

HINDE, R. A. (1963), 'The nature of imprinting', in B. M. Foss (ed.), *Determinants of Infant Behaviour*, vol. 2, Methuen.

HINDE, R. A. (1966), *Animal Behavior: A Synthesis of Ethology and Comparative Psychology*, McGraw-Hill.

HUNT, J. Mc. V. (1963), 'Piaget's observations as a source of hypotheses concerning motivation', *Merrill–Palmer Q.*, vol. 9, pp. 263–75.

HUNT, J. McV. (1964), 'The psychological basis for using pre-school enrichment as an antidote for cultural deprivation', *Merrill–Palmer Q.*, vol. 10, pp. 209–48.

HUTT, C., BERNUTH, H. V., LENARD, H. G., HUTT, S. J., and PRECHTL, H. F. R. (1968), 'Habituation in relation to state in the human neonate', *Nature*, vol. 220, pp. 618–20.

HUTT, S. J., HUTT, C., LENARD, H. G. BERNUTH, H. V., and MUNTJEWERFF, W. J. (1968) 'Auditory responsivity in the human neonate', *Nature*, vol. 218, pp. 888–90.

JAMES, W. (1890), *Principles of Psychology*, Holt, Rinehart & Winston.

KAGAN, J. (1967), 'On the need for relativism', *Amer. Psychol.*, vol. 22, pp. 131–42.

KAGAN, J., and LEWIS, M. (1965), 'Studies of attention in the human infant', *Merrill–Palmer Q.*, vol. 2, pp. 95–122.

KAGAN, J., and TULKIN, S. R. (1971), 'Social class differences in child rearing during the first year', in H. R. Schaffer (ed.), *The Origins of Human Social Relations*, Academic Press.

KAGAN, J., HENKER, B. A., HEN-TOV, A., LEVINE, J., and LEWIS, M. (1966), 'Infants' differential reactions to familiar and distorted faces', *Child Devel.*, vol. 37, pp. 519–32.

KAILA, E. (1932), 'The reactions of the infant to the human face', *Ann. Univ. Abo.*, vol. 17, pp. 1–114.

KARMEL, B. Z. (1969), 'The effects of age, complexity and amount of contour on pattern preferences in human infants', *J. exp. child Psychol.*, vol. 7, pp. 339–54.

KESSEN, W. (1963), 'Research in the psychological development of infants: an overview', *Merrill–Palmer Q.*, vol. 9, pp. 83–94.

KESSEN, W., and MANDLER, G. (1961), 'Anxiety, pain and the inhibition of distress', *Psychol. Rev.*, vol. 68, 396–404.

KESSEN, W., WILLIAMS, E. J., and WILLIAMS, J. P. (1961), 'Selection and test of response measures in the study of the human newborn', *Child Devel.*, vol. 32, pp. 7–24.

KLACKENBERG, G. (1956), 'Studies in maternal deprivation in infants' homes', *Acta Paediat.*, vol. 45, pp. 1–12.

KOHLBERG, L. (1968a), 'Early education: a cognitive-developmental view', *Child Devel.*, vol. 39, pp. 1013–62.

KOHLBERG, L. (1968b), 'Stage and sequence: the developmental approach to socialization', in D. A. Goslin (ed.), *Handbook of Socialization*, Rand McNally.

KOOPMAN, P. R., and AMES, E. W. (1968), 'Infants' preferences for facial arrrangements: a failure to replicate', *Child Devel.*, vol. 39, pp. 481–7.

KORNER, A. F., and GROBSTEIN, R. (1966), 'Visual alertness as related to soothing in neonates: implications for maternal stimulation and early deprivation', *Child Devel.*, vol. 37, pp. 867–76.

KOVACH, J. K., and HESS, E. H. (1963), 'Imprinting: effects of painful stimulation upon the following response', *J. comp. physiol. Psychol.*, vol. 56, pp. 461–4.

LAROCHE, J. L., and TCHENG, P. (1963), *Le Sourire au Nourisson*, Publications University of Louvain.

LASHLEY, K. S. (1951), 'The problem of serial order in behavior', in L. A. Jeffress (ed.), *Cerebral Mechanisms in Behavior*, Wiley.

LEVINE, S. (1960), 'Stimulation in infancy', *Sci. Amer.*, vol. 202, pp. 80–86.

LEVY, D. M. (1958), *Behavioral Analysis*, C. C. Thomas.

LEWIS, M. (1969), 'A developmental study of information processing within the first three years of life: response decrement to a redundant signal', *Monogr. Soc. Res. Child Devel.*, vol. 34, no. 9 (whole no. 133).

LEWIS, M., and GOLDBERG, S. (1969), 'Perceptual-cognitive development in infancy: a generalized expectancy model as a function of the mother–infant interaction', *Merrill–Palmer Q.*, vol. 15, pp. 81–100.

LORENZ, K. (1935), 'Der Kumpan in der Umwelt des Vogels', *J. Ornithol.*, vol. 83, pp. 137–213, 289–413.

LORENZ, K. (1966), *On Aggression*, Methuen.

MCCALL, R. B., and KAGAN, J. (1967), 'Stimulus-schema discrepancy and attention in the infant', *J. exp. child Psychol.*, vol. 5, pp. 381–90.

MCCALL, R. B., and KAGAN, J. (1969), 'Individual differences in the infant's distribution of attention to stimulus discrepancy', *Devel. Psychol.*, vol. 2, pp. 90–98.

MCCALL, R. B., and MELSON, W. H. (1969), 'Attention in infants as a function of magnitude of discrepancy and habituation rate', *Psychon.. Science*, vol. 17, pp. 317–19.

MCCLELLAND, D. C., ATKINSON, J. W., CLARK, R. W., and LOWELL, E. L. (1953), *The Achievement Motive*, Appleton-Century-Crofts.

MCGURK, H. (1970), 'The role of object orientation in infant perception', *J. exp. child Psychol.*, vol. 9, pp. 363–73.

MASON, W. A. (1965), 'Determinants of social behavior in young chimpanzees', in A. M. Schrier and H. F. Harlow (eds.), *Behavior of Nonhuman Primates*, vol. 2, Academic Press.

MEAD, M. (1962), 'A cultural anthropologist's approach to maternal deprivation', in *Deprivation of Maternal Care: A Reassessment of its Effects*, World Health Organization.

MILLER, G. A., GALANTER, E., and PRIBRAM, K. H. (1960), *Plans and the Structure of Behavior*, Holt, Rinehart & Winston.

MOLTZ, H. (1963), 'Imprinting: an epigenetic approach', *Psychol. Rev.*, vol. 70, pp. 123–38.

MOLTZ, H., ROSENBLUM, L., and STETTNER, L. J. (1960), 'Some parameters of imprinting effectiveness', *J. comp. physiol. Psychol.*, vol. 53, pp. 297–301.

MORGAN, G. A., and RICCIUTI, H. N. (1969), 'Infants' responses to strangers during the first years', in B. M. Foss (ed.), *Determinants of Infant Behaviour*, vol. 4, Methuen.

MOSS, H. A., (1967), 'Sex, age and state as determinants of mother–infant interaction', *Merrill–Palmer Q.*, vol. 13, pp. 19–36.

MOSS, H. A., and ROBSON, K. S. (1968), 'The role of protest behavior in the development of the mother–infant attachment', paper to the American Psychological Association, San Francisco.

ORLANSKY, H. (1949), 'Infant care and personality', *Psychol. Bull.*, vol. 46, pp. 1–48.

PIAGET, J. (1953), *The Origins of Intelligence in the Child*, Routledge & Kegan Paul.

PIAGET, J. (1955), *The Child's Construction of Reality*, Routledge & Kegan Paul.

PINNEAU, S. (1955), 'The infantile disorders of hospitalism and anaclitic depression', *Psychol, Bull.*, vol. 52, pp. 429–52.

PLOOG, D. (1969), 'Early communication processes in squirrel monkeys', in R. J. Robinson (ed.), *Brain and Early Behaviour*, Academic Press.

PRECHTL, H. F. R. (1965), 'Problems of behavioral studies in the newborn infant', in D. S. Lehrman, R. A. Hinde and E. Shaw (eds.), *Advances in the Study of Behavior*, vol. 1, Academic Press.

PRECHTL, H. F. R., and LENARD, H. G. (1967), 'A study of eye movements in sleeping newborn infants', *Brain Res.*, vol. 5, pp. 477–93.

PRECHTL, H. F. R., THEORELL, K., GRAUSBERGEN, A., and LIND, J. (1969), 'A statistical analysis of cry patterns in normal and abnormal newborn infants', *Develop. Med. child Neurol.*, vol. 11, pp. 142–52.

PREYER, W. (1882), *Die Seele des Kindes*, T. Grieben.

PROVENCE, S., and COLEMAN, R. (1957), 'Environmental retardation (hospitalism) in infants living in families', *Pediatrics*, vol. 19, pp. 285–92.

PROVENCE, S., and LIPTON, R. C. (1962), *Infants in Institutions: A Comparison of their Development with Family-Reared Infants during the First Year of Life*, International Universities Press.

PRUGH, D. G., and HARLOW, R. G. (1962), 'Marked deprivation in infants and young children', in *Deprivation of Maternal Care: A Reassessment of its Effects*, World Health Organization.

RHEINGOLD, H. L. (1956), 'The modification of social responsiveness in institutional babies', *Monogr. Soc. Res. Child Devel.*, vol. 21, no. 2 (whole no. 63).

RHEINGOLD, H. L. (1961), 'The effect of environmental stimulation upon social and exploratory behaviour in the human infant', in B. M. Foss (ed.), *Determinants of Infant Behaviour*, Methuen.

RHEINGOLD, H. L. (1968), 'The social and socializing infant', in D. A. Goslin (ed.), *Handbook of Socialization Theory and Research*, Rand McNally.

RHEINGOLD, H. L. (1969), 'The effect of a strange environment on the behaviour of infants', in B. M. Foss (ed.), *Determinants of Infant Behaviour*, vol. 4, Methuen.

RHEINGOLD, H. L., and ECKERMAN, C. O. 1970), 'The infant separates himself from his mother', *Science*, vol. 168, pp. 78–83.

RHEINGOLD, H. L., and ECKERMAN, C. O. (1971), 'Departures from the mother', in H. R. Schaffer (ed.), *The Origins of Human Social Relations*, Academic Press.

RHEINGOLD, H. L., GEWIRTZ, J. L., and ROSS, H. W. (1959), 'Social conditioning of vocalizations in the infants', *J. comp. physiol. Psychol.*, vol. 52, pp. 68–73.

RICHARDS, M. P. M. (1971), 'Social interaction in the first weeks of human life', *Psychiat., Neurol., Neurochir.*, vol. 74, pp. 35–42.

RICHMOND, J. B., and LUSTMAN, S. L. (1955), 'Autonomic function in the neonate', *Psychosom. Med.*, vol. 17, pp. 269–75.

ROSENBLATT, J. S. (1965), 'The basis of synchrony in the behavioural interaction between the mother and her offspring in the laboratory rat', in B. M. Foss (ed.), *Determinants of Infant Behaviour*, vol. 3, Methuen.

ROSENBLUM, L. (1971), 'Infant attachment in monkeys', in H. R. Schaffer (ed.), *The Origins of Human Social Relations*, Academic Press.

RUBENSTEIN, J. (1967), 'Maternal attentiveness and subsequent exploratory behavior in the infant', *Child Devel.*, vol. 38, pp. 1089–100.

SALK, L. (1962), 'Mothers' heartbeat as imprinting stimulus', *Trans. New York Acad. Sci.*, vol. 24, pp. 753–63.

SALZEN, E. A. (1963), 'Visual stimuli eliciting the smiling response in the human infant', *J. genet. Psychol.*, vol. 102, pp. 51–4.

SALZEN, E A. (1966), 'Imprinting and environmental learning', in L. R. Aronson, D. S. Lehrman, J. S. Rosenblatt and E. Toback (eds.), *Development and Evolution of Behavior*, vol. 1, Freeman.

SANDER, L. W. (1969), 'The longitudinal course of early mother–child interaction: cross-case comparison in a sample of mother–child pairs', in B. M. Foss (ed.), *Determinants of Infant Behaviour*, vol. 4, Methuen.

SANDER, L. W., and JULIA, H. L. (1966), 'Continuous interactional monitoring in the neonate', *Psychosom. Med.*, vol. 28, pp. 822–35.

SCARR, S. (1965), 'The inheritance of sociability', paper to the American Psychological Association, Chicago.

SCARR, S. (1969), 'Social introversion–extraversion as a heritable response', *Child Devel.*, vol. 40, pp. 823–32.

SCARR, S., and SALAPATEK, P. (1970), 'Patterns of fear development during infancy', *Merrill–Palmer Q.*, vol. 16, pp. 53–90.

SCHAEFER, E. S., and BAYLEY, N. (1963), 'Maternal behavior, child behavior and their intercorrelations from infancy through adolescence', *Monogr. Soc. Res. Child Devel.*, vol. 28, no. 3 (whole no. 87).

SCHAFFER, H. R. (1958), 'Objective observations of personality development in early infancy', *Brit. J. med. Psychol.*, vol. 31, pp. 174–83.

SCHAFFER, H. R. (1963), 'Some issues for research in the study of attachment behaviour', in B. M. Foss (ed.), *Determinants of Infant Behaviour*, vol. 2, Methuen.

SCHAFFER, H. R. (1965), 'Changes in development quotient under two conditions of maternal separation', *Brit. J. soc. clin. Psychol.*, vol. 4, pp. 39–46.

SCHAFFER, H. R. (1966a), 'The onset of fear of strangers and the incongruity hypothesis', *J. child Psychol. Psychiat.*, vol. 7, pp. 95–106.

SCHAFFER, H. R. (1966b), 'Activity level as a constitutional determinant of infantile reaction to deprivation', *Child Devel.*, vol. 37, pp. 595–602.

SCHAFFER, H. R. (1971), 'Cognitive structure and early social behavior', in H. R. Schaffer (ed.), *The Origins of Human Social Relations*, Academic Press.

SCHAFFER, H. R., and CALLENDER, W. M. (1959), 'Psychologic effects of hospitalization in infancy', *Pediatrics*, vol. 24, pp. 528–39.

SCHAFFER, H. R., and EMERSON, P. E. (1964a), 'The development of social attachments in infancy', *Monogr. Soc. Res. Child Devel.*, vol. 29, no. 3, (whole no. 94).

SCHAFFER, H. R., and EMERSON, P. E. (1964b), 'Patterns of response to physical contact in early human development', *J. child Psychol. Psychiat.*, vol. 5, pp. 1–13.

SCHAFFER, H. R., and EMERSON, P. E. (1968), 'The effects of experimentally administered stimulation on developmental quotients of infants', *Brit. J. soc. clin. Psychol.*, vol. 7, pp. 61–7.

SCHAFFER, H. R., and PARRY, M. H. (1969), 'Perceptual-motor behaviour in infancy as a function of age and stimulus familiarity', *Brit. J. Psychol.*, vol. 60, pp. 1–9.

SCHAFFER, H. R., and PARRY, M. H. (1970), 'The effects of short-term familiarization on infants' perceptual-motor coordination in a simultaneous discrimination situation', *Brit. J. Psychol.*, vol. 61, pp. 559–69.

SCHNEIRLA, T. C., ROSENBLATT, J. S., and TOBACH, E. (1963), 'Maternal behavior in the cat', in H. L. Rheingold (ed.), *Maternal Behavior in Mammals*, Wiley.

SCOTT, J. P. (1958), 'Critical periods in the development of social behavior in puppies', *Psychosom. Med.*, vol. 20, pp. 42–54.

SCOTT, J. P. (1962), 'Critical periods in behavioral development', *Science*, vol. 138, pp. 949–58.

SCOTT, J. P. (1963), 'The process of primary socialization in canine and human infants', *Monogr. Soc. Res. Child Devel.*, vol. 28, no. 1, (whole no. 85).

SCOTT, J. P. (1971), 'Attachment and separation in dog and man: theoretical propositions', in H. R. Schaffer (ed.), *The Origins of Human Social Relations*, Academic Press.

SEARS, R. R. (1944), 'Experimental analysis of psychoanalytic phenomena', in J. McV. Hunt (ed.), *Personality and the Behavior Disorders*, vol. 1, Ronald Press.

SEARS, R. R., MACCOBY, E. E., and LEVIN, H. (1957), *Patterns of Child Rearing*, Row, Peterson.

SEARS, R. R., WHITING, J. W. M., NOWLIS, V., and SEARS, P. S. (1953), 'Some child-rearing antecedents of aggression and dependency in young children', *Genet. psychol. Monogr.*, vol. 47, pp. 135–236.

SHIRLEY, M. M. (1933), *The First Two Years: A Study of Twenty-Five Babies*, University of Minnesota Press.

SLUCKIN, W. (1965), *Imprinting and Early Learning*, Methuen.

SOKOLOV, Y. N. (1963), *Perception and the Conditioned Reflex*, Macmillan.

SPEARS, W. C. (1964), 'Assessment of visual preference and discrimination in the four-month-old infant', *J. comp. physiol. Psychol.*, vol. 57, pp. 381–6.

SPITZ, R. A. (1945), 'Hospitalism: an inquiry into the genesis of psychiatric conditions in early childhood', *Psychoanal. Study Child*, vol. 1, pp. 53–74.

SPITZ, R. A. (1950), 'Anxiety in infancy: a study of its manifestations in the first year of life', *Int. J. Psychoanal.*, vol. 31, pp. 138–43.

SPITZ, R. A. (1965), *The First Year of Life*, International Universities Press.

SPITZ, R. A., and WOLF, K. M. (1946), 'The smiling response: a contribution to the ontogenesis of social relationships', *Genet. psychol. Monogr.*, vol. 34, pp. 57–125.

STEVENS, A. G. (1971), 'Attachment behaviour, separation anxiety and stranger anxiety in polymatrically reared infants', in H. R. Schaffer (ed.), *The Origins of Human Social Relations*, Academic Press.

TENNES, K. H., and LAMPL, E. E. (1964), 'Stranger and separation anxiety in infancy', *J. nerv. ment. Dis.*, vol. 139, pp. 247–54.

THOMAS, A., CHESS, S., BIRCH, H. G., HERTZIG, M. E., and KORN, S. (1964), *Behavioral Individuality in Early Childhood*, New York University Press.

THOMPSON, R. F., and SPENCER, W. A. (1966), 'Habituation: a model phenomenon for the study of neuronal substrates of behavior', *Psychol. Rev.*, vol. 173, pp. 16–43.

TINBERGEN, N. (1951), *The Study of Instinct*, Clarendon Press.

WAHLER, R. G. (1967), 'Infant social attachments: a reinforcement theory interpretation and investigation', *Child Devel.*, vol. 38, pp. 1079–88.

WALTERS, R. H., and PARKE, R. D. (1965), 'The role of the distance receptors in the development of social responsiveness' in L. P. Lipsitt and C. C. Spiker (eds.), *Advances in Child Development and Behavior*, vol. 2, Academic Press.

WATSON, J. B. (1925), *Behaviorism*, People's Publishing Company.

WATSON, J. B. (1928), *Psychological Care of Infant and Child*, Norton.

WATSON, J. S. (1966), 'Perception of object orientation in infants', *Merrill–Palmer Q.*, vol. 12, pp. 73–94.

WEISBERG, P. (1963), 'Social and nonsocial conditioning of infant vocalizations', *Child Devel.*, vol. 34, pp. 377–88.

WEIZMAN, F., COHEN, L. B., and PRATT, R. J. (1971), 'Novelty, familiarity and the development of infant attention', *Devel. Psychol.*, vol. 4, pp. 149–54.

WHITE, R. W. (1959), 'Motivation reconsidered: the concept of competence', *Psychol. Rev.*, vol. 66, pp. 297–333.

WILCOX, B. M. (1969), 'Visual preferences of human infants for representations of the human face', *J. exp. child Psychol.*, vol. 7, pp. 10–20.

WILCOX, B. M., and CLAYTON, F. L. (1968), 'Infant visual fixation on motion pictures of the human face', *J. exp. child Psychol.*, vol. 6, pp. 22–32.

WOLFF, P. H. (1963), 'Observations on the early development of smiling', in B. M. Foss (ed.), *Determinants of Infant Behaviour*, vol. 2, Methuen.

WOLFF, P. H. (1965), 'The development of attention in young infants', *Ann. New York Acad. Sci.*, vol. 118, pp. 815–30.

WOLFF, P. H. (1967), 'The role of biological rhythms in early psychological development', *Bull. Menninger Clinic*, vol. 31, pp. 197–218.

WOLFF, P. H. (1969), 'The natural history of crying and other vocalizations in early infancy', in B. M. Foss (ed.), *Determinants of Infant Behaviour*, vol. 4, Methuen.

YARROW, L. J. (1961), 'Maternal deprivation: toward an empirical and conceptual re-evaluation', *Psychol. Bull.*, vol. 58, pp. 459–96.

YARROW, L. J. (1967), 'The development of focused relationships during infancy', in J. Hellmuth (ed.), *Exceptional Infant*, vol. 1, Special Child Publications.

Acknowledgements

Thanks are due to the following for permission to use illustrations in this volume.

Figure 1 W. H. Freeman & Co. for *Scientific American*

Figure 2 *Merrill–Palmer Quarterly*

Figure 3 *Merrill–Palmer Quarterly*

Figure 4 *Zeitschrift für Experimentelle und Angewandte Psychologie*

Figure 5 Tavistock Institute of Human Relations

Figure 6 American Psychological Association

Figure 7 Society for Research in Child Development

Figure 8 American Association for the Advancement of Science

Figure 9 British Psychological Society

Figure 10 British Psychological Society

Figure 11 Society for Research in Child Development

Figure 12 Harper & Row

Index

Accommodation, 23
Activity level, 165, 166, 169, 170
Adams, G., 57
Ahrens, R., 67, 68, 70
Ainsworth, M. D. S., 84, 109, 112, 115, 118, 133, 141, 142, 147, 164
Ambrose, J. A., 64, 72, 73, 83, 104
Ames, E. W., 45, 47, 50
Approach, 36, 143, 149, 151
  selective, 123–8
  to unfamiliar, 122
Arousal, 63 ff., 108, 150, 165
  and maternal punitiveness, 161
  modulation of, 158–60
Atkinson, J. W., 99
Attachment, 110, 123, 132, 139, 141
  and age, 112, 115–18, 136
  breadth of, 109, 144–6
  concept of, 106–8
  conditions for, 118–19
  and critical period, 120–21
  determinants of, 111–14
  development of, 114 ff.
  and exploration, 141–4
  individual differences in, 113–14, 136–8
  intensity of, 117, 136–41, 142
  models of, 144–6
  number of, 133–4
  objects of, 35, 133–6, 151
  onset of, 118 ff., 129, 134, 138, 151
  operational criteria for, 114–15
  patterns of, 108–11, 115
  proximity as goal of, 145, 146
  and species, 111–12
  specific, 31, 133
Attention, 36, 44, 92 ff., 99, 171
  maternal, 142, 160
Autism, 76–7
Avoidance, 103, 108, 123–8, 151
  of proximity, 146, 148, 150, 152
Axelrad, S., 102, 148

Baer, D. M., 19, 20, 102, 162
Baldwin, A. L., 21
Bandura, A., 22, 90
Banks, J. H., 86
Bartoshuk, A. K., 94
Bateson, P. P. G., 101
Bayley, N., 82, 169, 171
Behavioural synchrony, 174
Bell, R. Q., 51
Bell, S. M. V., 164
Bergman, P., 168, 169
Berlyne, D. E., 45
Bernuth, H. V., 56, 94
Bijou, S. W., 19, 20, 162
Birch, H. G., 168, 169
Birns, B., 169

Bower, T. G. R., 43, 94, 98
Bowlby, J., 25, 106, 108, 115,
116, 133, 144, 145, 146, 154
Brackbill, Y., 57, 64, 74, 162
Brain damage, and crying, 62
Brennan, W. M., 45
Bridger, W. H., 94, 169
Bridges, K. M. B., 29
Brody, S., 102, 148
Bronshtein, A. I., 38
Bronson, G. W., 121, 147, 149
Brossard, L. M., 74
Brown, J. L., 168
Bruner, J. S., 94

Caldwell, B. M., 15, 88, 89, 120,
138
Callender, W. M., 115
Campbell, D., 142
Caretakers, 138
number of, 138, 147
proximity of, 60, 111
substitute, 115, 130
Caron, A. J., 95
Caron, R. F., 95
Casler, L., 155
Central processes, 91
Central representations, 99,
131, 141
acquisition of, 91–7, 127, 130
presence of, 104, 105, 128, 129
Central structures, 20, 21, 22
Charlesworth, W. R., 95
Chess, S., 168, 169
Clark, R. W., 99
Clayton, F. L., 55
Cognitive capacity, 31, 158
Cognitive models, 91
Cognitive operations, 130, 131
Cognitive organization, 23, 103,
123 ff.
Cognitive structure, 21 ff., 31,

119, 146, 153
Cognitive theories of
development, 20–26
Cohen, L. B., 96
Coleman, R., 155
Complexity, 51, 95
perception of, 44–6, 49
Conditioning, 17, 19, 43, 90
operant, 19, 74
of vocalization, 75
see also Reinforcement
Contact
with mother, 121, 140
perceptual, 35, 36, 114
physical, 108, 110, 113, 143
Contingency, 20, 74, 162–63
Cox, F. N., 142
Critical period, 36, 101
and attachment, 120–21
see also Following response
Crowell, D. H., 57
Crying, 61 ff., 79, 80, 109, 165,
167
and autism, 76–77
eliciting conditions of, 63–5
function of, 62, 65–7, 73
organization of, 61–2
rhythmic pattern of, 62
specific inhibitor for, 63
terminating conditions of,
63–5

Darwin, C., 29, 67
Decarie, T. G., 74, 113
Dember, W. N., 46
Dennis, W., 147, 154, 156, 161
Dependence, 34
emotional, 35–6, 106
physical, 33, 106
Deprivation, 30, 120, 122
maternal, 153–5
perceptual, 155–8

Detachment, 138–41
Discrepancy hypothesis, 99–101
Discrimination, 90, 115, 124, 127
    of mother, 82 ff.
        experimental studies on, 86–9
        observational studies on, 82–6
Distress, 66, 103, 111, 117, 143
Dollard, J., 34
Drive, 33–7, 136

Earl, R., 46
Eckerman, C. O., 139
Effectance motive, 163
Emerson, P. E., 35, 113, 116, 118, 122, 133, 134, 135, 136, 156
Escalona, S. K., 33, 148, 168, 169, 170, 173
Expectancy, 163
Experimental technique
    familiarization, 100
    simultaneous presentation, 92
    'vestibulator', 64
    visual preference, 44, 47, 54
Exploration, 110, 127, 139, 157, 170
    and attachment, 141–44, 145, 151–2
Eyes as stimulus, 54, 68, 69, 79, 103

Face as stimulus, 48 ff., 57 ff., 103
    critical properties of, 51, 55, 69, 70
    familiarity of, 71
    mother's, 68, 86
    orientation of, 51–4

perception of, 48 ff.
preference for, 49–50
recognition of, 49
scrambled, 51, 55, 59, 100
smiling at, 67
Familiar, 97, 103, 129, 142, 147
    and novel, 95–7, 99, 126
    people, 84, 87, 123, 131, 150
    and strange, 117
    see also Familiarity, Unfamiliar
Familiarity, 85, 92, 96, 105, 143, 149
    dimension of, 124, 126
    and smiling, 67, 71
    see also Familiar
Familiarization, 93, 100, 103
    short-term, 97
    technique, 54, 100
    see also Habituation
Fantz, R. L., 43, 44, 47, 48, 49, 50, 51, 52, 54, 55, 92, 93, 95
Father, as attachment object, 35, 134
Fear, 143, 147, 151
    of strangers, 103, 130, 138, 171
        and child-rearing practices, 147
        development of, 146–51
        intensity of, 147, 148, 152
        and methodological problems, 148–51
        onset of, 121–3, 129, 146–8
    see also Strange, Stranger
Feedback, 24, 63, 91, 144, 145, 170
Fisichelli, V. R., 62
Fitzgerald, H. E., 86
Following response, 32, 108, 110
    visual, 102

Foss, B. M., 64
Frank, L. K., 24, 25, 26, 144
Freedman, D. A., 77, 113, 137, 147
Freedman, N., 77
Freezing, 148
Freud, S., 15, 34
Freudian hypotheses, 15, 16

Galanter, E., 91
Geber, M., 84
Gellhorn, E., 170
Gesell, A. L., 18, 19, 24
Gewirtz, J. L., 20, 21, 72, 73, 75, 76, 162, 171
Gibson, E. J., 90, 97, 98
Goldberg, S., 158, 163
Goldfarb, W., 120, 154
Gordon, T., 64
Gottesman, I. I., 78, 137
Grausbergen, A., 27, 62
Gray, M. L., 57
Gray, P. H., 102, 121
Greenfield, P. M., 94
Griffiths, R., 82
Grobstein, R., 66, 160

Haaf, R. A., 51
Habituation, 40, 54, 92 ff., 158, 162, 171
  see also Familiarization
Harlow, H. F., 35, 36, 143, 173
Harlow, R. G., 155
Harris, J. D., 92
Haith, M. M., 46, 94
Hebb, D. O., 99, 129, 147, 155
Henker, B. A., 55, 171
Hen-Tov, A., 55, 171
Heredity, 17, 18, 22, 78
  twin studies in, 137
Hershenson, M., 45, 47
Hersher, L., 138

Hertzig, M. E., 168, 169
Hess, E. H., 36
Hinde, R. A., 102, 120
Hospitalism, 154
Hospitalization, 115
Hunt, J. McV., 24, 38, 95, 96, 99, 105, 129, 147, 150
Hutt, C., 56, 94
Hutt, S. J., 56, 94

Imprinting, 34, 36, 101–3, 120
Incongruity, 129, 147, 150
Individual differences, 19, 62, 147, 164, 167–72
  and attachment, 113–14
  in intensity of attachments, 136–8
  patterns of, 168–72
  in signalability, 73–8
Infant care, 14–20, 147
Information processing, 38, 42, 58, 123, 124
  capacity for, 21, 69, 80, 150
Innate releasing mechanism, 68
Institutional infants, 72 ff., 104, 118, 138, 153 ff., 170
  see also Hospitalization
Interaction between infant and mother, 66, 107, 109, 136, 138, 167
  for 'cuddlers', 113
  and developmental stages, 158
  perceptual, 37–8
  and sensitivity, 164
  sequences of, 80, 172
  and vocalization, 84
Internal representations, 21, 23, 37, 141, 152

James, W., 14
Julia, H. L., 165, 166

Kagan, J., 55, 100, 105, 160, 171
Kaila, E., 67
Karelitz, S., 62
Karmel, B. Z., 46
Kessen, W., 24, 26, 63, 169
Kibbutz infants, 73
Kinaesthetic stimulation, 84
Klackenberg, G., 155
Kohlberg, L., 21
Koopman, P. R., 50
Korn, S., 168, 169
Korner, A. F., 66, 160
Kovach, J. K., 36

Lampl, E. E., 148
Laroche, J. L., 171
Lashley, K. S., 26, 27
Learning, 20, 34
  discrimination, 90
  motor, 21
  'no-trial', 22
  perceptual, 90 ff., 101, 102,
    127
  social, 112
Lenard, H. G., 27, 56, 94
Levin, H., 36
Levine, J., 55, 171
Levine, S., 161
Levy, D. M., 168
Lewis, M., 55, 158, 163, 171
Lind, J., 27, 62
Lipton, R. C., 154
Lorenz, K., 13, 29, 30, 101
Lowell, E. L., 99
Lustman, S. L., 169

McCall, R. B., 100
McClelland, D. C., 99
Maccoby, E. E., 36
McGurk, H., 54
Mandler, G., 63
Mason, W. A., 159

Matching process, 105
Maternal
  attention, 142, 160
  attitudes, 165
  deprivation, 153–5
  punitiveness, 161
  responsiveness, 136, 172
  see also Mother
Maturation, 18, 19
Mead, M., 134
Melson, W. H., 100
Memory, 91, 104, 128, 129, 163
Miller, G. A., 91
Miller, N. E., 34
Model,
  neuronal, 91, 103
  systems engineering, 24–6,
    144–6
Moltz, H., 102, 120, 161
Monotropy, 133
Moore, R. W., 45
Morgan, G. A., 148, 149
Moss, H. A., 66, 164, 171, 172
Mother, 103, 104
  central representation of,
    127 ff.
  contact with, 121, 140
  face of, 68, 86
  as a haven of safety, 143, 151
  perceptual exposure to, 97
  proximity of, 67, 106, 114,
    132 ff., 141 ff.
  recognition of, 82 ff., 89, 98,
    99
  responsiveness to, 84, 85
  sensitivity of, 158, 164, 168
  separation from, 109, 116,
    143
  stimulation by, 137, 156, 158,
    162
  and stranger, 82
  substitute, 115, 116, 130

Mother – *continued*
  surrogate, 32, 35, 36
  see also Attachment,
    Interaction, Maternal
Mother learning, 21, 112
Muntjewerff, W. J., 56

Najarian, P., 154
Neonate, 27, 38, 41, 43, 56
  hearing of, 38, 40, 56
  pupillary reflex in, 39
  signalability of, 77–8
  visual activity of, 47, 160
Nevis, S., 51, 52
Novel object, 96, 124, 152, 158
  and familiar, 95–7, 99, 126
Novelty, 89, 104, 142, 144
Nowlis, V., 36

Object, 32
  acquisition, 118, 131
  choice, 133–6
  permanence, 43, 128
  see also Social object
Observational learning, 22, 90
Observational techniques, 85
Olver, R. R., 94
Orientation
  of face, 51–4
  social, 77
Orienting response, 42, 91
  habituation of, 40
Orlansky, H., 15

Pacers, 46
Parke, R. D., 36, 112, 159
Parry, M. H., 124, 125, 126
Pavlovian conditioning, 17, 90
Perception, 168
  face, 48–56
  form, 44, 49
  movement, 46–7

in neonates, 38 ff.
  selective, 43–8
  solidity, 47, 55, 69
Perceptual constancy, 42, 43,
  89, 98–9
Perceptual deprivation, 155–8
Perceptual differentiation, 115,
  127
Perceptual exposure, 21, 97,
  104
Perceptual interaction, 35, 37–8
Perceptual learning, 90 ff., 101,
  102, 127
Perceptual and motor
  integration, 127
Perceptual organization, 42–3
Perceptual salience, 35, 104, 127
Petrova, E. P., 38
Piaget, J., 22, 23, 24, 25, 43, 67,
  128
Pinneau, S., 155
Ploog, D., 32
Pratt, R. J., 96
Prechtl, H. F. R., 27, 62, 94,
  167
Preferences, of infants, 33, 46,
  49, 50, 95
Preyer, W., 29, 38
Pribram, K. H., 91
Provence, S., 154, 155
Proximity, 60, 111, 138, 141
  avoidance, 108, 146, 148,
    150, 152
  of mother, 67, 106, 118, 132,
    145
  seeking, 107 ff., 131, 146
  of stranger, 114, 150
Prugh, D. G., 155
Punishment, 36, 90, 161

Reaction patterns, 168, 169
Recall, 129, 131

Recognition, 49, 58, 82 ff., 96, 129, 131
    of mother, 82 ff., 98, 99
Reinforcement, 87, 90
    contingent, 20, 74, 163
    continuous, 74, 87
    differential, 21
    intermittent, 74
    see also Conditioning
Response decrement, 92, 158
    see also Habituation
Responsiveness, 117, 128, 168
    auditory, 56–7
    differential, 56, 83, 85, 86
    maternal, 136, 172
    to mother, 84, 85
    positive, 123, 131, 149
    selective, 56, 127
    to stranger, 117, 149
    visual, 38, 124
Rheingold, H. L., 48, 75, 76, 112, 139, 140, 142, 143, 155, 156, 157, 162, 164
Rhythm, 165, 167
    in crying, 62
    endogenous, 26–8, 64
Ricciuti, H. L., 148, 149
Richards, M. P. M., 28, 163, 164
Richmond, J. B., 169
Robson, K. S., 66
Rosenblatt, J. S., 174
Rosenblum, L., 102, 133
Ross, H. W., 75, 76, 162
Rubenstein, J., 157

Salapatek, P., 148
Salk, L., 56, 57
Salzen, E. A., 67, 103
Sander, L. W., 165, 166
Sayeg, Y., 156
Scarr, S., 78, 137, 148

Schaefer, E. S., 169
Schaffer, H. R., 35, 84, 105, 113, 115, 116, 118, 119, 122, 124, 125, 126, 127, 130, 133, 134, 135, 136, 138, 146, 147, 149, 150, 151, 155, 156, 170, 171
Schemata, 22 ff., 91, 96, 99
Schneirla, T. C., 174
Scott, J. P., 36, 61, 122, 133, 159
Sears, P. S., 36
Sears, R. R., 15, 36
Secondary drive hypothesis, 33–7, 136
Selective approach–avoidance, 123–8
Selective perception, 43–8
Selective responsiveness, 29, 56, 71
Sensitive period, 102, 120
Sensitivity, 38–42, 63
    mother's, 164, 168
Separation, 138, 139
    protest, 115 ff., 129, 130
Sex differences, 171, 172
Shirley, M. M., 29
Signal, 62, 66, 112, 158
    strength, 73
'Signalability', 73–8
    in autism, 76–7
    and heredity, 78
    of neonate, 77–8
Silfen, C. K., 47
Skinnerian conditioning, 19
Sluckin, W., 102, 120
Smiling, 29 ff., 74, 79 ff., 102 ff., 171
    developmental changes in, 69–73
    eliciting stimuli for, 67–9
    and familiarity, 67, 71

Smiling – *continued*
  function of, 67, 73
  in institutional infants, 72
  selective, 71, 72
Social behaviour, 28–31
Social class, 160
Social learning, 112
Social object
  impact of, 48–57
  construction of, 128–31
  see also Object
Social orientation, 77
Social relationship, 30, 106
Social stimulation, 170
Sokolov, Y. N., 91
Spears, W. C., 45
Spencer, W. A., 94
Spitz, R. A., 67, 68, 122, 148,
  154, 155
State, 144, 167–8, 170
Stayton, D. J., 164
Stettner, L. J., 102
Stevens, A. G., 138
Stimulation, 36, 65, 151, 153 ff.,
  169
  homogeneity of, 161
  kinaesthetic, 84
  maternal, 137, 158, 162
  phasing of, 163–7
  quantity of, 153–8
  reciprocity of, 163–7
  speed of, 150, 151
  timing of, 162–7, 168
  variety of, 161–2
  see also Stimulus
Stimulus, 21, 32, 40, 71, 78, 124
  complexity of, 95
  intensity of, 161
  supra-optimal, 68
  see also Stimulation
Strange
  and familiar, 117

  fear of, 123, 129
  situation, 142, 144
  see also Fear, Stranger
Stranger, 83 ff., 142 ff.
  anxiety, 148
  and mother, 82, 116
  proximity of, 114, 150
  response to, 104, 117, 123,
  128, 129, 149
  see also Fear of strangers,
    Strange
Systems engineering models of
  attachment, 24–6, 144–6

Tcheng, P., 171
Tennes, K. H., 148
Theorell, K., 27, 62
Thomas, A., 168, 169
Thompson, R. F., 94
Tinbergen, N., 68
Tobach, E., 174
Tulkin, S. R., 160

Unfamiliar, 122, 127, 152
  environment, 143, 144
  stranger as, 128, 144
  see also Familiar

Visual
  contact, 114
  fixation, 39, 47, 50, 55
  following, 39, 102
  perception, 38–40, 124, 160
  preference technique, 44, 47,
    54
  see also Perception,
    Perceptual
Vocalization, 109
  conditioning of, 75

Wahler, R. G., 87, 88
Walters, R. H., 36, 112, 159

Watson, J. B., 17, 19, 24
Watson, J. S., 51, 53
Weisberg, P., 75, 76, 162
Weizman, F., 96
White, R. W., 163
Whiting, J. W. M., 36
Wilcox, B. M., 55
Williams, E. J., 169

Williams, J. P., 169
Wittig, B. A., 142
Wolf, K. M., 67
Wolff, P. H., 27, 36, 61, 62, 63, 65, 71, 85, 130
Wolfson, J. H., 86

Yarrow, L. J., 83, 85, 153